Between Skins

Between Skins

The Body in Psychoanalysis –
Contemporary Developments

Nicola Diamond

WILEY-BLACKWELL

A John Wiley & Sons, Ltd., Publication

This edition first published 2013
© John Wiley & Sons, Ltd 2013

Wiley-Blackwell is an imprint of John Wiley & Sons, formed by the merger of Wiley's global
Scientific, Technical and Medical business with Blackwell Publishing.

Registered Office
John Wiley & Sons Ltd, The Atrium, Southern Gate, Chichester, West Sussex, PO19 8SQ, UK

Editorial Offices
350 Main Street, Malden, MA 02148-5020, USA
9600 Garsington Road, Oxford, OX4 2DQ, UK
The Atrium, Southern Gate, Chichester, West Sussex, PO19 8SQ, UK

For details of our global editorial offices, for customer services, and for information about
how to apply for permission to reuse the copyright material in this book please see our
website at www.wiley.com/wiley-blackwell.

The right of Nicola Diamond to be identified as the author of this work has been asserted in
accordance with the UK Copyright, Designs and Patents Act 1988.

Library of Congress Cataloging-in-Publication Data
Diamond, Nicola.
  Between skins : the body in psychoanalysis–contemporary developments / Dr. Nicola
Diamond.
    pages   cm
  Includes bibliographical references and index.
  ISBN 978-0-470-01942-9 (cloth)
1. Body image. 2. Human body. 3. Somesthesia. 4. Body schema–Psychological
aspects. 5. Mind and body. 6. Psychoanalysis. I. Title.
  BF175.5.B64D53 2013
  155.2–dc23
                                                    2013000738
A catalogue record for this book is available from the British Library.

Cover image: © Edvard March/Corbis
Cover design by Richard Boxall Design Associates

Set in 10/12pt Sabon by SPi Publisher Services, Pondicherry, India
Printed and bound in Singapore by Markono Print Media Pte Ltd

1   2013

Contents

Introduction

When Selma first came to see me she was suffering a severe case of vaginismus.[1] Her vaginal walls were in a state of involuntary constriction and this had been a lifelong developmental complaint. She was 22 at the time and, embarking on her first serious relationship, her anxiety about her 'condition' had intensified.

She had been through a battery of medical tests and investigations but no organic cause could be found. Selma described to me how she had been a very shy and timid child who would, as she put it, 'hide under mum's skirt' when any stranger arrived at the house. She explained how she was tied to her mother's 'apron strings' and cried incessantly at nursery. Separation had been a struggle from the first, and after two years of therapy she continued to seek out comfort in the safe and familiar.

An incident had occurred when she was five that stuck out in her memory. When she was with her father on one of his weekend visits (her mother and father had separated when she was three) she fell over while they were in the park and cried. Although not badly injured, she was withdrawn and preoccupied for days after.

In the analysis Selma described her fears. As a child, she feared spiders and small animals. As an adult this fear had continued; she was scared of cats and asked if there were any in the building before entering into the analysis. She feared anything that had not become part of the familiar – the alien and other – and most of all she feared damage being done to her bodily integrity. For example, at seven she had been on a picnic for her birthday party but had got so 'paranoid' about an ant that she

Between Skins: The Body in Psychoanalysis – Contemporary Developments,
First Edition. Nicola Diamond.
© 2013 John Wiley & Sons, Ltd. Published 2013 by John Wiley & Sons, Ltd.

believed had crawled into her anal orifice that she spent most of the event in tears and refused to sit down on the grass from that day forth.

From her early clinging to her mother and anxiety of separation in her anxious, insecure attachment style, she very readily felt unprotected and associated danger and lack of protection with her father with whom she did not live or feel close to, a fear which she then generalized to include all male figures. This insecurity of attachment that overlay her primordial fear of harm to her bodily integrity became a preoccupying narcissistic fragility as she began to experience what she described as 'strange' sensations, which made her feel uncomfortable, and her reaction was to tense up. These feelings were undoubtedly sexual and from early on she did not like them. She remembered as a girl of 10 seeing a sex scene with a boy touching a girl and she had to switch off the television. 'The feelings were unbearable'; she could not risk any sexual feelings, and her anxiety developed into a way of shutting herself off from anything sexual, culminating in her inability to open up to a man. The fear of irreparable damage if she let in the other was too great. However, before her analysis it was not possible to be conscious of this, so she expressed the relational experience somatically, shoring herself up once and for all, or so it seemed.

Selma described how she had always felt less trusting of men and when she started relations she would 'clam up'. The previous counsellor had suggested that she had experienced abuse, but there was no evidence of this in her experience or history, and I came to the conclusion that this was going nowhere, that is searching for a concrete event as a cause rather than understanding the qualitative relational disturbance being expressed. I said to Selma: 'You say "clam up" – it is also like that with your vagina which states "no entry – all trespassing is prohibited"'.

The therapy was long, involving an exploration of her fears of irreparable damage by the other, working on separation from the primary family (by leaving home, as this was one of the achievements during the analysis) and challenging her defences by opening herself little by little to sexual sensation and a sexual relationship with her partner which was now experienced as threatening but not intolerably so. Selma struggled with the relational fears that were connected to bodily ones – being taken over – invaded and destroyed – by the other and so on. Conjointly with this relational reworking (through the dynamics in the analytic relationship), she also addressed her phobic responses by a gradual counter-action involving bodily self exploration with and without her partner. In consequence, the vaginismus slowly reduced its rigid grip and greater muscular flexibility become more possible; the vaginal contractions proved to be much more than simply a habituated involuntary reflex response.

This brief extract from one of my clinical cases raises some questions. How is it that a relational closure in the context of others becomes a lifelong contraction in the vaginal walls? How is it that a relational experience with others is expressed as somatic condition? What is the link between the experience of separation, affective and sensual states, meaning and the body? How does an attachment and sexual history coalesce in a physiological state and response?

As an experienced clinician focused on working with 'psychosomatic' or 'conversion' states, I have become increasingly frustrated with the way bodily symptoms are not well understood and not adequately addressed as a form of communication in their own right. From an academic standpoint the theoretical impasses in the psychoanalytic and psychosomatic literature and research are still only too plain to see; dualistic forms of thinking where divisions between mind/body and world are still upheld. I believe there is the need for a more relational understanding of the formation of bodily symptoms: how somatic expression is a communication of which the subject is unconscious. The body is capable of complexity, and biology is more malleable and can be transformed by an interpersonal and social field.

I have thus embarked on this ambitious interdisciplinary investigation into the nature of the body as a way of: (1) fundamentally challenging persisting dualisms; (2) putting forward an alternative and possibly more viable model of the body; (3) offering something to our understanding of 'conversion' and 'psychosomatic' symptoms that are seen in the clinic and are present in everyday life; and (4) hopefully encouraging a more creative exchange between the disciplines so that links between the different fields can be made.

Why *Between* Skins?

'Between skins' is about the way we exist with one another, how bodies connect, how biological processes communicate and how the skin as an exposed surface has direct contact with the field of others. This book investigates how relations with others and the social world can really get under and inside our skins.

The reference to 'between skins' is both to the skin as an exteriorized surface in intimate relation with others (and with the wider social environment) and to the 'interior' of the body, which is also profoundly affected by social interaction and environmental relations. What is implied is that any lining of or process in the body, whether derived from 'without' or 'within', can be rendered vulnerable to relational exposure.

Between Skins exploits the metaphor and the lived materiality of 'between skins', in order to show how skin-to-skin contact becomes a relational space where an affective connection is created between persons and the outside world: how so-called internal bodily processes do not inhabit a pure interiority but are altered by 'outside' influences from the very beginning and how the skin in both senses as an interior and an external surface is in the world and thereby becomes intertwined with the relational field of others and with social models of the body.

Reference will be made throughout to Merleau-Ponty, a philosopher and phenomenologist, a true revolutionary and innovative interdisciplinary thinker who explored the intersection between the life sciences and was sympathetic to psychoanalysis. He likened the body to a glove turned inside out, dedicated as he was to exploring the structure of inside and outside in respect to body and social field. He depicted the way the body is – in the world – and how the world of others inhabits the very heart of bodily life. This book will work to show how Merleau-Ponty's trope can be used to describe the lived materiality of the flesh.

Between Skins opens up inside to outside and vice versa and asks the following questions: How do biology and the field of the social interconnect? How is psyche linked to body and world? How do others get literally and metaphorically under our skins, live in our sensations, affect our bodily experience and processes? How do feelings and meanings structure bodily perception, motility and function? How do cultural images and forms of life organize bodily experience and process?

This Book Sets Out To . . .

Between Skins signposts a paradigmatic shift that has taken place in psychoanalysis and allied disciplines. This is the move from a one-person psychology to a relational as well as a multi-personal perspective. The book foregrounds how this shift in focus translates into a new model of the body. What will emerge is a rigorous challenge to individualistic accounts of the body in order to show how the body (including biology) is social in nature.

The fact of our interpersonal being as both intersubjective and intercorporeal implies a radical departure from a one-person, one-body approach. Intersubjectivity and intercorporeality will be explained and illustrated as the book unfolds, but put most simply these terms describe how subjective and bodily states are fundamentally interpersonal and that feelings, meanings and even neurobiological processes are open to others and profoundly influenced by them.

The biologist Jacob von Uexküll has been seminal in conceiving the organism in relation to its environment. He showed how organism and environment are fundamentally interdependent and proposed that biology and language/meaning systems coexist. Exploring what is known as biosemiotics, he observed the growing and greater complexity of semiotic systems, especially in human societies (Uexküll 1926, 1957).

Starting from the connection between body and environment, and not the organism in isolation, implies a paradigmatic shift in an understanding of biology. It is a fundamentally different way of thinking about the relation between internal and external processes, inside and outside, bodily self and others, temporal–spatial relations and about the relation of the body to semiotic or signifying processes. The brain is not located in a vat but situated in a body and world, and this radically challenges the way the mind–body–world question is addressed.

Links with Psychoanalysis and Why Psychoanalysis?

In Anglo-American psychoanalysis the way the interior of the body connects to the external world and how the outer world relates to inner experience is the basis of much theorizing. So, for example, 'internalization', 'incorporation', 'projection' and 'expulsion' are terms that are commonly used. The experience of receiving communications like a 'projection' or a 'counter-transference' in the clinical literature is increasingly described as somatic in affect and in effect. However, such an approach has, traditionally, unwittingly resorted to a binary of inside/outside where there exists no aperture from within the organism, psyche or subject for a relation with the outside environment and world of others. Without this issue being worked through, the 'projections' of feelings and bodily states end up having to jump over an unbridgeable gulf.

Between Skins, in exploring the radical nature and consequences of an intercorporeal approach, will focus specifically on how biology can be rethought from within psychoanalytic models of understanding. Why psychoanalytic models of the body? Because psychoanalysis potentially offers a non-reductionist view, involving complexity, and processes that do not rely on consciousness or awareness and where memory, emotion, image, fantasy and meaning play a crucial role in bodily experience.

Psychoanalytic models attempt to understand the relation between biology and how we become emotional about our bodies. It examines the ways we represent, imagine and fantasize about the body, and hence gives meaning to bodily experiences. In this respect psychoanalysis provides an analysis of the multiple layers of bodily experience and process. Such a complex understanding is required for exploring the peculiar nature of bodily symptoms that are seen in the clinic and that exist in everyday experience. These symptoms can present with alterations in sensation and often function but have no known organic aetiology or are not adequately understood by a reduction to an organic causation alone.

In examining figure(s) of the body in psychoanalysis, interdisciplinary connections will be created between attachment studies, the neurosciences, philosophy and the social sciences. As part of this project, it will be necessary to challenge the residual dualism that stubbornly persists in psychoanalysis and even to some extent arguably in neuroscience.

In this book I identify a persisting dualism in psychoanalysis, one which splits the body off from the so-called 'mind' and world and which in consequence renders psychic life and the representation of the body reified and abstract. Through the exploration an alternative figure of the organism will emerge, which shows how biology does not belong to a closed system but is open to affect, memory, meaning, the field of others and the cultural world. The materiality of the body and the importance of somatic experience and expression will be reinstated with a difference. For the soma will be situated in a relational context and therefore be inseparable from others, affective communication and meaning.

Towards Sociality

In addressing the interpersonal field of micro-relations in depth, macro-relations can no longer be ignored: they set the scene of the wider context. Ultimately there is an extensive sensory field, where sensory-affective communication takes place between bodies and sensory information is constructed and transmitted by cultural, multisensory media and other organizational sites.

These sensory transmissions are actively received as sensory communications in bodily ways and these communications inform bodily experience. In referring to 'sensory transmissions', my emphasis is on non-verbal communication systems. The power and importance of linguistic expression is recognized, but my aim is to understand language more broadly, not as linguistic processes alone.

This project of relating the body to culture connects with other recent writings. Lafrance (2009), Manning (2009) and Pile (2011) all draw on psychoanalysis as a more satisfactory way of linking the body with sociality, particularly by way of the skin as the zone of exchange(s). My work continues with this theme but with specific application to the clinical context and to furthering interdisciplinary connections.

Embodied Cultural Differences

There is no neutral body. Others profoundly affect us and leave their marks which live on somatically. Before we are born contexts are already there, preparing to define us, and the moment we take a breath and are visible and tangible to a world, cultural markings are already at work, engendering, discriminating by colour and bodily type, classifying and so on.

The relation between body and inscription will be what *Between Skins* sets out to better understand and account for: how these social delineations get inside us and under our skins. In challenging the overarching and determining power of the a priori biological bedrock (prior to experience and as a founding given order), what will be revealed is an aspect of the body more open to protean potential, the way bodily processes in their function and form can be open to influence, alteration and transformation.

Relating to the Clinical Field

By applying the developing analysis of embodiment to clinical examples throughout, I will explore how somatic states and the social intersect in lived experience. The aim is to open up ways of analysing the body's symptoms in the consulting room and in the social world at large. My work both as an academic in psychosocial studies and as an experienced clinician in psychoanalytic and related work makes it possible for me to develop conceptual understanding and to explore the links between theory and clinical reality.

Sexuality in relation to the body has a central place in psychoanalysis. In this exploration sexuality will be addressed, but not exclusively. On the one hand I shall question the way current Anglo-American trends in psychoanalysis leave out the body and sexuality. On the other hand, I view embodied motivational processes more broadly and in their complexity, and shall also address the relationship between attachment and sexuality. My approach to understanding the psychosocial formation of somatic symptoms will be multifaceted.

The Structure of the Book

Finally, some comments on the structure and style of this book. An organism is traditionally viewed in terms of a body whose content is held in and sealed off from the outside world by a skin. *Between Skins* begins with the interior of the body – the vital order, that is the internal bodily processes that are essential for life (Part II) – and moves on to the skin as the protective sac (Part III). However, as the book progresses this conventional structure – from the inside to the outside of the body – is reversed, or inverted, to reveal how the outside world is in fact not sealed off but already inside and endemic to the body's interior, that is the outside is already inside.

Furthermore, the skin that initially resembles a fortress and functions like a barricade, with the inversion, starts to look radically permeable, letting the outside in and leaking vital contents into the world. Here the skin is no longer defined by what it contains, is not referred inwards but is left simply facing outwards, now utterly exposed in its absolute exteriority to relations with others, the containing envelope transformed, turned inside out. With this restructuring there also emerges another bodily figure, which is no longer located in a fixed place, all closed up, but instead is relationally situated within an environmental field, existing as more plastic and protean in nature.

The body of the book at first replicates the traditional bodily structure only to invert and eschew it, reinscribing and advocating in the very act of writing a new and different bodily configuration. The manifested textual body – form and structure – thus reiterates the book's content, its core theme and argument.

Human development is not simply linear; it can jump ahead of itself with a sudden leap forward and then possibly regress backwards, and so on. So, in a related vein, a non-linear developmental movement forwards and then backwards at times characterizes the act of writing in this book.

The book opens with an introduction to contemporary developments in an interdisciplinary context, setting the scene for where the analysis will eventually go. This context is to help the reader gain an overall picture so that detailed points can be understood within a wider frame.

For a true leap forward, we have first to take a step back, for traditional impasses have to be faced and thoroughly worked through. This takes the form of persisting mind/body dualisms in psychoanalysis. From these impasses there is a foundational reworking, a shifting of basic premises and therefore the possibility for a genuine forward development towards a new emerging bodily figure. So the uneven development ends up doing the job that has to be done, that is, to make sure the old problems are rigorously challenged and are properly unravelled along the way.

The aim here is to show up the failure in the traditional approach to the body question, in order to offer a convincing and viable alternative. The aim of this journey, with all its twists and turns, is to engage with the complexity of the field and to attempt to readdress the body in psychoanalysis, to link this with contemporary interdisciplinary developments and clinical actualities.

A 'grand project' of this type will inevitably fall short; the claims and arguments made are necessarily tentative and are offered as provocations with the aim of inciting controversy and debate to further thinking and possible links between disciplines.

Note

1   When referring to clinical cases throughout I use an approach that is employed by some French psychoanalysts and termed a *bricolage* (Levi-Strauss refers to *bricolage* as drawing on materials at hand to create new ensembles: see

Levi-Strauss 1968). In this context, this occurs when a composite figure is created out of material cleverly drawn from different analytic cases and combined with fictional narrative. This ensures that names, places, situations and individuals cannot be identified, while at the same time the analytic expertise in collecting 'material fragments' and re-narrating them ensures the integrity and clinical validity of the individual case study.

Part I

The Framework
Neuroscience and Interdisciplinary Connections

1

Introducing Interdisciplinary Connections

Interdisciplinary Connections

Here I signpost interdisciplinary links. The more detailed clarification and explanation of concepts and themes will become clearer later on. The exploration of interdisciplinary connections will, hopefully, be of interest to the interdisciplinary fields relating to neuroscience, philosophy and cultural studies, but I shall aim to contribute specifically to the fields of psychosocial studies and relational psychoanalysis.

While making various disciplinary connections, it is impossible to do justice to each specialist field; being a Jack(y) of all trades and master of few makes it difficult to please each specialization. One's strength, it is hoped, is to be found in the *links* made *between* disciplines and in the opening up of the borders and the blurring of boundaries where possible.

It may at first appear odd to make links between such apparently different disciplines as philosophy, neuroscience, psychoanalysis and social and cultural studies, yet I would argue this is not the case. A relationship between the disciplines and their view of the body can be established, though this does not imply that the different approaches are always readily compatible. The aim of this book is to weave these distinctive fields into a creative exchange with one another in order to stimulate further debate and developments. It does not set out to claim definitive answers.

Philosophy is both a study of ontology (an understanding of the being of things) and a way of unpacking founding axioms. Philosophical investigation can be carried out on any discipline in order to identify and expose its founding assumptions.

Between Skins: The Body in Psychoanalysis – Contemporary Developments,
First Edition. Nicola Diamond.
© 2013 John Wiley & Sons, Ltd. Published 2013 by John Wiley & Sons, Ltd.

Definitions of the body are frequently based on presuppositions that derive from philosophy and can be exposed as such. Mind/body divides have a basis in metaphysical thinking and such philosophical notions can be found in neuroscience in spite of scientific claims to the contrary. Likewise psychoanalysis and the social sciences can be influenced by dualistic divisions.

Dualism has dominated Western models of mind and body, and these models need to be challenged if a view of the body free of the dualist impasse is to be advanced. I shall look at the residual dualism in psychoanalysis. The main term to be introduced in Parts II and III is *propping*. This is a term coined by the French psychoanalyst Jean Laplanche and derived from the German word used by Freud, *Anlehnung*. Put simply, propping describes how the sexual drive and the more complex psychical representation of the body initially emerge out of the biological body processes, at first by leaning and finding support in, and then by deviating from, them. This results in a sexual drive 'proper' which is more closely linked to psychical/'mental' forms of representing the body. I explore how the term 'propping', despite being used as a border term to link body and psyche, does not in fact overcome dualism but resurrects the undissolvable divide.

The term 'propping' is important, as it also impacts on other important formulations, for example the work of the French psychoanalyst Didier Anzieu, who accounts for the emergence of the skin ego. Part III will be devoted to a discussion of his work and the skin envelope. The popularity of the propping concept as way of resolving the body/mind problem spread to social, cultural and film studies, so critical discussion of this term has relevance for these fields as well. I shall try to show up how dualism is a problem and how it can be worked through from within psychoanalytic thinking, drawing on interdisciplinary developments to support my argument.

In providing a preliminary overview of the context for writing the book, I have already introduced terms that may be unfamiliar and not yet adequately explicated. These are terms that describe interpersonal reality, like 'intersubjectivity' and 'intercorporeality'. Later I shall also refer to the 'mirror neurons'. These specialized neurons, it is claimed, provide a neurobiological basis for intercorporeality. I ask readers to bear with me: these concepts in their complexity will be explained as the argument unfolds.

For now suffice it to say that all such terms describe how the body, and even the biological processes, are bound to others. Mirroring and observing the actions of others is the way we learn about our own bodies. Furthermore it is through the other that biological processes and affective bodily experiences become patterned and structured. I explore how the interpersonal and social field is primary and profoundly influences the biological processes.

What is identified in this book is the emergent relational ontology regarding the body that cuts across the apparent disparate disciplines of philosophy, neuroscience, psychoanalysis and psychosocial and cultural studies. I have referred to this interdisciplinary development as a paradigmatic shift, a Copernican turn for these disciplines, that has resulted in a move away from the view of a physical body cut off from the psyche and the world towards that of a bio-psychosocial body.

There is the twentieth-century turn that brought about the paradigmatic shift described above, which philosophical developments made possible. As early as 1917 the German philosopher Edmund Husserl identified *intersubjectivity*. This is taken up by the philosopher Martin Heidegger, whose book *Being and Time* (1927; Heidegger 1962) examines the interpersonal field and intersubjective being. Maurice Merleau-Ponty developed an understanding of bodily being as profoundly bound up with others, referring to intercorporeality in 'the child's relations with others' (1951; Merleau-Ponty 1964).

Since then Anglo-American and European researchers in developmental and cognitive psychology, psychoanalysts and neuroscientists have described and expanded upon relational models of the body. These different fields (including the philosophical) are in fact all connected in that they share the relational paradigmatic shift regarding the body.

In developmental psychology Colwyn Trevarthen (1978, 1979) is well known for importing the term 'intersubjectivity' from phenomenology and relating it to the early non-verbal bodily relation between infant and caretaker. Meltzoff and Moore (1977) refer to intercorporeal gestural mirroring in empirical research on infant–adult interaction.

Merleau-Ponty's observation of intercorporeality has profoundly influenced neuroscientists, the most well known being the Italian neuroscientists Rizzolatti, Gallese and Iacoboni, and led to the discovery of the mirror neurons (Rizzolatti *et al.* 1996; Gallese *et al.* 2004; Iacoboni 2005). It is claimed that the neurobiological basis of intercorporeal being is to be found in the functioning of the mirror neuron.

In French psychoanalysis Jacques Lacan (1977b) had already proposed the mirror phase in 1936 (published in English 1966), and Merleau-Ponty, who was sympathetic to psychoanalysis, took up Lacan and described how intercorporeal being is the basis for the body image (in French, 1951; Merleau-Ponty 1964). Later, from different traditions in psychoanalysis Anglo-Americans Atwood and Stolorow (1984) related intersubjectivity to the analytic relationship, and Schore (1994) linked neuroscience and attachment to explore the biological relational basis in the early attachment relationship. In British attachment theory and Anglo-American relational psychoanalysis, a focus on intercorporeal and intersubjective approaches has flourished.

Intercorporeal and relational models have likewise influenced psychosocial and cultural studies, notably through the work of Massumi (2002) and the rise of the 'affective turn', which, arguably, has brought affectivity and the body into the limelight of social analysis.

Between Skins charts the move from dualistic thinking and the earlier psychoanalytic theories of propping to an emerging multidisciplinary and relational model of the body. The connections sought between the different disciplines is in no way spurious, for there are shared philosophical problems and revolutionary shifts that lie at the foundations of the different disciplines.

The problem is that there has been uneven development: the old dualistic models keep returning and the radical implications of the paradigmatic shifts have not been sufficiently understood. My purpose here is to show how links can be legitimately made between the disciplines to reveal a more viable body model.

Finally in such a context, where the body is not an island but tied to a relational field, what also needs to be considered is the relation between the body and language. This was referred to early on as biosemiotics and in later thinking as non-verbal and bodily forms of social communication.

Philosophical Concerns in This Enquiry

This work will address the ontological presuppositions that exist in the models of the body which are examined. It is worth looking at philosophical assumptions that underlie basic axioms, for when a set of suppositions are accepted unquestioningly they are taken for granted as givens, as mere assertions. Investigating the beliefs that lie at the basis of a paradigm enables us to reflect and evaluate their status.

In *Being and Time* Heidegger (1962) points out that regional ontology, whether in the life sciences or the humanities, makes assumptions about the nature of the 'Being' under study. There are assumptions in science about the 'Being' of biology, as there are assumptions in psychoanalysis as to the 'Being' of the psyche. Heidegger notes how fundamental ontology which raises the general question of what 'Being' is underlies every regional ontology. Therefore an investigation of the very question what Being is has some relevance to every discipline.

As part of the journey ahead I deal with the fact that, despite revolutionary shifts, the mind/body and body/world splits persist as a residual dualism. This is an interdisciplinary problem, but I shall address this particularly in psychoanalytic models of the body. One of my main tasks will be to work through the impasses set up in these dualistic models. I hope to add something to the debates that still rage, but this book does not set out to be an exhaustive study or to resolve the issues. It will, however, raise core concerns.

In my entry on 'Biology' in *Feminism and Psychoanalysis: A Critical Dictionary* I wrote:

> Since the eighteenth century, biology has referred to the scientific study of organic life, the logos founding the law of nature. Biology can either be an

open-ended scientific discipline, the 'study of life', or it can refer to a fixed and determined biological order. From its inception, psychoanalysis has made reference to the biological sciences. As a physician and neurologist, Freud was familiar with the natural and physical sciences of his day, and particular influences like Darwinism, and the physicality school of Brücke, Bois-Raymond, Helmholtz and others are well documented . There is a tension between the Freud who is in search of a biological bedrock and the Freud who develops a field of psychoanalytic enquiry. (Diamond 1992: 22)

One of the themes of this book is that if biology is understood as chiefly 'logos founding the law of nature', in other words as holdfast biological bedrock, the consequences are that biology remains fixed and determinate, a law entire unto itself. Such a figure of biology shows itself as not malleable to change. This will be contrasted with another model of biology, more open from the first, where it has insufficiencies from the beginning and is dependent on a relationship between two or more person-bodies where organism and environment are interdependent (Uexküll 1926).

The more open model, I suggest, allows a link between biology and semiotics and more complex language-based systems. Once the full implications of the more radical and open biological model are taken on board, the dualistic view is called into question and the biological bedrock model is fundamentally rewritten and reworked at its very foundations.

My aim is to foreground how the somatic terrain is much more open than has previously been understood, how somatic capacities can be altered by interaction with the fields of others and how this affects the development of bodily processes, their form and mode of expression. I suggest that the bodily symptom that is presented at the clinic and in everyday life in fact reveals a developmental interpersonal and social history. Reference to the 'psychosomatic condition' can be replaced by the term 'sociosomatic symptom'.

The Irreducible Organic Component and How It Figures for Us

Despite the inevitable interpenetration of the biological and social domains, there is always the 'facticity' (Heidegger) of the body: death is imminent, bodily processes can break down as pathological cell and tissue processes manifest themselves as cancer, for example, and so on. Merleau-Ponty referred to the irreducibility of the body that sets limits to existence that no one can ultimately control.

So despite the focus on somatic aperture, on biological plasticity and on the ramifications of interdisciplinary developments that open the body onto a relational field, there is always an aspect of the body that is irreducibly organic and cannot ultimately escape death. This aspect is inevitable, leaving the human being and all living beings ultimately helpless and entirely vulnerable.

One of the possible meanings of the Lacanian 'real' is an aspect of the body that resists any form of comprehension, is fundamentally irreducible and ungraspable. Whereas I refer to the body that defies processing control or meaning and can never be tamed, to unbound body states that can be unleashed and can roam wild. These are associated with body phantasmagoria, the most macabre and estranged body experiences, reflecting the extremes of alterity, where any stabilized body identity is lost. Alexandra Lemma (2010) points out that the unbounded grotesque body is well explored in the phantasmagoria of the flesh in David Cronenberg's films.

Neuroscience: One of the Important Bed-Mates

In the flourishing field known as neuropsychoanalysis, headed by key thinkers and researchers like Mark Solms and involving many important neuroscientists and psychoanalysts, there are both tensions and differences in perspective as well as the attempt to produce a coherent and integrated model. One tension is the discrepancy between a one-person body and two-person body model and in this context between taking the individual organism as the primary unit of analysis, in contrast to the focus on what goes on between organisms. In the first model the biological determinants and psychic dynamics 'internal' to the organism take precedence, while in the second model intercorporeal relations play a central role and the impact of environmental influence is highlighted. It is the latter model that I favour and foreground in this book.

In addressing psychoanalysis and neuroscience I do not take neuroscience as the master discourse and I do not limit the analysis to neurobiological descriptions of dynamic brain processes. Instead I focus on a genuine interdisciplinary approach to psychoanalysis, drawing on social science and philosophy as well as neuroscientific findings. I also recognize the fact that psychoanalysis in its richness and complexity can at times inform neuroscience, and not only vice versa.

I will try and avoid neuroscientific reductionism which can lead to the following problems: (1) describing physiological, neurological and anatomical processes and features in depth as a way of explaining phenomena: as a method on its own, this does not explain the psychobiological experience, its phenomenology and meaning; it does not capture bodily perception and certainly none of its complexity; (2) the body is regarded too much as a reactive system to stimuli and hence descriptions of brain processes can be too mechanistic.

I reiterate the importance of exploring how meaning can play an active role in bodily experience and process. The broader role of semiotics and

language (understood in a broad sense and not reducible to linguistic phenomena) in body processes will be a key area in my exploration. It is not
enough to resort to what I consider reifications of 'psyche' or 'mind' as
meaning creators. This does not adequately take into account the way the
social field and the world of others influence meaning-making.

In exploring interdisciplinary connections between neuroscience and
psychoanalytic, social and philosophical thinking, I acknowledge the controversy as to the viability of such a project. With the recent upsurge of
popularity in neuroscience within psychoanalysis and in areas of the
social sciences there has been scepticism as to the scientific status of such
applied neuroscience and questions regarding its usefulness in social and
psychoanalytic studies.

In response to such concerns, I have tried to avoid the usual pitfalls, challenging neuroscience as master discourse, and any reductionism, while
opting for a genuine interdisciplinary enquiry. However, beyond this, hypothetical models are part of any scientific exploration and evidence in the
natural sciences is always being debated. The use of neuroscience in interdisciplinary research and by those who are not neuroscientists is evidently on
more rocky ground, and scientific claims for evidence can be poorly made
and substantiated.

The claims put forward in this book are suggestive. The neurological–
social relations proposed are made to get the creative connections flowing
further, to encourage debate, criticism and further research by specialists in
the field(s). In this book the line between an imaginary and actual neurology
is not clear-cut, but what is clear is the importance placed on the biosocial
relation for understanding life and how it is lived.

Challenging a Top-Down Approach

In neuroscience the brain is central but always inextricably bound to body
processes. As Jaak Panksepp (1998) implies, the brain is not suspended in a
vat but exists in a body and a world. Despite the fact that in neuroscience
there can be a tendency to localize brain functions, it is, of course, understood
that in actuality these can be considered only in the context of processes
across the brain and in complex brain–body dynamic relations.

In terms of brain functions, thinking has been related to synaptic links and
the neural connections made. The cortical brain is described as connected to
'higher' social cognitive functioning but these processes cannot be regarded
apart from the so-called subcortical brain where basic emotions are said to
be located and are directly linked to affective bodily states, routed in body
processes. These affective and bodily states have been aligned to the 'instincts'.

'Instincts' as a term relates to the translation of Freud and the resulting
Anglo-American readings of Freud. Neuroscientists such as Jaak Panksepp

(1998) have discovered a number of neural emotive-motivational systems and this challenges Freud's more limited dual classification of the life and death drive. In respect to brain development the subcortical brain processes related to primary motivational systems are developed in an interactive nurturing context and later become 'integrated' into higher cortical processes.

This book challenges an over-mentalist approach: 'brain' is not an equivalent for 'mind'. In neuroscience the reification of the brain takes place when a top-down brain approach is advocated, a point of view that I question and do not subscribed to. As I have implied, the localization of brain functions has to be viewed in the context of brain–body processes. There are complex bidirectional loops involving sensory information from the environment, influences from sensory muscular and neural body processes, and interactions within complex brain dynamics.

Antonio Damasio and Gerald Edelman, both eminent neurobiologists, offer convincing arguments for the dependence of the brain on the body (Edelman 1992; Damasio 2000). Memory is not simply localized in the brain but exists throughout brain–body systems in interaction with the environment.

To counter the fallacy of a top-down approach: recent explorations into major organs such as the heart and the stomach have identified neural cells that are likened to brain cells in the heart and along the entire lining of the gut (Lacey and Lacey 1978; Gershon 1999; Lorimer 2001; McCraty 2004). Memory function and emotion have been related to the heart and the stimulation of hormonal changes in the body, while enzyme secretions generated by the stomach send messages to the brain concerning hunger, stimulations of hunger which may have no relation to the actual biological need to eat.

In highly developed robotics the patterning of sensorimotor coordination is possible only if memory systems are distributed throughout the 'organism' which gives insight into the human body situation (Pfeifer and Bongard 2007; Pfeifer and Hoffman 2010).

The Brain–Body Map

The figure representing the layout of the body in relation to the sensorimotor cortex of the brain is typically caricatured as a man with huge hands, lips and tongue. This is known as the homunculus (Figure 1.1). The brain's sensorimotor cortex strip is where the body map is said to lie (Figure 1.2). In the homunculus the exaggerated body parts reflect the concentration of sensory nerve endings, which lead to heightened sensitivity, in certain parts of the body. This brain map is routed through bodily processes and is precisely a brain–body map. For the brain–body map receives sensory and

Figure 1.1 Brain–body map, or sensory homunculus. Photo © Natural History Museum, London.

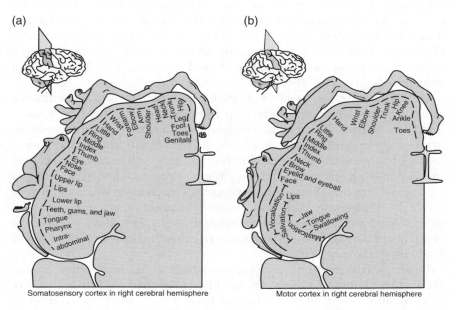

Figure 1.2 Brain–body map showing (a) somatosensory cortex in right cerebral hemisphere; (b) motor cortex in right cerebral hemisphere.

motor-neural information from the body and is also influenced by the way the body is mirrored and imaged.

The sensorimotor cortex strip is one of the most interesting areas of the brain related to the representation of the body. The brain–body map is the neurobiological correlate of Freud's body ego (Freud 1974 [1923]; Damasio 2000) which, I argue, is linked to the sensory body and is a construct. Figure 1.1 shows a body already influenced by representation. That it is represented as a man is, of course, related to the influence of social representations of the body; gender comes into the picture as the representation of the male body continues to enjoy hegemony in the way it is often used to stand for human-kind, both male and female. The enlargement of the hands and lips relates to these being very sensitive areas; however, the genitals could arguably take up more representational space. Also, alterations can be brought about in the brain–body map, as there is neural plasticity (a fact which I shall make much of in this book).

How the body is stimulated and the use of body part(s) can alter sensitivity. There is a potential for any part of the body to become 'invested' and an exaggerated focus of attention a point Freud makes clearly. Developmental experiences can alter sensitivity in areas of the body, and this arguably has an effect in bringing about subtle changes in the brain–body map.

Although there is some basis in argument for a genetic brain map (Melzack 1999), the map is not determined by a genetic body map alone: there is significant neuroplasticity, as recent neuroscientific research has discovered (Ramachandran and Blakeslee 1999; Ramachandran and Rogers-Ramachandran 2000; see Part III). Price (2006) argues that congenital amputees are profoundly influenced by the image of the body derived from others, and proposes a developmental model where the body image derived from others plays a key role in the formation of the body map.

How the body is used, such as in motility and comportment, can influence the body map. The brain–body map is 'normally' influenced by sensory input derived from the interaction between body and environment. However, in cases where there is a loss of a limb, and therefore fresh sensory input is lacking, treatment using artificial limb and trickery with mirrors can activate the action–body memory and the mirror neurons, thereby creating a 'corrective' corporeal image–sensory feedback mechanism which can reduce lower limb phantom pain and thus alter sensory perception of pain (Ramachandran and Rogers-Ramachandran 2000). This illustrates how the visual image derived from the environment can influence the construction of the brain–body map.

Finally, a comment on the brain–body map: it has been referred to in the singular, but in fact there can be a number of them, or rather a variety of configurations in play. As the question of body image in relation to the body map is addressed, this possibility of different and changing body images becomes apparent. The suggestion is that versions of the body influence brain–body mapping.

I shall consider the way the body is mirrored by the external environment, including how others play a role in this and in the development of the body image throughout the life span and the effects this has on the map. The brain–body map is not fixed. It can alter and can itself generate change. This is the effect of neural plasticity: the brain-body map(s) is not a static phenomenon.

Psychoanalysis: The Brain–Body Map and Body Image

I am interested in looking at the relationship between the neuroscientific exploration of the brain–body map and body image in the light of psychoanalytic insights regarding body image. As early as 1923 Freud noted that the neurobiological correlate of the body ego is located in the 'cortical homunculus' which lies across the sensorimotor cortex (see Figure 1.2 and Part III):

> The ego is first and foremost a bodily ego; it is not merely a surface entity, but is itself the projection of a surface. If we wish to find an anatomical analogy for it we can best identify it with the 'cortical homunculus' of the anatomists, which stands on its head in the cortex, sticks up its heels, faces backwards and as we know, has its speech-area on the left hand side. (Freud 1974 [1923]: 16)

Neurobiological findings do suggest that this body-image 'ego' can be influenced by the mirror image and the mirror neurons imply that that this body-action image is based on the observation of others. The claim that mirror neurons are the neurobiological basis for an intercorporeal process links up with Merleau-Ponty's observation of the mirror image derived from others and Lacan's description of the mirror phase. I thus identify interdisciplinary connections for an understanding of the interpersonal and social formation of body image, and suggest a possible relation with brain–body mapping, a point that will be more adequately fleshed out and discussed in Part III.

Lacan's understanding of the idealized and constructed nature of the image helps explain how body representations may exaggerate, alter and morph into something else, making body image potentially dysmorphic and changeable in experience. From a neuroscience perspective Ramachandran and Blakeslee (1999) comment on the way neural plasticity permits rapid change to take place in brain–body mapping.

The psychiatrist and psychoanalyst Schilder's earlier contribution to an understanding of body image is invaluable. Schilder combined Carl

Wernicke's concept of the somatopsyche and Sir Henry Head's (1920) postural model of the body with Freud's (1974 [1923]) idea that the ego is primarily a body ego to arrive at his own formulation of the fundamental role of the body image. In *The Image and Appearance of the Human Body* (1950 [1935]) Schilder argues that body image can be related to sensorial body states and makes it clear that the body image cannot be reduced to a reified mental experience.

Schilder proposes a dynamic body image which is not fixed and has plasticity. Furthermore the body image is not static but for Schilder exists in lived motility, and is informed by kinaesthetic, visceral and other sensorimotor messages from the body. I embrace this aspect of Schilder's approach: his body image is not an abstract phenomenon in the realm of pure ideation; on the contrary, it is living and sentient, relating to motility and sensory states. Schilder's body image, like the brain–body map, is a multisensory construct.

Body Image versus Body Schema

Whereas Schilder relates the body image to body schema and therefore does not make an absolute distinction between image and motility, Gallagher and Cole (1998 [1995]) have argued for clarity in definition, noting the confusion between Schilder's body image and Head's postural schema. They wish to separate out body image from (postural) body schema. Although Gallagher (1986) has argued that a clear conceptual distinction between body image and body schema is helpful in working out functional differences, he also emphasizes that the conceptual distinction should not imply that at the behavioural level image and schema are unconnected or that they do not sometimes affect one another.

One of the key issues for Gallagher and Cole is that the body schema maps the body for motility and functions automatically, without our awareness, sub-personally and non-consciously governing our posture and movement, whereas they wish to designate body image as perceptual, intentional and conscious. In other words, body schema is the basis of movement as such and body image the basis of subjective experience. In Gallagher and Cole's formula, body schema has consistency in being basic to ongoing functional motility and the body image can perceptually alter according to 'subjective' state.

Why I Do Not Adopt Gallagher and Cole's Terminology

Although Gallagher and Cole's work is respected, there are various reasons why I shall employ another frame of reference and different terms. I would argue that complexity sets in when we consider a virtual geography that can alter and vary, and is not separable from motility. The many examples of clinical symptoms discussed throughout this book testify to the inseparability of lived body states.

Further, Gallagher and Cole's thinking is situated in a cognitive framework, and so clear-cut definitions of terms introduce complications when the framework adopted is not that of cognitive psychology. In contrast to Gallagher and Cole's view, when body image is approached from a psychoanalytic perspective it is not mainly conscious or subjective. In Freud body image is unconscious as well as having a conscious aspect. Merleau-Ponty refers to the pre-reflective, and in this context the sense of body 'self' resides neither in a third-person nor a first-person perspective but can exist in an ambiguous position between embodied subject and other.

My approach is sympathetic to both Freud, who argues that body image can also be outside conscious awareness, and Merleau-Ponty, who believes that body image is not owned in a simple way by a unified 'I' but is predicated on the perspective of the other. A definition of body image that derives from and is endorsed by contemporary perspectives in psychoanalysis, phenomenological philosophy and neuroscience describes how body image(s) is (are) fundamentally influenced by others.

Body image is derived from the other (Lacan 1977a [1936]) and the space of the field of the Other,[1] mirrored from 'outside', as inevitably bound to otherness. Lacan refers to the Other as a position no actual person can occupy. I use the term here to emphasize how the body is always predicated on an otherness which it cannot appropriate as owned and to indicate how the body is subjected to an irreducible exteriority that is always there: there is always a look coming from the outside field which cannot be eradicated. Because I adopt a two-person and multi-person approach, subjectivity is never truly autonomous; intersubjectivity and intercorporeality are always in play. I shall argue that the third comes first, in the sense that otherness from the first defines the body; the perspective of the first person-body depends on and derives from a third-person perspective.

The work of Lacan and the use of the mirror metaphor can be seen as supporting the pictorial view of the body image, as can later findings regarding mirror neurons. Although the visual basis is coterminous with motor-neuron simulation in mirror neuron activity, Gallese, as we shall see, also relates tactility to mirror neuron simulation.

Furthermore, in regard to psychoanalytic understanding I shall also argue that there are grounds for relating the visual body image to touch and tactility, which give rise to what Benthien (2002) refers to as the primacy of the 'sensation ego'. It will be made clear what Benthien means and I shall consider the interpersonal basis of the experience of body sensations.

In lived body terms, there is evidently a complex relationship between body representation and sensory and motor effects. Neuroscientific work on phantom limb and related phenomena has noted how changes in body representation produced in the brain–body map can have a profound influence on sensory body states. I suggest that alterations in brain–body representations can have an effect on motor skills and body movements.

I define body image uniquely and am interested in the relation between body image and body comportment, the more so given that I focus on how body representation should not be reified and conceived as an ideational construct alone. I want to understand how a body construct is not only visual but can also be kinaesthetic and, depending on the circumstances, can relate to body movement as well as sensation.

In conclusion, I respect Gallagher and Cole's terms, but distinguish my enquiry from theirs. Hence I define my concepts differently. I wish to retain the interrelationship between body perception and body action. I shall refer to the neuroscience-based sensorimotor cortex brain–body map, with the proviso of its greater complexity and its links to the psychoanalytic body ego. The brain–body map as I use it takes on board the relationship between the sensorimotor cortex strip as the homunculus gestalt with its links to the body ego/image phenomenon. In the sensorimotor cortex the visual image of the body can involve kinaesthetic changes and has links to the action body.

In my definition, the body ego cannot be reduced to a mental abstraction (which, it is evident, occurs in some of the psychoanalytic literature). By drawing on Schilder's observations of body image but linking this to the body ego and in turn relating the body ego to the sensorimotor cortex strip, it is possible to consider multisensory input – involving not only visual mirroring but also tactility, taste and the olfactory and thermal sense. It is also interesting to speculate on the possible relationship between certain alterations in the brain–body map and shifts that take place in body ego phenomena.

Working Towards a Brain–Body Mapping

When we deal with neuroscience and human complexity some degree of imaginary geography is always at work in the creation of the brain–body maps. The 'ego-body-centric' location is necessarily contentious (Kinsbourne 1998), as what is being dealt with is a complex of interacting brain processes and brain–body dynamics, and then there are the phenomenological descriptions of experience. The truth is the exact relationship between experiential phenomena and neurobiological process is never self-evident.

Nevertheless, in respect to the general functioning of the brain–body map, neuroscientists, as noted, have related this map to alterations in sensory and motor states. The sensorimotor strip(s) can generate sensory and motor experience and is wired up to sensory and motor neural pathways which are connected to designated areas of the body. Stimulus is both fed back to the sensorimotor cortex and generated by it. *I am interested in the way*

*interpersonal and social 'messages' influence the body feedback and
generative brain–body map.*

In considering the virtual generative brain–body map terms like
'representation' are used. In neuroscience 'representation' requires more
conceptual discussion and elaboration. As yet neuroscience does not benefit
from the complex understanding and nuanced sense that such a term has in
psychoanalytic and philosophical debates.

However, as already noted, psychoanalysis suggests that a body image can
be reduced to an abstracted, pure idea status, albeit complex, relating to
memory, fantasy and the like. I think Merleau-Ponty can help challenge this
tendency to render the image as entirely abstract, rejecting the reified notion
of 'idea' implied by traditional debates on representation that presupposed
'idealism' (he likewise rejected the inverse claims of a mechanical material-
ism). With Merleau-Ponty a representation cannot be separated from lived
body states and, of course, a relational field.

Avoiding Mentalist Reduction

When exploring psychoanalysis I shall note that the focus is on the body as
represented in image and fantasy. What will be identified as a key problem
is the way these representations are understood to exist in the psyche/mind,
whereby a split is created between the body as soma in the material world
and the mind as the realm of ideation and symbol.

Could such an argument have a case if we translate mind to brain? Would
it be true to say that the body as image/representation exists in the brain
which can be likened to mind? *Between Skins* argues against this conclusion.
(1) By referring to the brain we are in the world of physicality and the body
and not in a dualist terrain of a disembodied psyche/mind. (2) The brain exists
in the body. The sensorimotor cortex strip is complexly linked to different
parts of the brain and sensorineural body processes/systems. (3) As indicated,
all this takes place in relation to the world, to the social field of others and to
the field of sensori-semiotic communications and construction.

Moving Towards a Brain–Body–Ego Relational
Perspective: An Imaginary Lived Geography

In referring to psychoanalysis and developing the understanding therein, I shall
address the formation of the body-skin ego phenomena and the way the gestalt
configuration which is construed in the first six months of life can be altered
developmentally depending on the type of relations with others (including
attachment styles). Depending on the quality of mirroring and multisensory
communication from others, the gestalt effect, it will be suggested, varies.

In perturbed relations a more chaotic and fragmented body ego can become more dominant and fundamentally disruptive, undercutting any idealized gestalt effect and the establishment of any relative stability in body gestalt. It is suggested that alterations in the body gestalt can affect the brain–body map which can not only bring about changes in sensory states but do so in motility as well, in so far as it is possible that body movement can be affected by disturbances in the body gestalt. This body gestalt is in turn affected by relational and emotional trauma and/or developmental failures/deficits.

My conjecture is that when the gestalt idealization is profoundly disrupted throughout development, or by later trauma or even injury, bodily being is necessarily affected. This impacts not only the body ego and image but also sensory body states, including the very integration of sensory and even expressive movement involving such areas as motor coordination, motility, posture, balance and style of comportment. There will be clinical examples and discussion of such phenomena throughout this book (see Part III).

And Finally

One of the views put forward is that compartmentalized rigid thinking is not helpful or appropriate when examining the brain–body–world relationship. It is important not to confuse conceptual distinctions for the purposes of clarification with the actuality of lived corporeal complexity.

In the chapters that follow I shall explore how relations with others, how we live in and use our bodies, semiotic and social ways of constructing the body through sensory communications (through gesture, touch and social imaging) all influence bodily experience. I shall develop a semiotic understanding of bodily processes and sensory states.

Note

1   I do not use strictly a Lacanian definition of the Other (reference will be made to his schema later). The point I am making here is that others are not defined by likeness as based in the self-same; others affect and effect us because they are unfamiliar, different, there being no self-referential point in this schema. I mean by 'other' the way the world of others retains otherness and the way the body of the actual other conveys something unknown and unfamiliar. The body of the other also expresses social forms of significance that are greater than the individual and that powerfully subject every actual body to a social will and to meanings that are not under the individual's control.

2
Nurture/Nature

In this chapter I shall briefly outline the shift to a relational body ontology – the relation of organism to environment and of biology to interpersonal relations, the move towards intersubjectivity and intercorporeality, the emergence of intercorporeality in the context of developmental psychology, with philosophical underpinnings. This approach will be returned to and further developed in later chapters.

The Complex Interdependence of Organism and Environment

A temporal dimension is necessarily part of the process when development is acknowledged as endemic to organism and environment interaction. When do interpersonal, environmental and cultural influences begin? Can we get to a pure nature that is said to exist prior to experience? This is a chicken and egg question which is not helpful in so far as it arrests time into a before and after. It also creates a separation between biology and experience as if they could be independent of one another. Likewise a false a priori split is created between biology and cultural inscription. 'Femininity', for example, does not function as a cultural stamp which is superimposed or added at a later date, but rather is somatically lived, from belching to 'farting', to forms of appetite, to ways of talking, walking, dancing and so on (see also Young 1990).

When biology interacts with environment, change and transformation take place. In actual life there is the passing of time and biology is experience-dependent. Biology and experience become interwoven and are

Between Skins: The Body in Psychoanalysis – Contemporary Developments,
First Edition. Nicola Diamond.
© 2013 John Wiley & Sons, Ltd. Published 2013 by John Wiley & Sons, Ltd.

fundamentally inseparable. Biology and experience cannot be extrapolated from one another in lived time, except for analytical purposes. Theoretical distinctions can be made for clarity of argument but they must not be confused with lived situations. Such analytic tools taken too literally create oversimplification and distortion.

Environmental and interactional experience is already underway, within the very first weeks of life. As soon as the baby is in the world, experience is shaping nature, and there are many biological processes which are dependent on environmental experience and intervention. Furthermore, certain qualitative types of interchange are required for development to take place. In fact, there is already interaction in the womb (see Piontelli 2002). Genetic and environmental interaction occurs where temporal sequencing is complex. Some genes are activated after birth with experience, and dependent on quality of affective interaction.

There is also the case of intergenerational transmission of affective biological states where trauma and disturbance in attachment can play a key role (Fraiberg *et al.* 1975). The power of intergenerational transmission in families and across generations is based on the way unprocessed affect (unrevised trauma) can result in non-verbal behavioural/mood states picked up by the infant of the following generation, and this can result in psychobiological deregulation and compulsion to repeat in action and body-based behaviour.

When neuroscientists study brain activity they are most commonly dealing with subjects who have been exposed to some form of life experience. This is certainly the case with human subjects and often with animals. The raw biological data have in these contexts already undergone a developmental period.

In contemporary neuroscience importance is placed on the subcortical brain (popularly known as the primitive brain) where the 'basic' biological urges, the so-called instincts and primary emotions, are generated. However, these 'primitive' processes necessarily undergo development in the context of interactional experiences and environmental influences throughout the life cycle, resulting in their development and integration into the 'higher' cortical brain functions, where more complex symbolizing, language and culture play a key role.

From this perspective, emotions develop and become integrated with greater reflective, social and symbolic capacities in the cortex of the brain. The degree of integration of the reflective capacities with affective states will depend on the quality of interaction experienced in early development and in later experience. However, no bio-affective states remain pure and unmediated; the physical-affective states are formed in the nurturing process and in various ways, depending on context.

Allan Schore's (1994) recognizes the importance of right brain procedural memory in interaction with environment processing. This emotional right brain body development does the basic seminal groundwork and is required for what is to follow in higher cortical and left brain processing.

Bowlby, the psychiatrist and psychoanalyst with a special interest in the biological and evolutionary sciences and founder of attachment theory and research, was aware 'that there is potential in the healthy neonate to enter into an elemental form of social interaction' (Bowlby 1969: 7). Despite the tensions in his work between a one- and two-person-body approach, Freud noted as early as 1895 that a baby aiming to satisfy any biological need is dependent on a response from a caretaker, who provides what he calls 'a secondary function of the highest importance, that of communication' (Freud 1895: 315).

Bowlby (1969) emphasizes organism–environment interaction and considers the dichotomy between the innate and the acquired to be a false one. A biological trait, whether morphological, physical or behavioural, is a result of interaction with the environment. Some traits may become more stable, often due to evolutionary outcome; others are more unstable, malleable and modifiable in the context of cultural influences (Diamond 1998: 206).

However, even with more stable evolutionary traits, the environment defined more broadly can be seen to play a significant part. Evolutionary biologists refer to the natural environment and to genetic adaptations and modifications ensuring greater likelihood of the survival of species. However, our environment also includes the social environment and with humans there is great social complexity involving radical changes to survival needs in that environment. For example, the effects of urbanization, changing geography and environmental provisions have a profound effect on what is required for survival. We are not dealing with an unmediated natural environment but with a highly complex social one which contextualizes the natural environment and is inseparable from it. Evolution is in this sense socially inscribed and cannot be considered as an unfolding force of nature, as a law unto itself. The relation between evolution and social relations over extensive periods of time is an area insufficiently understood and worthy of further study.

In regard to physical illness and disease with known organic aetiology, the significance of experience in the early interpersonal environment is evident. René Spitz's studies of 'hospitalism' (1946) and Robertson's films (e.g. 1953) reveal the power of attachment and separation, showing that children who are deprived of love and affection are more susceptible to disease and have a higher mortality rate. Spitz looked at orphanages which provided for the child's basic material needs but no emotional love or continuity in affective care, while Robertson's studies showed the disastrous effects on a young child of early hospital separation. When the child was left to be looked after by hospital staff and the parents were not allowed to visit, the toddler would shift from fury to apathy, then despair and withdrawal. If the withdrawn state had continued it had the potential to develop into marasmus, a failing to thrive syndrome which also led to a lowering of immunological resistance to illness and disease. Lower immunological defence and higher mortality rates were found to be associated with emotional neglect and a lack of attachment love and care.

In adults, when a spouse dies and one is left in a state of attachment loss and suffers from unresolved mourning, the latter can develop susceptibility to disease and a reduced immune response, resulting in earlier onset of illness and death. The one who is left 'joins' their lost partner in death more quickly than might be expected.

Attachment, Developmental Psychology and Intercorporeality

Schore's work (1994, 2003a, 2003b), which explores the interaction between attachment and biological development, has blossomed in popularity, particularly in the field of psychotherapy. He observes how the development of neurons in the brain and the connections made are dependent on the early attachment relation and the intercorporeal brain–body relation between caretaker and baby; how affective communication occurs in the non-verbal affective exchange between the caretaker and baby and how this alters biological processes; how hormones, the nervous system, growth, homeostasis – in fact the affective bioregulation of somatic states are dependent on the early attachment relationship and indeed on relations throughout the life cycle.

Schore without a doubt embraces a two-person-body approach and offers an analysis starting from an interpersonal approach where findings on attachment on intersubjectivity as a bodily communication are fully acknowledged. There is no adherence to a binary in his model as brain, body and world are intertwined. He focuses on developing the idea that affect is psychobiological and is modulated and regulated in the dance between parent and baby. This is through touch, mirroring, sound and other sensory means of communication, before words have definite meaning. He observes how mother and baby alter each other's somatic states and the brain's neural development, the impact that the mother has on the developing infant and also how this process continues throughout life (see Figure 2.1). Intimate relations continue to have psychobiological effects which profoundly affect later development.

In exploring the early relationship Schore emphasizes the development of the right (emotional) brain and the early relationship. He also places importance on the eventual relational links and the established integration of the right and left hemispheres. He addresses the way autobiographical memory is linked to the experience of subjectivity, as does Damasio (2000). For Schore autobiographical memory is also linked to procedural emotional non-verbal memories of bodily self in relation to others. It is rooted not only in states of consciousness but also in unconscious memory, which gives rise

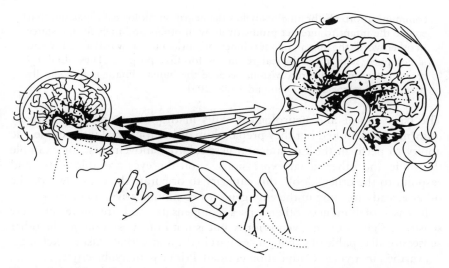

Figure 2.1   The affective-neural interaction between mother and baby. Adapted from C. Trevarthen (1993) The self born in intersubjectivity: the psychology of an infant communicating. In U. Neisser (ed.), *The Perceived Self: Ecological and Interpersonal Sources of Self-Knowledge*. New York: Cambridge University Press, pp. 121–173.

to the pre-reflective emotional body, or know-how. It is this level of embodied memory where change has to take place if the 'compulsion to repeat' is to be shifted. Schore offers an implicit critique on a 'mentalist' model which locates affective change in mental processing alone.

I embrace Schore's work and in particular his emphasis on the interdependence between the attachment relationship and affective biological processes. His explanations are based on the interaction of the bioneural processes in relations with others, and he describes in detail the bioneural processes and dynamics of brain functioning. In contrast, my main focus is not on in-depth descriptions of physiological, neurological processes as a way of explaining phenomena, but rather on the link between biology and semiotics in interpersonal experience and in this context how the world of others gets under our skin and inside our body. In my view, in-depth descriptions of neurobiological processes on their own do not tell us about the phenomenology of experience and the meaning of these affective biological states for the person of for other people.

Trevarthen supports the basis of Shore's biorelational model, noting that biology is orientated towards sociality:

Trevarthen and Aitken . . . document biological findings that the human infant is predisposed to relating to others, to intentionally seeking out contact and communication. The brain already has the neuro-physiological capacities that enable the infant to interact productively with others and their feeling states In other words the human infant is inherently orientated towards sociality and is equipped with physiological resources for that purpose. These findings recast the nature/nurture division, because the human infant is biologically predisposed to sociality. (Diamond 1998: 205)

The basic motor and neurological skills in the infant are still relatively unformed and limited but they prepare him or her for social intercourse, the ability to perform the fundamental gesticulatory movements, for example the smile and other facial expressions. Soon the eyes are able to fix and respond to the other's look, this capacity to orientate the eyes towards the other already forming in the emergence of communicative interaction.

In cases of blindness other senses 'compensate' and are more intensely sensitive. Sight is often given priority but is not in fact essential as the other senses are all capable of playing a key part in the non-verbal sensory exchange. Trevarthen in a video compilation entitled 'Primary Intersubjectivity', has an observation study depicting a mother singing to her baby who is lying down next to her but mother and baby are evidently not touching.[1] Instead the intonation of the mother's singing voice is reflected in the movements of the baby's arms. The baby's arm movements are exactly attuned to the mother's voice. The baby's arm movements, like those of a conductor, vibrate with the music and the pulse is shared.

In developmental psychology it was Trevarthen who coined the phrase 'primary intersubjectivity' (1979). He actively drew on phenomenology and cites Habermas (1979). However, it was the phenomenologist and philosopher of the body Maurice Merleau-Ponty (1964) who, after Husserl (1960) referred to intersubjectivity, directly linked it to lived bodily experience with others. Merleau-Ponty saw intersubjectivity as an embodied pairing, mirroring as well as mimicry, and he coined the term 'intercorporeality'.

Intercorporeality: The Philosophical Contribution, Developmental Psychology, Mirror Neurons

In 'The child's relations with others' (1964) Merleau-Ponty describes how the child finds his or her body in the other's body. The infant finds itself in the other's expressive actions via initially mimicking the adult's facial and bodily behaviour, whereby 'I live in the facial expressions of the other' (Merleau-Ponty 1964: 146). Merleau-Ponty is in this sense a proponent of the idea that the other comes first (hypothetically prior to and) as a condition for forming a relation to the 'self', which for Merleau-Ponty is always a bodily self.

Later developmental thinkers Meltzoff and Moore (1977) refer to an 'innate intercorporeality' and support Merleau-Ponty's claims, noting how 42 minutes after birth a baby can mimic the other sticking out the tongue, before it knows where its own tongue is located. In *Attachment and Intersubjectivity* we stated:

> In our approach, we have emphasized the importance of moving away from the position that begins from the 'I' and then tries to find out about the world of others. We noted how this position fails to discover the other, unable as it is to get out of an enclosed state instead we have proposed that it is the other that comes first and, as we shall see, the infant first takes the position of the other. As Merleau-Ponty would say … the infant at first lives and feels in the facial and bodily gestures of the other (1962: 46). (Diamond and Marrone 2003: 133)

This moves away from the one-person body primary position to the relational two-/multiperson intersubjective, corporeal perspective as the starting point. Impressively, Gallese, a key figure in the neuroscience research of mirror neurons, announced at the Twelfth Neuropsychoanalysis Congress in Berlin in 2011 that the other comes first and that the sense of bodily self derives after that fact.[2]

Merleau-Ponty claims in 'The child's relations with others' that 'in perceiving the other, my body and his are coupled, resulting in a sort of action that pairs them' (1964: 118). This is confirmed and developed by the neuroscientific study of the mirror neuron system. The neuroscientists Marco Iacoboni and Dapretto (2006) and Rizzolatti *et al.* (1996) put forward the mirror neurons as the neurological basis of intercorporeality. Mirror neurons within a monkey's premotor area F5 fire not only when the monkey performs a certain class of action but also when it observes another monkey or the experimenter perform a similar action (Rizzolatti *et al.* 1996).

The mirror neurons in the brain, in the parietal motor circuits, produce a neural matching mechanism whereby the observer of another's actions is simulated in the motor-neural pattern and the claim is that the affect accompanying the action is simultaneously evoked. The other's actions are mapped in neuron activity. Our neural systems are in contact with the other and their actions resonate in us (see Diamond and Marrone 2003: 134–135). Gallese's later research focuses on touch and the way the touch of another simultaneously is motoneuronally mapped (Gallese *et al.* 2004). This can be related to Freud's understanding of identification. Mirror neurons, as specialized neurons, are not exclusive to brain activity but the research is still developing.

Intercorporeality implies and presupposes a different understanding of space. Heidegger (1962) describes the way Euclidean geometry is a dominant paradigm, and in this model physical space has discrete entities with measurable space between them. A one-person-body paradigm adopts such an assumption: the person-body is located in space as a discrete body, another person-body is likewise located and there is a measurable distance between them. The idea of a discrete organism entirely apart from another organism and environment is based on the same principle. In psychoanalytic accounts of projection and counter-transference a notion of intersubjectivity is required. Without this we would be left with an unviable model where there would exist two discrete bodies in space and the affects from one to the other would have to mysteriously jump over an unbridgeable gulf.

In *Being and Time* Heidegger (1962) states that human beings do not live together like water in a glass, for water inside a glass does not 'inhabit' the glass, as water and the glass exist as *partes extra partes*. The water is absolutely inside the glass and the glass is absolutely outside. In contrast to person-bodies, they affect one another, they are in active, sentient relation; a chair leaning against a wall is not the same as when two bodies touch one another. Heidegger says that we dwell in one another, inhabit one another affectively.

Merleau-Ponty draws out how the body is situated (not located) in a relational affective space, how we dwell in one another bodily. Neuroscientists like Gallese draw directly on Merleau-Ponty to address the neurobiological basis of intercorporeality. Likewise Schore's work in attachment and neuroscience explores the intercorporeal affective biological relation between baby and other and the developmental consequences this has for becoming a body. This book will attempt to advance an understanding of biolife as intercorporeal dwelling.

Biology and Sexuality: Regulation and Deregulation of Biorelational Processes

The neuroscience approach tends to assume homeostatic principles as norms of functioning. Schore's type of work stresses affect regulation in attachment relations and dysregulation, as in the case of trauma and attachment disturbances. In the focus on affect regulation as a positive developmental achievement little emphasis has been placed on exploring the field of sexuality. I shall work to correct the focus, so that dysregulation and sexuality in relation to the body are rightfully addressed.

By situating the 'body work' in psychoanalysis, I embrace the relevance of sexuality. Fonagy (2011) notes that contemporary Anglo-American psychoanalysis has largely lost interest in sexuality. Whereas the trend has been to address sexuality insufficiently, I will flag up the relation between soma and sexuality.[3] In 'Beyond the pleasure principle' (1920) Freud relates sexuality to an increase and intensification of excitation which produces what is termed 'the marginal effect', the transgressing of thresholds and facilitating of deregulated states.

Research in the neuroscience of attachment has tended to emphasize the way 'good enough' attachment interaction can facilitate affective regulation of somatic states and dysregulation, in so far: (1) as this relates to the normal and necessary imperfections of the 'good enough' attachment interaction, and (2) as a specific effect of neglectful and/or intrusive/abusive trauma and insensitive parenting, that is as a result of fundamental disturbances in the attachment relationship. Attachment-based neuroscience and neuropsycho-analysis has had a tendency to somewhat neglect the somatically disruptive potential of sexuality, the way sexuality can, as Fonagy (2007) points out, radically perturb regulation of somatic states and emotion.

In this book I shall work to create a more complex picture, which includes how regulated and deregulated somatic states are established and how deregulation of somatic states can relate to both traumatic dysregulation in the attachment field and the domain of sexuality, and how sexuality and attachment trauma can overlap and produce changes in the somatic field.

Notes

1   In a privately circulated video compilation entitled 'Primary Intersubjectivity'.
2   Personal communication with Vittorio Gallese.
3   Sexuality has a specific importance in relation to deregulated body states and to loss and perturbations in body identity. This is why my argument is that the biological processes readily err from their so-called proper course. It is also the case that states of alterity and *Unheimlich* are intensified within the sphere of sexuality as also occurs in attachment trauma. My point is that sexuality in its complexity is of the body. Not all areas can be sufficiently addressed in the scope of this book. For a further exploration of sexuality and its bodily vicissitudes see my forthcoming 'Exploring some vicissitudes of feminine sexuality'.

3

Bodily Expression and Language Relations

The relationship between bodily expression and language is a complex one. Historically there has been a dominant tendency to reduce bodily communication and to elevate linguistic communication to language proper. In this book I reapproach and address afresh the body and its relationship to language and open up an understanding of language and what is meant by the symbol and symbolization.

Traditionally language has been aligned to speech and to words and linguistic ability, based on the influence of Ferdinand de Saussure's (1916) contribution from structural linguistics, and on structural and poststructural developments. This in turn has influenced debates in psychoanalysis on symbol formation and psychic development. Structural linguistics and theories of language have not only influenced psychoanalysis but also developmental psychology, philosophy, psychosocial and cultural studies and even neuroscience in the way language function and speech are understood.

Historically a dichotomy has emerged between the body and language which cuts across debates in psychophysiology, socio-cultural studies and psychoanalysis. This book challenges such a divide between body and language and reworks the relationship, linking soma to a broader and more open definition of language.

Affective Bodily Relations

Within psychosocial and cultural-media studies there has been increasing criticism of a theoretical focus on social meaning based on signification to the neglect of the body in its physiological effects and affects. Brian

Between Skins: The Body in Psychoanalysis – Contemporary Developments, First Edition. Nicola Diamond.
© 2013 John Wiley & Sons, Ltd. Published 2013 by John Wiley & Sons, Ltd.

Massumi's chapter 'The autonomy of affect' in his *Parables of the Virtual* (2002) has had a massive impact on current developments in thinking, leading to what has been referred to as the 'affective turn' in psychosocial-related research.

Massumi describes how responses to a short clip of film played with and without verbal commentary elicited different reactions, noting that the affective pleasurable response evoked by visual sensory-based stimuli was distinct from the more cognitive-based response to the 'factual' clip which had a verbal voice-over, which made this clip appear more socially organized and linguistically structured. From this observation, Massumi suggests that bodily/physiological affective responses to non-verbal sensory stimulation are different from linguistic/language-based socially coded responses. He argues that bodily affective states express intensity and operate differently from socially structured linguistic forms of communication.

From this distinction between sensory states as affective intensities and social linguistic structures a debate has emerged in psychosocial and film/cultural studies which differentiates between the body as affective intensity and as socially encoded linguistic meaning. Massumi's work is interesting but complex, and some of the interpretations of what he says have in my view led to an unhelpful divide between body and language (see Leys 2011).

I would challenge both sides of the debate. In this book I emphasize the fact that affective bodily states are never pure and unadulterated, asocial, 'in nature' or 'at source', for affective somatic responses are in a temporal retroactive process, always and already influenced by a relational field of others and of social sensibility. Furthermore, language need not be reduced to linguistic and highly organized structures. I would broaden and redefine language to encompass sensory, bodily and non-verbal expression, including visual and musical forms of meaning-making, identified as 'semiotic' flow. Meaning can involve non-sense and need not imply the closure of sense or rigidity.

This book challenges a clean divide between affective intensity and social meaning. I explore affectivity as necessarily interpersonal (as evident in Massumi[1]) and as part of a wider social relational field, as developmentally in process between bodies and across the life cycle. I turn now to the developments in understanding that help open up the field of language to bodily semiotics and allow for greater fluidity in process.

Bodily Proto-Conversation: Sensory Semiotics as the Basis for Language

Based on the earlier observation of intercorporeal relations, Trevarthen (1978, 1979, 1990) in his studies of infant–parent interaction views the non-verbal, sensory dance of turn-taking between bodies as both the forerunner of linguistic acquisition and the more richly affective proto-conversation:

What I want to remind us of is the rich nature of language. The 'proto-conversation' that Trevarthen (1979) refers to is a form of language. Sensibility and less structured sense making is emergent in the non-verbal exchange. In the interaction between caretaker and infant, communication takes place through gestures, movements and sounds well before the baby can articulate words. The non-verbal cannot simply be subsumed to verbal language. Thinking and action develop together. (Diamond 1998: 207)

Trevarthen (1990) argues, as do Meltzoff and Moore (1977), that gesture is not to be confused with a reflex action, from the very 'first' there is the orientation to be social. Babies single out human faces from objects very early on. The motivation is to interact and soon rudimentary sense is beginning to be shared. Trevarthen identifies mimicry as anticipating the formation of semantic meaning and the temporal pacing and spacing of turn-taking as the precursor of syntax construction in linguistic development. *Language in this context is broadened, going beyond linguistic limitations, to include an open and enriched affective bodily field.*

Trevarthen (1990) criticized linguistic philosophers like Peirce and psychologists like Piaget for an over-cognitive, logistic and intellectualist approach to language development. He argues that the early emotional and bodily non-verbal, semiotic proto-conversation is more fundamental and acts as the ground for language acquisition, informing linguistic ability.

This claim does not undermine the validity of the research into the logical and cognitive abilities in infant development promoted by Gergely (Fonagy *et al.* 2002) and others; it rather shows that language acquisition has a primary basis in affective somatic/sensory-based interaction. In such a model it is clear that language is defined more broadly than as linguistics. Affective sensory modes, gesture, touch, mirroring and sound intonation are modes of expression whereby shared meanings emerge (see also Stern 1977, 1985). Shared ways of making sense imply that such semiotic meanings become part of the public sphere and are part of the cultural repertoire.

Bodily Expression as a Form of Language

Merleau-Ponty (1962) argues that the gesture is a form of speech, and notes that cultures create different gestural signifiers:

It would be legitimate to speak of 'natural signs' only if the anatomical organisation of our body produced a correspondence between specific gestures and 'given states of mind'. The fact is that the behaviour associated with anger or love is not the same in Japanese and an occidental. Or, to be more precise, the difference in behaviour corresponds to a difference in the emotions themselves. It is not only the gesture which is contingent in relation to the body's organisation, it is the manner itself in which we meet the situation and live it. The angry Japanese smiles and the Westerner goes red and stamps his foot or else goes pale and hisses his words . . . What is important is how they use their bodies, the simultaneous patterning of body and world in emotion. The psycho-physiological equipment leaves a great variety of possibilities open, and there is no more here than in instinct a human nature finally and immutably given . . . It is no more natural and no less conventional to shout in anger or to kiss in love . . . Feelings and passionate conduct are invented like words. (Merleau-Ponty 1962: 189)

Merleau-Ponty is adamantly against a vulgar Darwinism or any crude form of social-biological reductionism in the style of Desmond Morris. Such an approach refuses to take into account the complexity of bodily language and modes of cultural expression.

Merleau-Ponty argues that there is no crude natural sign as far as the body is concerned and that the physiological equipment is radically open to many possibilities of affective expression (affective used purposely here) which are simultaneously formed with the gesture and are the articulation of the body in its cultural specificity. It is the use of the body (see Mauss 1936 [1934], the forerunner of Merleau-Ponty), the manner of expression and the affective states themselves that alter according to context.

In 'The body as speech and expression' (1962) Merleau-Ponty argues that the means of expression – the bodily gesture or other enactments – are not separate from that which is expressed – there is no state of contemplative thought that lies elsewhere – but rather the means of expression brings the expressed – the feelings and meaning – into being. For Merleau-Ponty the gesture or other bodily expression can function like the word, is a type of language, as the word is no mere clothing for thought but brings it into being and makes the thought possible. Likewise the bodily expression/ gesture is the means of expression which simultaneously produces the emotion and makes meaning possible. Meaning is made in the expression of body and world (Diamond 2004).

I have purposely referred to 'affect' in this discussion, though 'emotion' has been used in the translation of Merleau-Ponty's text. There is a long-standing debate that concerns itself with distinguishing affects from emotion and then in turn meaning (see also note 1). I have cautioned against confusing terminological distinctions used for the sake of conceptual clarification with actual ontological claims. If it is a matter of conceptual clarification alone, there is then the recognition that in actual situations – that is, lived experience and bio-psychosocial processes – there is no static and fixed moment, for in actual experience the processes are inseparable and do not take place linearly.

Put most briefly, the debate takes a number of forms in the history of literature, philosophy and popular culture. At its simplest, the affects (or sometimes reference is made to feelings) are distinguished from emotion and then meaning. Affect is unprocessed[2] and emotion relates to the social moulding and meaning to a closure in sense, often in words or speech.

I think Merleau-Ponty cuts across these analytic distinctions by making it impossible for there to be a pure state of bodily affect that remains untainted, that somehow lies untouched elsewhere and exists as prior to expression, which is in fact already and always underway. 'Contamination' has already temporally taken place, as has the inevitable exposure to others and to sociality.

Absence, the Symbol and the Somatic

In psychoanalysis in the theory of symbol formation, absence and separation play a crucial role. There is the fact that the symbol comes into being when the object is *in absentia*. Symbols all around – whether images, words or artefacts – present what is not in fact present. They are symbols precisely because they signify and then have poetic licence.

For the infant it is only when there is an experience of the absence of (m) other that she is wanted, when there is some sense that she has gone missing. In the longing for the missing piece memory gets activated; in the missing non-presence the symbol stands in for what is not. In the rudimentary version of the psychoanalytic story, representation in the absence of the object takes place through a word and/or image.

Lacan refers to the *objet petit a* in order to clarify that the missing piece can never be found; it was missing from the first. A way of explaining this most simply is to point out that it is only in the moment of missing, in the experience of a lack and a loss that the baby wants and is propelled to imagine and configure out of nothing – to represent, to eventually find a symbol. So the symbol is based in the experience of the lack, the gone (*Fort* in German), not something present. This experience of absence has to leave its mark for the infant to enter the field of the symbol (in non-psychotic trajectories), that in most psychoanalytic accounts is presumed to leave a trace in the psyche (the psyche or mind, or even brain, depending on the metaphysical and conceptual preference). What goes unsaid in all this is why the body as such is left out of the account. It is assumed that mind or psyche can be in the realm of idea and can engage with non-being, can grapple with ideas, can contemplate; likewise it is assumed that it is the brain that thinks and in this regard it is only the mental sphere that is required.

The body in this model is presumably a pure materiality, at worst stuck in a brute presence, and at best not capable of being involved in a thinking process. Certainly if the symbol is associated with the capacity of abstract thought and the body is defined as its brute presence, then never the twain shall meet. It is evident that metaphysical presumptions are at work.

What I have set out to show is how the registering of absence can and does directly involve sensory body processes and how touch can be considered a form of language. This part of the work is important in addressing the relation of the symbolic field to bodily process and expression. In this context an understanding of the symbolic is redefined, so the work of the symbol is not solely aligned to speech and the linguistic sphere but encompasses a sensory semiotic and is somatically accessed.

The registering of absence in relation to bodily processes needs to be tackled if the field of symbol and language is to be broadened to include bodily being. In opening up the debate I aim to explore the relation of biology to semiotic and developed symbolic systems, placing emphasis on bodily expression and its relation to signification. It is not the case that in the beginning was the word.

In the area of cultural studies I hope to contribute to the development of the theory of inscription as a form of body writing; to find a way of making sense of the tattoo metaphor for a writing on the palimpsest skin, viscera and senses; to transform a literal description of an engraving to one that makes more transcribing sense.

The importance of body writing necessarily relates to debates in cultural studies regarding inscription. It is not a matter of separating biology from inscription, an a priori, fully constituted biology upon which social inscription is superimposed like a stamp at a later date, for I would argue that we live cultural experiences somatically, and that relations with others and rituals alter how we sleep, dance, eat, make love and die. Likewise, the soma is how gender gets lived. Many social modes of differential markings are fundamentally bodily and cannot be extrapolated from the body context.

In the Beginning Was the Body: Lakoff and Johnson

In the *Philosophy of the Flesh: The Embodied Mind and its Challenge to Western Thought* (1999) Lakoff and Johnson have arguably put forward the most pertinent theory for the origin of language. Their theory is well known: they identify the body as the foundation for language and observe how many metaphors that are used in everyday language derive from bodily states, for example 'rule of thumb', 'the heart of the matter', 'he broke my heart', 'she's laid back'.

Lakoff and Johnson claim that metaphorical thinking is fundamental and that there is no simple way of escaping metaphorical forms of expression. So although there is a bodily basis, it is only and already construed through the metaphors of the body we live by. The idea of the bodily basis of language has a second qualification. There is no first moment of a body 'doing its stuff' on its own; it is already altering in relation to environmental influences, including others and the sensory-somatically-based communication this brings. Furthermore, the body functions, processes and structures themselves are, as this book sets out to show, influenced by non-verbal meaning-making and the creation of sense and non-sense through the proto-conversation which colours every bodily activity and arguably contributes to the production of body-based metaphors. It becomes a false chicken before the egg problem: language (including the proto-conversation) and bodily being evolve together.

Lakoff and Johnson state: 'We will suggest, first, that human concepts are not just reflections of an external reality, but they are crucially shaped by our bodies and brains especially by our sensory-motor system' (1999: 22). However, it is possible to extrapolate the sensorimotor system from environmental influence only hypothetically. In actuality, if the implications of the interdependence of organism and environment are taken to their radical conclusion, the first moment has already been lost. Therefore the body-in-the-world is the starting point.

In the journey that follows I shall show how metaphors from others and the cultural field – from the world – supplement and support the biological sphere where it is found to be lacking. I shall argue with regard to the relative plasticity of a number of biological processes against the idea of the sufficient and fixed preconstituted biological bedrock prior to being in the world and thereby challenge the false extrapolation of body from world which creates an untenable singular bio(-logos) determination which can result in an implausible dualistic model.

Psychoanalysis highlights a model in which forms of body representation are seen to derive from body function and structure. This is described as an analogous relation. I shall show the pitfalls of this formulation and how it installs rather than resolves a dualism. My aim is to offer a more viable alternative model.

A simple predetermined a priori biological bedrock model is to be challenged. The fundamental interpenetration of the biological and social is to be foregrounded and plasticity is identified for a number of body processes – in both functionality and structure building. Plasticity is part of bio-life and involves a more indeterminate and open process; it is therefore in contrast to what has been termed bio-logos. In opening the biological field, the connection of body function and form to semiotic and symbolic relations is to be made and the link between bio-life-the interpersonal world and cultural field is proposed.

I shall show how the lived materiality of bodily being can express a relational life in a semiotic language, sometimes involving a more elaborate and symbolic form of articulation. This will allow me to account for how body symptoms I encounter in the clinic can be read as a form of communication. In this context the bodily symptom can display what is going on in interpersonal and social relations; as noted, this can involve different degrees of meaning elaboration.

Somatic Access to the Symbol

This book makes a distinction between somatic access to rudimentary symbol capacity and complex symbolic processing. In the first case, the body in the symptom does partake in the expression of meaning and affect. This is viewed as a form of semiotic non-verbal communication. It includes somatic semiotics from early relations and more culturally derived influences, expressing fears, anxieties, desires organized around body functions and basic concerns around body-skin integrity and failure.

Depending on early interaction and the development of bodily processes, somatic-sensory expressions may or may not be adequately assimilated to the non-verbal level of semiotic expression. The point I am making is that this depends on the quality of the interaction and the development of brain–body processes that ensues. However, in most circumstances a form of somatic semiotics is the norm, as is a degree of somatic integration into linguistic processing. However, it is common for a person to present a bodily symptom that expresses a somatic-semiotic meaning without their having any idea what the significance is. None or few affect–meaning links may be present to conscious awareness.

The philosopher Nietzsche refers to the body as the unconscious. In accordance with this idea I am exploring bodily semiotic expression as unconscious communication. When there is greater secondary linguistic elaboration of non-verbal states then conscious access is more readily available. In contrast, in cases where there has been less reflective verbal processing, and environmental trauma has been related to bodily symptom formation, conscious access to the symptom's meaning can be non-existent. Nevertheless, in such circumstances somatic-semiotic expression is still characteristic of the bodily symptom, but remains unknown to consciousness. There have been misunderstandings on this point, leading some psychoanalytic thinkers to conclude that there is a deficit in body meaning; this is not necessarily so.

In my thinking I make a distinction between somatic access to the symbol and a more complex symbolic process. The latter has similarities with what in mainstream psychoanalysis is referred to as symbolic process. In this kind of symptom the non-verbal semiotic process is more worked through, and as in a more traditional approach there can be further development through linguistic processing. Meaning and affect can in turn become more accessible to consciousness.

This book puts forward different degrees and types of symbol processing and development. There is an explicit exploration of the way the somatic-sensory field accesses the symbol, how there is already in the non-verbal sphere a semiotic formation, where meaning and the effect of absence and difference leave their mark and are at work. The linguistic field of expression further defines, refines and elaborates, but is not exclusive to what will be included in the broadened domain and definition of language.

The 'Maternal' and the 'Other'

Reference is made throughout to the maternal other, the field of others and, perhaps most importantly, to otherness and alterity, the latter being crucial in any interpersonal approach which recognizes the problematic nature of personal bodily identity – where in the hearth of 'owness' there exists an alterity that is irreducible, that cannot be mastered, controlled or eradicated.

As noted, I do not begin with a primary preconstituted bodily I. On the contrary, it is the other that comes first and the infant first assumes the position of another, not I. Any first person-body position is both predicated upon and derived from this other field. Lacan refers to the Other. In principle this Other is relevant for any discussion concerning alterity and otherness. Reference to the Other is about 'the Other', which no human being can be or become, as that would be to dissolve otherness into pure identity and ownership, into the self-same, and there would be no other of the other (otherness) anymore. There is so often in the 'misguided' human experience the illusion of human omnipotence, an idealized and aggrandized position where one believes that it is possible to have it all, to be above it all and to be all, that is become a kind of demigod. Inevitably we all come down from such heights with a big fall, like Humpty-Dumpty who falls apart.

Otherness or alterity refers to the other which, like the Other, always remains other and cannot be subsumed into the same. However, the particularities of the Lacanian Other has not been actually implied. To avoid confusion it needs to be said that, while Lacanian insights are appreciated, this book is not inserted into a Lacanian terminological system and does not adhere to some of his founding presuppositions. In Lacan the Other is related to the phallus as master signifier.[3] Obviously no one can ignore the phallic signifier in a paternalistic heterosexist hierarchical economy where the body as gendered is so inserted, but there are some fundamental differences in the framework I propose. In a certain kind of psychoanalytic understanding, the phallus as signifier becomes the signifier of difference per se that acts as the necessary third term, breaking up the maternal dyad. However, why should the *phallic* signifier be the signifier of difference as such? What is not adhered to is the idea that the phallic signifier has a necessary given ontological or epistemological status, as the founding of *all* differences, the logos.

There are different and varied forms of sexuality; arguably the phallus does not have to be the signifier of sexual differentiation. There is a *potential* for different ways of signifying difference. Admittedly any master signifier would ultimately be irreducibly other, but the reference to the phallus is swapped for the breast as the signified unobtainable object, but in playing the same function no change in fact takes place.

Rather than focusing on a single key body signifier, I suggest that there are varied ways of signifying bodily differences in the complex field of social relations which create both diversity and, unfortunately, hierarchy (where power and control exist). In regard to hierarchy, racism, for example, rallies the master signifier as the *white* signifier – which creates illusions of power and denial of lack.

In this context construing skin colour and body configurations in discriminatory ways can be likened to the function of the *phallic* signifier; but in its different form as *white* signifier specific prejudicial differences are formed, figuring the body surface and features in ways which are characteristically racist. In doing this discriminating between bodies goes beyond gender and leads to further prejudices. This kind of social specificity does matter and needs to be accounted for.

When referring to the maternal a generic and broad-ranging definition of otherness is implied.[4] Implicit in the maternal, I suggest, are already a plethora of differences which are endemic to the mother – culture, gender, race, class and so on. These differences live on in her and are expressed in her relation to the infant. There is no such thing as a lone baby, nor is there simply the existence of the parent(s) and baby, for there is the differentiated field of a range of proximal others including siblings, grandparents and so on. Then there are the wider cultural differences and influences which are already in play within the earliest dyadic relationship.

Difference and otherness in this formula are already potentially at work and underway in the maternal field. Differences per se are not predicated on the phallic signifier alone and the theoretical work that has challenged the logocentric view of the phallus has been taken on board, as have the developments which consider the 'origin' of difference and diversity in the field of sexuality in a more expansive field.[5]

Notes

1 Distinctions have been made between affect, feeling and emotion. Although the creation of discriminations of this kind has a historical legacy in the debates within the humanities and a legitimate place in descriptive analysis, I do not adhere to such terminological divisions in this book, nor would I claim ontological grounds for any such distinctions. Shouse (2005), in reading Massumi, regards affect as distinctive as an intensity that is not structured through linguistic meaning, whereas feelings relate to personal biography and emotion to socially coded modes of expression and are thus both narrated and bound to meaning. From both a theoretical and a clinical perspective affectivity cannot be separated from historical trajectories whether individual or otherwise (general historical movement) nor,

most importantly, from social forms of articulation and expression, with the proviso that expression can be sensory and non-verbal and more open and fluid.

Merleau-Ponty argues that affect is not pure but is in the process of becoming in the acts of expression which can be bodily, such as gesture, and the means of expression are necessarily always already interpersonal-social and context-bound. Massumi's thinking, informed by Bergsonian, Nietzschean and Deleuzian developments, is complex and distinctly philosophical: affect relates to the virtual and does not operate on a time line (Husserl) or in clock time. In Massumi affect is potentially disruptive and destabilizing of fixed meanings, but it is not separable from the interbodily field (intercorporeal) and what I have referred to as 'proto-language' (sensory, non-verbal and musical modes of expression). Where Massumi suggests that language is more fixed and circumscribed by the word and speech, I would broaden language to include habitual, socially coded meaning and more unbound modes of semantic play. In my schema affective intensity can be aligned with Freud's 'marginal effect' and a sensory musical semiotics that is more playful and works more towards unbinding. Thus deregulation coincides with disruptive and destabilizing in Massumi but is still part of the broader definition of language.

In the model I propose affective intensity does not exist outside language as such, but relates to less bound modes. I refer to the sensory and musical but linguistic expression can also potentially derail and resist closure. In the exploration of musicality and rhythm in sensory modes of communication, what affectively moves is part and parcel of sensory and non-verbal modes of relating. In my reading, post-phenomenological debates regarding temporality and Nietzsche's eternal recurrence as becoming are relevant. The affective as potential is in a state of anticipation rather than realized. It is a virtual phenomenon to the social modes of expression (that are never fully realized), since they are also in the eternal process of becoming. Temporality in this model is always on the move, in the process of passing. There is no pure original before moment and the contamination by experience of a social field has both already happened and is always in the process of happening. In psychoanalysis, the equivalent understanding of temporal process is identified in descriptions of deferred action – afterwardsness and *Nachträglichkeit*. This is key to the experience of trauma and indeed bodily trauma, which will be addressed later in the book.

2   Unprocessed affect has been understood in the psychoanalytic and developmental literature to be bodily and unmediated by symbolic meaning-making (associated with linguistic thought and word expression). This model presumes a dichotomy between, on the one hand, the body and primitive affect and, on the other hand, linguistic processing in mental thought. According to this model, thinking involves the mental sphere only and not the body. This notion of 'mentalization' and 'symbolization' will be taken up as a problem in this book. For now I wish to point out that this model assumes that affect, if it is bodily and no more, is necessarily unprocessed and in an unmediated state. Because I do not work with this dichotomy between the body and the mind, I argue against the idea of the unmediated affect. In my view unprocessed affect is always mediated by a relational field. I distinguish rather between different degrees of processing. I suggest that there are different types of bodily enactment which show up different degrees of processing/working through. For example, in the compulsion to

repeat through bodily actions, as in the case of trauma and intergenerational trauma, I contend that stories – albeit somewhat fragmented and non-coherent (to ego function) – are enacted. There is disorganization, the sense is less bound and it is certainly the case that a secondary active processing has not been taken up so the person is not aware of why they are feeling and behaving bodily in a certain way.

However, the body can communicate interpersonal experiences by a bodily act, can express meaning through a non-verbal use of language. Coherent meaning and understanding are not there but deregulating and unstable bodily expressive states are and these, I argue, are based on forms of bodily semiotic transmissions. In such cases snippets of action narrative exist in sensory modes of expression which the body take-over presents in the form of a repetitive acting out. The themes literally repeat like the regurgitation of something that cannot be digested by the bodily ego and is more aligned to the primary processes, to use Freudian terminology. There are then differences in the quality of processing and making into sense. However, this does not mean that the body and its affects are unmediated: they are thoroughly interpersonal and involve a semiotic process.

3   Even in a phallic-based economy where the masculine is positioned as more than the woman in the fantasy, it is so because of the social organization of vision and profoundly embedded meanings. The phallic metaphor in such a system in fact circulates and is not confined to the construction of the penis or the masculine body as woman can be phallic as can objects and material possessions in the fantasy. Verhaeghe and Declercq note that the phallus signifies lack in the Other, implying that which is incomplete and failing, and refers to the phallus as a kind of prosthesis, even an incomplete prosthesis (2002: 59). Behind the ruse lies the lack. The phallic function in fact always leads us to lack. It is arguably a fantasy to believe that the phallic signifier is the delineator of all difference(s).

4   Kristeva explores bodily semiotics in the maternal field where differences are in play but are less fixed and delineated, more fluid and rhythmic. This is of interest, as is her understanding of the abject body state, where it is undecided as to what is alien/other and what is mine. Given my focus in this book on states of alterity in body symptom formation, I acknowledge Kristeva's (1980, 1982, 1984) contribution. Whereas Kristeva expands understanding but still adheres to a Lacanian framework, I do not. In the schema I propose, a sensory semiotics is not debased, since in my thinking language is not reduced to linguistics and speech or subsumed and consumed into a phallic definition of the symbolic.

5   Sam Weber (1982) playfully refers us not to the phallus but the thallus in order to take the phallic metaphor away from a binary definition of difference and closure. The thallus is a term for mushroom roots. These roots open up to differential pathways that lead to further diverse proliferations, taking us into a more open and various field of differences. Derrida in the *Geshlecht* papers (1983, 1987a, 1987b, 1993) revisits Heidegger, who has been key in addressing the nature of Being and existence, Heidegger's philosophical contribution implicitly influencing Lacanian developments of the Freudian subject and field, and post-phenomenological, poststructural developments since.

In the Geshlecht papers Derrida wonders about Heidegger's inadequate addressing of sexuality and the body in regard to the human being-there-in-the-world (*Dasein*). Merleau-Ponty offers the necessary corrective to Heidegger in examining embodied existence, including a specific exploration of sexuality. However, Derrida points out that Heidegger by the way reference to *Geshlecht*, leads to innovations from within Heidegger's work.

Derrida refers to Heidegger's hypothetical 'originary différ(a)nce', how it describes thrownness into existence. Thrownness is described as a movement that disperses and disseminates, rather like seeds bursting out and scattering in all directions. *Geshlecht* in German not only refers to sex and gender but also to race, class, lineage, family, generation and so on, as a way of characterizing the possible plethora of socially embodied differences that are disseminated. This implies that much variety can come into play that has the potential to branch out to open diverse pathways as well as there being many ways of creating social forms of discrimination and closure whereby binary hierarchies can demarcate bodies and segregate.

In the movement towards divergent directions, the suggestion is that bodily being is open to many possibilities. In regard to sexuality there is the potential of multiple pleasures and many kinds of sexualities. This embraces Freud's 'polymorphous perversity' and the kind of emerging sexualities and practices that defy traditional binary classifications.

Whatever the mythical story of emergence, the emphasis is on potential complexity, multiplicity and variety. As otherness is not only considered phallic, master signifiers can be configured in varying ways and the possibility of key hegemonic differences are not reducible to the phallic signifier but are specified by the historical cultural situation. In this highly differentiated context the definition of the maternal is more freed up. The other need not be positioned in a phallic economy and in this regard stands as that which is other of the other, resisting absorption into the self-same.

4

Setting the Scene
The Problem of the Binary Divide

This chapter offers a brief overview of areas in mainly Anglo-American psychoanalytic thinking that have contributed to the creation of unhelpful binary divisions between body and mind. Dichotomies have been established between the inside of the psyche and the outside world which result in cutting not only the mind off from the body, but also the mind from the world. In this context the status of the somatic sphere in relation to symbol formation and the social field remains a problematic area in psychoanalysis.

The issues that will be raised regarding the persistence and difficulties in dualistic and binary thinking derive not only from my academic research in psychoanalysis but also from how this Anglo-American style of psycho-analysis is applied in practice. I have also observed the pitfalls of dualistic understanding in my years of clinical training and personal analysis and in the clinical supervision I have received.

Arguably, with all the developments that have taken place in object relations, relational psychoanalysis, neuroscience and attachment, such binaries have been resolved and dissolved, and indeed this book can be situated in this apparent 'progressive' context. However, dualistic and binary thinking do not go away so easily. The body problem in psychoanalysis needs to be discussed. It is important to both identify and work through the source of a residual dualism, otherwise binary divisions return to haunt us insidiously.

As has been noted, there is a strand of Freud's thinking which advocates a one-person-body perspective, which starts with both the study of the singular organism and the premise that the vital order is integral to the individual organism and exists as a series of biologically fixed functions that arise from interior sources. What such a model insufficiently attends to is

Between Skins: The Body in Psychoanalysis – Contemporary Developments,
First Edition. Nicola Diamond.
© 2013 John Wiley & Sons, Ltd. Published 2013 by John Wiley & Sons, Ltd.

the interrelation between interceptive and exteroceptive experiences and the interdependence of organism with environment, including the influence of others and the social field on emergent somatic processes.

Inside versus Outside in Early Klein

In psychoanalysis the Kleinian school has been profoundly influential. It is a model which places particular emphasis on internally generated experience. The origin of this idea can be traced back to bodily sources. Susan Isaacs' paper 'The nature and function of phantasy' (1948), which formed the early basis of Klein's thinking, describes how phantasy life emerges from internally generated sensory experience. 'The earliest phantasies, then spring from bodily impulses and are interwoven with bodily sensations and affects. They express primarily an internal and subjective reality' (Isaacs 1948: 93). She further states: 'Phantasies do not, however, take origin in articulated knowledge of the external world; their source is internal, in the instinctual impulses' (93). 'The earliest (primary) phantasies in the infant initially spring from bodily impulses and bodily sensations (primary phantasy being the mental representation of instinctual urges)' (Diamond 2001: 46). Isaacs does note that there are external stimuli (1948: 84), and although they are considered narrow and limited there is some experience of external reality. So Isaacs does acknowledge some influence from external experience, but this is secondary; her point is that instincts and body sensations fundamentally derive from innate and internal experience and sources.

In this model, body processes are viewed as 'instinctual impulses'. As soon as a more elaborate imaginary process occurs, the realm of mental representatives is introduced. The instinctual processes are internal to the organism. It could be claimed that Isaacs' views are early formulations and do not reflect more modern ideas, but for now the point simply is that old problems do not readily go away; they are the basis of assumptions that still circulate. For fundamental change it is necessary to raise questions at source and to rework basic premises.

Definitions of the internal and subjective derive from the idea that bodily sensations, instincts and affects are internal experiences. However, many of the so-called internally derived bodily sensations, affects and instincts with which psychoanalysis is concerned are from the first exposed to environmental stimuli; in fact, the neuroscience attachment literature shows how many somatic processes – biological, neural and hormonal – in fact require environmental stimulation for development (Schore 1994), and are indeed orientated towards seeking out contact with external experience and in particular with others (Trevarthen 1978, 1979).

Despite the fact that contemporary developmental thinking is now acknowledged by Kleinian theory, when it comes to the language of 'instincts and phantasy' an interiorized model of the body can so often return through the back door. To name the obvious: hunger involves seeking out a feeding relation and a provision of one. It is difficult to retain a clear-cut autonomy of bodily sensations – feelings or impulses as they from the beginning are the outcome of an interaction with the environment and with another human being.

The Context of the Freud–Klein Controversies, 1941–1945

In the Freud–Klein controversial discussions of 1941–5, Edward Glover, in contrast to Isaacs' view, placed 'experience before phantasy' and argued that 'to regard phantasy as primary neglected the basic significance of reality factors that were involved in laying down memory traces of sensory experiences' (Hayman 1994: 351). Hayman notes that Glover's view emphasizes environmental influences. I summarize the view as follows:

> sensory experience did not arise directly from an internally generated source, but was always mediated by contact with the world (i.e. a feed [a feeding relation]) which in turn gave rise to the memory trace . . . linked to past experience, that made up the raw material from which phantasy was built. (Diamond 1998: 198)

In this view, body processes are not interior physical states which then become internal mental states, but are internal–external somatic experiences, the outcome of relation. The inside relates to the outside field of the other. However, such formulations are underdeveloped.

In both Isaacs' and Glover's models external reality is not theorized. For Isaacs it is an unmediated, 'objective' reality as opposed to a pure subjective reality and internally generated experience. Phantasy emerges from the mind's eye, based primarily on more or less insulated body states and an innate state of paranoia. For Glover, the experience of reality is simply assumed; there is no discussion of semiotically embodied communication or the impact of symbolic social systems on development. However, the 'memory trace' as the outcome of relation and the feeding experience are linked, an important point that will be taken up in later chapters.

Arguably, in Klein the interior view of the instinctual source has never been entirely resolved. Of course there has been the impact of Bion's work which has opened up Kleinian thinking to a more relational model. The notion of the baby and mother in the nursling relation is crucial here. The mother acts as a maternal container, in which the beta elements – the raw somatic elements – are transformed into alpha function by the mother's capacity to help the baby metabolize and transform primitive affect into thinking.

Persistent Dualism in Developments of Bion and Psychosomatics

Bion's theory of thinking (1962) has become significant in contemporary British psychoanalytic understanding. Bion describes the transformation of raw somatic beta elements into thoughtful alpha function. This is achieved by the mother's capacity to process her baby's experience. In developments of Bion, emotional thinking has been understood to imply that thought contains affect. This is to tolerate in thought the no-breast and the experience of absence, anxiety and fear of irreparable loss. This is no mean feat and something that even years of analysis can still leave difficult to bear.

However, the problem with the formulation of thought as container is the tendency towards a theory of mentalization. It has become increasingly popular in the British context to refer to the transformation of somatic beta elements into alpha thinking as a form of mentalization. This is observable not only in Fonagy and Target's earlier work but also in Kleinian developments that explain alpha functioning as thoughts in the developing mind (Garland 1998). A version of mentalization can also be found in McDougall's thinking (see below).

However, the exact status of the soma in and after this process is left unclear. How exactly does the soma get transformed and integrated into symbolic experience by this transition from beta somatic elements into alpha thought? Unless such questions are asked and addressed, the formulation can easily fall back into a mind/body division. I wish to allow for the transformative somatic in the alpha process without falling into a dualistic jump from body to mind and then leaving the body out of the account. For this, it is relevant and important to identify how the soma is taken along with the processing and transformation of experience.

Joyce McDougall describes psychosomatic phenomena from a psychoanalytic perspective. She draws on Pierre Marty and colleagues' (1963) work on psychosomatics and she is very influenced by Bion's ideas. In some of her formulations McDougall (1982) returns to a binary split. She compares thought to air and the body to grains of sand and one of her key arguments for psychosomatic disturbance is that there is insufficient 'psychic elaboration' processing, a deficiency in 'alpha function'; the psyche is effectively underdeveloped and primitive somatic affect is discharged into the body. This argument is most clearly stated in her earlier writing.

In her primary analysis of alexithymia (no words for emotion), McDougall (1982, 1986) describes a form of 'concrete' thinking whereby the somatic symptom is of central concern to the patient. All affect appears to go into somatic discharge and the patient complains about physical pain and discomfort, but fails to unconsciously associate and elaborate meaning.

McDougall argues that the somatic discharge is direct, as the psyche and its capacity for elaborating and symbolizing is bypassed.

Although the description is insightful for specific types of presentation of somatic states in certain patients, the problem in the formulation is the assumption that thinking is solely psychical and mental. Owing to such an assumption, there is too much generalization that psychosomatic states by their nature end up devoid of meaning and symbolic expression and erring on the side of 'concrete' functioning.

The alexithymic psychosomatic symptom is in direct contrast to the hysterical conversion symptom. The hysterical symptom identified by Freud and Breuer is where the somatic symptom is said to function as a metaphor and to disguise symbolic meanings. However, psychoanalysis has difficulty explaining the process of 'conversion', often resorting to a dualist framework. In psychoanalytic treatment there has been a growing trend away from identifying Freudian conversion phenomena to the more McDougall-type interpretation of psychosomatic disorders. Joyce McDougall's understanding of psychosomatics is recognized as important and has validity for understanding an array of somatic symptoms that lack associative richness and meaning; the problem lies in the dualistic thinking that underlies McDougall's explanation. Later in this book I shall offer an account of alexithymia, but one which avoids the pitfalls of a dualist account.

However, this shift in symptom focus which characterizes the contemporary climate is not simply related to changes in presenting clinical cases; an argument can be made for the continuing presence of conversion-like symptoms in the clinic. People may not present, in the same way as in Freud's day, a non-organic paralysis with rich associations leading off from the symptom, but a varied array of somatic disorders are now seen, for example certain cases of eating disorder, somatic hypochondria and organ dysfunction, that are not bereft of associative depth and significance.

As noted in the Introduction, one of my clients, Selma, had a rare condition of hysterical vaginismus: contraction and swelling of the vaginal walls (involving the pelvic floor muscles). She had 'clammed up', as she put it. In the analysis we explored her refusal to let the other in, to let go and open up. She had literally installed a no-entry barricade, but once her fears of losing her body integrity in orgasm (the fear of being overwhelmed by an invasive other linked to early childhood experiences) were worked through, little by little she began to enjoy sex and intimacy. As little as a year into the therapeutic work the symptom lessened, no longer fixed, and coitus began to be possible on occasion. Although there was a while when the condition reduced and then flared up again, it did, however, eventually dissipate. This is an example where a relation between affective meaning and somatic state is coterminus and there needs to be a way of accounting for this relational link.

I suggest that the 'modern' psychosomatic style of thinking cannot adequately account for semiotic and symbolic bodily expression when it does occur. It would seem that there is a too ready leap to mind when addressing alpha function; in contrast, the body as such remains stuck – as a field of raw primitive sensation and affect. The body being dumb to symbolic achievement, it can at best express archaic states of being (McDougall 1986, 1989).

An 'Over-Mental' View in Anglo-American Psychoanalysis

In this book I query contemporary models in psychoanalysis that use an 'over-mentalist' approach to processing experience. 'Mentalization', strictly speaking, refers to a mental awareness of other minds, points of view, feeling states; it relates to a certain relational capacity to understand others. However, in my critique of an over-mentalist model, I am questioning the idea that for emotional change what is required is a mental shift alone (understood as transforming affects into mental thoughts).

This over-mentalist model can be identified in parts of Fonagy and colleagues' (2002) earlier work where they deploy more traditional cognitive models of development with an account of 'reflective function' in attachment research while making reference to Bion's (1962) ideas. In their work it is mostly a problem of terminology, in particular the word 'mentalization', which in my view is misleading. Their approach does not in fact advocate a dualist model. As noted, however, over-mentalist accounts can be found in certain post-Kleinian developments of Bion's alpha function, and histori- cally in the French tradition of psychosomatics (Marty and M'Uzan 1963; Marty *et al*. 1963; Marty 1990). These approaches have arguably suffered from the problem of mind/body dualism and from an over-mental explanation for psychic change, most readily identified in Joyce McDougall's (1982, 1986) developments in her formative work on psychoanalytic psychosomatics.

In *Attachment and Intersubjectivity* (2003) Diamond and Marrone question the concept of mentalization. As did Fonagy at his presentation at the Neuropsychoanalysis Conference in Berlin (2011), where he argues that the body has been excluded from forms of psychoanalysis.[1]

Fonagy and Target's more recent writings (see 2007) correct an over- mentalist view. Using contemporary work from cognitive science, they argue for an embodied mind tied to relations with others and language. Although the cognitive psychology route differs somewhat from the orientation in this enquiry, Fonagy and Target's more recent thinking moves towards an embodied approach which is complementary and in accordance with what this book advocates. Their work and thinking have been crucial for furthering and developing understanding in the field.

I argue that it is necessary to question an over-mentalist model for emotional change. For when behaviour is pulled towards a compulsion to repeat, thought as a mental activity is not enough to change experience and action. To address compulsive patterns effectively requires an understanding of how profoundly driven these behaviours are and the inescapable bodily component.

Fonagy and Target note at various points that what is involved is much more than a conscious and mental process; instead there is 'an automatic procedure unconsciously invoked' (Fonagy *et al.* 2002: 27). Affects are in fact 'pre-reflectively processed . . . with the non-verbal interpersonal basis of working models of self and others' (Fonagy and Target 1997: 680–681). This suggests that the process is tied to interpersonal body-based experience and memory.

Rather than the focus being on a mental process per se, it now is on interpersonal non-verbal bodily know-how, where patterns of emotionally driven behaviour pre-reflectively inform current interactions. This can lead to what is referred to as forms of acting out repeating, compulsive, disturbed patterns of relating.

In *Attachment and Intersubjectivty* Diamond and Marrone note that Fonagy and Target acknowledge even in their earlier thinking that reflectivity can be adequately achieved only when it manages to effect procedural bodily memory, interpersonally based know-how (2003: 143). It would seem that it is this enactment mode that needs to be tapped in a reflective process, for an acting out to be transformed into an 'acting in', otherwise the psychic change does not reach the body-driven baggage.

For now, suffice it to say mentalizing is not enough. If affective change and working through are to happen, alteration in non-verbal know-how has to take place fundamentally. So even in Bion's language, there needs to be a way of understanding: (1) the way somatic beta elements are relationally inscribed in non-verbal communication and as procedural memory, and (2) how somatic processing is also involved in transforming beta elements.

Body versus Speech in Lacan

Unlike his British counterparts, Lacan, a key thinker in French psychoanalysis, does not refer to an ill-defined external reality but instead to the imaginary symbolic and the real. For Lacan there is a symbolic system that constructs the world through symbols. This symbolic is not a property located in the individual psyche but is endemic to the social field in which we live. In contrast, the imaginary is the field of idealized images and the real is a register beyond the symbolic and relates to that which cannot be represented in language, such as irretrievable loss. I mention Lacan as he elaborates the subject's relation to the field of language much more fully than British colleagues. However, his work has also led to an impasse regarding the relation of the somatic to the symbolic. His thinking, which was influenced by Saussure's structural linguistics, regards language as based in the field of word and speech alone.

As the symbolic is related to the word and speech, which configures a field of differential relations of signifiers into a system of terms, the flesh as such does not itself signify; at most it is capable of simple signs in the symptom, which Jacques Alain-Miller (1992) compares to animal signs: by this he means that the body is poor in symbol.

Alain-Miller (2012) refers to *jouissance* as bodily enjoyment and the effects of the signifier, and here he differentiates between a body phenomenon and a body event. What is important about the body event as an unconscious symptom is not the sensuous nature of the body per se but the mark of speech and the act of the signifier that strikes the body (with the impact of the real in severing the symptom from meaning). There is a lot to address in this important contribution; however, the binary divide of body and speech is still present and therefore has relevance for our critical discussion. Lacan, who focuses predominantly on the specular, the unseen and word/speech in defining language, was not particularly sympathetic to Merleau-Ponty's work on the body as speech, and the complex role of touch and tactility in body experience. It would appear that the overemphasis on linguistic models in Lacan has left the soma spoken for.

In this chapter I have taken a flying look at key thinking in the field of psychoanalysis where impasses have been created regarding the status of biology and the somatic in relation to mind, world and language. This is to demonstrate that despite 'progressive' developments dualistic and binary thinking still exists in psychoanalytic thinking and where in the Anglo-American context over-mentalist models have taken root. The challenge this book raises to a persistent dualism is therefore of relevance not only historically but for current practice and debates in the field.

Note

1   In his address Fonagy (2011) argues that it is attachment theory that is the brand of psychoanalysis responsible for the exclusion of the body. It is true that attachment theory, in prioritizing attachment, has neglected sexuality, but it is also true that with the general trend in psychoanalysis on the pre-Oedipal mother and earlier primitive states of anxiety there has been a more widespread neglect of Oedipal sexuality. This would include even some Kleinian developments that Fonagy does not draw our attention to. Also, the focus on attachment as the problem theory in psychoanalysis suggests that it is attachment that has neglected the body, rendering other psychoanalytic approaches free of criticism. This is misleading since attachment is the one approach that has more generally most included the body in its theorizing and research. From Bowlby to Schore there has been the recognition of the organism environment relation and the intimate connection between attachment and affective neurobiological processes.

Part II

The Vital Order

Moving Away from Interiority and Biology as Bedrock

5

The Vital Order and the Biological Functions
Going Back to the Fundamental Problem

The status of psychosomatic life has troubled psychoanalysis and the medical profession. Complaints of physical symptoms – pain, alteration in sensation, functional change and somatic conditions – have either been left with no known origin or at least no clear-cut organic aetiology. Such symptoms, nevertheless, can debilitate restrict, consume and preoccupy the person. In spite of all the developments in understanding, the relation of the somatic to the patient's psychic life, symbolic world and social relations has continued to be an issue for psychoanalysis. Dualisms persist and exert their influence as age-old problems to this day.

It is still apparent across the psychoanalytic literature that there exists an insistent divide between the fixed order associated with the somatic sphere and the domain of a free roaming fantasy life associated with psychic activity. Conversion hysteria in Freud recognized that an idea could alter somatic function and sensation and in that regard there was a challenge to any absolute divide between the mental and the somatic, but what did Freud mean when he said the drive *exists on the border* between soma and psyche? Furthermore, how does the body–psyche directly link up with an environmental field?

Biology versus Sexuality: An Untenable Division?

As noted, developments within neuroscience, including neuropsychoanalysis and attachment-based neuroscience, claim to resolve the traditional psychoanalytic dualism; however, such dualisms continue. In the psychoanalytic sphere Laplanche (2002) states that the neurosciences are still dealing with the biology of self-preservation organized around homeostasis as the ideal

Between Skins: The Body in Psychoanalysis – Contemporary Developments,
First Edition. Nicola Diamond.
© 2013 John Wiley & Sons, Ltd. Published 2013 by John Wiley & Sons, Ltd.

norm, and he includes here the more recent research which focuses on attachment and affect regulation. He argues that this approach operates in the 'self-preservative terrain'.

In contrast, the arena of sexuality and drive is related to excess excitation and the transgression of thresholds, which is disruptive and contradictory for the organism. Here infantile sexuality and the scandalous nature of the drive are located and are viewed as entirely different from a genetic and self-preservation-orientated biology.

Laplanche's point is important and what he says about sexuality and excess excitation holds true. The problem here is that when a too clean divide between a self-preservative biology and a psychoanalytic domain proper (for the drive) is upheld, the argument becomes confused. For instance Laplanche (2002) refers to a genetically programmed sexuality ruled by hormones in contrast to an infantile indeterminate sexuality where the 'hormonal origin is *absent in man* from birth to pre-puberty'. I understand that hormones do not determine, but to say that they are absent as such is an overstatement.

In order to clarify a distinction a point is made too fiercely and this, I would argue, occurs precisely because the status of biology remains problematic. Hormones are associated with a fixed determined set-up and therefore have no place in the sphere of a free roaming drive and sexuality. There is no space to concede that hormones are not simply automated but are activated by intimacy wishes, fantasy memory and so forth. If biology is understood as a predetermined, fixed system then it can never be integrated with the drive.

In such debates the argument is that the field of sexuality has nothing to do with the body as such, *when really the issue is how it is that the more imaginative, metaphorical and driven aspects of our sexuality do in fact become bodily manifest and biologically transformative.* Even when at points Laplanche notes the existence of a more malleable biology, he still views this as self-preservative by nature and therefore opposes self-preservation and biology to the drive and sexuality. This helps identify how in ever more sophisticated developments there is a return to dualism. If the dualist basis is not tackled face on, it weaves itself back in and the age-old divide carries on with all the implausibility that goes with it.

What will become evident in the argument of this book is that the so-called self-preservative is not stuck in an a priori biological programme, but also has to be built and constructed and, like sexuality and drive, it is subject to the impact of the other and is the outcome of a developmental process. The question is more how it is that the self-preservative tendencies can be so easily eschewed by the erring of the drive and more imaginative constructs of the body. As this book will show, homeostasis can be readily tipped into overdrive; an intact skin boundary can transform into an-ill defined sack that loses definition affecting motility and sensation. Constructs of the body are not all in the mind, and the more precarious body states can alter self-preservative tendencies.

What needs to be explained is how the drive, infantile sexuality and biology are in fact interwoven and how binary distinctions continue to preclude this possibility. It is not good enough to jump from body to psyche/mind in order to link biology to symbolic thinking. In this chapter I go back to the fundamentals in psychoanalysis in order to address the roots of the problem and to find a way to rework basic premises.

Introduction to Jean Laplanche

In the Anglo-American context James Strachey's translation of Freud has contributed to a particular reading of Freud. 'Freud rarely uses the term "instinct", however, although in the English translation the German *Triebe* ("drive") has been replaced with the word "instinct", which has led to a biologistic reading of Freud in the English-speaking countries' (Diamond 1992: 23). 'Biologistic' here refers to a definition of the 'instinct' as a biologically determined impulse that has a fixed source aim and object.

Laplanche argues that the English translation subordinates drive to that of a fixed biological 'instinctual' process, so the specificity of the drive is omitted. It is evident that in Freud's works, whatever the translation, the account has complexity. The key works are 'Instincts and their vicissitudes' (1915) and the 'Three essays on sexuality' (1905), although Freud developed this theme throughout his works.

French readings of Freud have not encountered the same pitfalls as their English counterparts, in that *Triebe* has not been reduced to *Instinkt* and the distinctive nature of the drive is made apparent. *Triebe* (drive) is seen as specific to human sexuality and as having no fixed source aim and object. Nevertheless the exact relation of the drive to the biological processes has, arguably, never been adequately clarified.

The internationally respected psychoanalyst Jean Laplanche is well known for his rigorous, scholarly reading of Freud and has had a profound impact on French and English psychoanalysis. His detailed reading of Freud has led to the dictionary *The Language of Psychoanalysis* (1983), which he compiled with his colleague Jean Pontalis and which has become a standard encyclopedia on psychoanalysis. Since 1988 Laplanche has been the scientific director of the French translation of Freud's complete works. Emeritus professor at the University of Paris, he died in May 2012.

By the time he wrote *Life and Death in Psychoanalysis* (1985) Laplanche had broken away from the French analytic tradition of Lacan, and had moved towards making his writing accessible to an Anglo-American audience, particularly Freudian schools. His writings have been well received and influential in the English-speaking world, including in the fields of media, film and cultural studies. Laplanche's rigorous reading of Freud is one reason why *Life and Death in Psychoanalysis* has been so influential, informing psychoanalytic developments including Didier Anzieu's work on *The Skin Ego* (1989), which will be addressed in Chapter 12. It describes in depth the body/psyche model that can be traced in psychoanalysis, and clearly shows where all the pitfalls in the argument lie.

However, the purpose of exploring *Life and Death in Psychoanalysis* is not to critique Laplanche. The rigour and depth of his reading of Freud capture the crux of the problem and sow the seeds for the revolution in thought. Laplanche distils Freud, drawing out the discovery of a psychoanalytic understanding of psyche, and in this sense he typifies a general trend in Anglo-American psychoanalysis to move away from the biological and the somatic towards an understanding of the mental/psyche.

My aim is to deploy Laplanche's detailed analysis to show up both the premises of a residual dualism as well as to find a way out of the impasse. The purpose is to revisit psychoanalytic foundations to show up their problematic nature, to free the paradigm from its own frame of reference. To attempt to bypass or to simply invent a new paradigm would only keep old problems intact and hence alive and kicking.

Setting Up the Solution Finds the Problem

In *Life and Death in Psychoanalysis* Laplanche offers an in-depth reading of the differentiation of *Instinkt* and *Triebe* in order to clarify Freud's thinking. Spelling out the roots of binary thinking that still haunts psychoanalysis to this day, *Life and Death in Psychoanalysis* views the analytical distinction between instinct and drive as worth preserving and seeks to bridge the gap between the biological functions and the drives and their symbolic representation. It does this by developing from a rereading of Freud the notion of propping, a middle/border term which is meant to account for the genesis of the psychic-sexual register out of a former vital order. As a middle term, it necessarily implies a distinction between two registers, 'the vital register . . . in opposition to the sexual register' (Laplanche 1985: 16).

The vital register involves the biological functions essential for the 'exigencies of life' (as Freud would put it), these include respiration, ingestion, excretion, thermal control, and the like, often aligned to self-preservative functions, mainly considered as including many visceral and internally stimulated body processes. As will become evident, these biological bodily processes are commonly viewed as internal as opposed to external processes and as a fixed and predetermined state of affairs – a perspective I shall be increasingly questioning. When the term 'vital order' is used, it will refer to this understanding of internal biological processes essential to life, but it will also become apparent that vital order can change its sense and take on a more radical meaning of a biological set-up that I shall be advocating as an alternative model.

Laplanche sets out to avoid the idea that organic functions and the drive are two disconnected realms, hence the emphasis on propping, which allows for the emergence of the drive without denying the instinctual realm. Propping attempts to solve a traditional impasse between soma and psyche; it extends Freud's metaphor of a delegated mandate, in which 'the biological stimulus finds its delegation, its representation in psychical life as drive' (Laplanche 1985: 13), but without falling into the trap of reducing the drive and the field of representation to a mere reflection of organic functions. The term propping (*etayage* in French) has been employed in the translations of Freud's writings, but according to Laplanche its use has been unsystematic. Laplanche wishes to reclaim a consistent sense for the term and prefers it to the word in use, *anaclisis*, because 'propping' retains 'the rigorous conceptual value which the German word *Anlehnung* – meaning to find support or propping in something else' (Laplanche 1985: 13) – maintained in Freud's original scripts. Propping declares a movement of derivation in which the drive and representation are said to emerge by leaning, being propped up by the instinctual functions while also simultaneously deviating and dissociating from that biological order.

Thus the first part of the movement means that the emergent drive starts life by being grounded in the vital biological processes, finding support in those 'bodily functions essential to life' (Laplanche 1985: 16). The vital order is defined here as the order of life and is given by nature: 'A pre-formed behavioural pattern whose arrangement is determined hereditarily' (10), which is fixed and repeatable as a series of mechanistic 'chain reactions ending in a permanent discharge of tension' (13).

The source/stimulus acts as an automatic 'triggering device', resulting in the 'corresponding mechanism' (Laplanche 1985: 14). A definite source, impetus, aim and determinate object make up these bodily functions. The source is located in a somatic process, from which arises the stimulus. In hunger, the impetus is a specific humoral or tissue imbalance creating a state of tension at its source, the digestive system. The aim performed by a 'notary scheme' (10), a search for the breast, its nipple for feeding, in order that the object of need be found – milk and consequent nourishment – resulting in a satisfaction with the release of physiological tension.

Such fixed body functions act as the initial ground for the first stage of propping. However, propping is claimed to initiate a double movement, the drives leaning and deviating from the instinctual processes. With the moment of detour, there is a movement of derivation, characterized as metonymic and metaphoric in its slide and slippage from the biological vital order to that of the domain of sexuality, the drives, having no determinate source, aim or object. However, as soon as sexuality relates to the drive and representation, it becomes a psychic fantasy, a mental act.

The problem is that if there is a rigid distinction between the instinctual vital order and the psychical-representational sphere, sexuality is left to be all in the mind, so to speak. This leaves two orders rather than a graduation from one to another and with an account which cannot adequately explain how the fixed vital/somatic order can express roaming desire and sexual meanings.

The main propping account states there is a gradual process whereby the drive and the psychic sphere do emerge out of the fixed vital order. At first, the drive is modelled on the function, the difference being barely perceptible (Laplanche 1985: 17), a sensual stimulation with the warm flow of milk; in the slide from milk to breast, a displacement of 'that first object' (20) is said to takes place.

The sexual object is no longer 'identical to the object of the function, but is displaced in relation to it' (Laplanche 1985: 20), by a 'relation of essential contiguity, which leads us to slide almost indifferently from one to the other: from the milk to the breast as its symbol' (20). As noted, the object of the need is forever lost for the drive; it is replaced by a fantasm (the fantasmatic breast), a symbolic breast that cannot be re-found in the presence of the satiating milk. Because the fantasy is based in absence, rather than the satiating object (milk), it is viewed as existing in the psychical-mental field. Laplanche describes how the feeding aim, ingestion, is transposed via a certain slippage from the body instinctual order to the psychical drive state, but then how there is 'no longer an associative chain through contiguity' (1985: 18), for in its place there forms 'a scenario . . . fantasy' (20) which borrows 'from the [biological] function its register and its language, but adding to ingestion . . . the term cannibalism' (20). And then associated meanings can come about, like preserving within oneself, destroying, assimilating.

Such associations are viewed as part of a fantasy structure, transcribed on a psychical level, a mental act (Laplanche 1985: 20). The process of ingestion provides manners of expression for an incorporation, which extends them into an 'entire series of possible relations' (20), where incorporation is no longer confined to food and the digestive system, for 'psychic incorporation as a taking in of the other involves an entirely new meaning – a psychical act' (20).

Here what is noted is very interesting: the act of incorporation can in fact 'encompass other bodily systems and orifices' (Laplanche 1985: 20); it extends from digestion to other body functions and orifices. This is the kind of psychoanalytic discovery about the somatic field that I wish to emphasize in this book, the relative mobility of body processes and their possible relations. Furthermore, it would seem that the significance of incorporating the other can be expressed in somatic states and is not relegated to a psychic-mental act alone. What needs to be explained is how the body is taken up in this more open system. If the vital functions can tip over the threshold into the marginal effect which it is agreed occurs, then they are no longer tied to a fixed biological order, which is, however, where Laplanche situates the vital biological processes.

I am interested in addressing a more open biology which then can take on a metaphorical and more multidimensional sense; my emphasis would be on the act of incorporation being an act of incorporating the other involving the possibility of bodily sensations, functional changes and, instead of words, a somatic act. The emphasis here is on the relational meaning articulating the functional processes according to its own logic.

The example that follows is illustrative not so much of sexuality as of attachment disturbance. As will later become clearer, excess and the marginal affect are both open to deregulation and hyper-arousal, with emerging sexual excitation and with fundamental perturbations in the bodily–other attachment set-up. In both cases the biological functions err from their presupposed 'proper' limit and pathway of expression.

Samantha had a sensitive gut condition, where her symptoms were gastric reflux, digestive difficulties and pain. This condition dated back to babyhood but she came to me for therapy when her condition reactivated. I asked her about medical checks for hiatus hernia and ulceration and, yes, she had been through the barrage of tests and had no such conditions. There had been at one time a bacterial inflammation and that had subsided, but still this part of her body seemed to be the target for her discomfort and pain.

I always encourage patients to go for medical checks if they have a key symptomology, because in so many cases it shows that the discomfort they experience, the functional changes they suffer and the peculiarity of sensations either have no identifiable organic aetiology or that the symptoms they experience are somewhat atypical and exaggerated and in that sense differ from a standard medical understanding.

In the first sessions, some key themes came up. The mother had cared for Samantha only when she was physically ill; Samantha described her mother as highly self-centred, the type of mother who was always setting others up to fulfil her own wants. Samantha's enmeshment with her mother became obvious, and as an adult she was still getting over and was preoccupied with the dynamics of her relationship with her mother, taking on the feelings of her mother and others (likened to mother) and, most of all, all the negative states projected onto her that Samantha absorbed but that were not assimilated.

It appeared that Samantha's capacity to filter was poor and everything flooded in. Her entire digestive tract then became hyperactive and she suffered from an overactive peristalsis. The build-up of acid was a build-up of noxious other, and her own affective states intermingled. She became unable to hold in any more, and tried to throw up the toxic waste-mother.

Excess: The Marginal Effect as an Increase in Excitation Relating to Emergent Sexuality

Returning to the main propping model and the focus on the marginal effect in its relation to emergent sexuality, there is arguably too clean a distinction maintained between a biological sexuality – 'A biological scheme which would secrete sexuality from pre-determined zones exactly as a physiological set-up gives rise to nourishment' (Laplanche 1985: 21) – and a sexuality linked to fantasy and to psychic mental representation that revolves around the absence of an object, that is the breast as fantasm.

Yet a so-called biological sexuality all the time gets entangled in the 'psychic' meaning and 'mental representation'. From my point of view, there is the need to account for the way mental representations are somatically lived. The fact that the soma can be involved makes a pure mental realm simply untenable. Take one of my male clients who suffered from premature ejaculation. His physiology was in normal functioning order, yet his fears about living up to his masculine aspirations resulted in him falling short, failing to adequately penetrate or to please the other by coming on entry. The fact is that psychic meaning and ideas about the self can be lived as sensation and can alter somatic function.

Therefore it is a relief to discover another logic at work where the clear divide between biological bedrock and psyche gets undercut by another description, for what is also described is how the sexual excitation arises as a 'concomitant marginal effect' 'as soon as the intensity passes beyond certain quantitative thresholds' (Laplanche 1985: 22). Here Laplanche notes that Freud describes how a source in a purely physiological sense is soon replaced by a source that is indirectly produced as soon as anything occurs in the body beyond a quantitative threshold. For this somatic shift to occur there has to be a physiological flexibility – let's say plasticity – and for this to be so the vital somatic field cannot be completely stuck in a fixed and closed system.

So even the fundamental vital order, the basic biological functions essential for life – eating, sleeping, breathing, excreting, secreting and so on – can be directly involved with excess excitation and movement. It is no longer a matter of the erotogenic zone as a privileged site for stimulation. This is because, as Laplanche acknowledges, Freud made explicit that localizable excitations extend to any cutaneous region of the body, even to internal ones. It is, of course, also the case that agitation, anxiety and intellectual effort can become the source of marginal effects.

What is to be emphasized here is that the body functions and sensations are clearly open to this kind of indirect stimulation; organs and skin can be subject to the marginal affect. Again what needs to be emphasized is that this marginal effect of intense excitation is somatic and physiological (but not in a restricted sense) and what I am arguing in this book is how somatic expression can be directly bound to metaphorical sense and meaning.

> Simon came to analysis with a series of somatic complaints, including palpitations and a pain in his heart. He believed that he was suffering from angina and went for a series of medical examinations, but nothing was found. The pain was sometimes excruciating and in the first six months of therapy we discovered that he had a 'wounded heart'. Before this formulation was made, before words were spoken, his heart had been hurting, telling us about his pain.
>
> The fact Simon had felt 'understood' helped him find some solace by sharing his burden. Later he noted, 'I am bleeding. I lost my love. I tried to get on with my life, functioning as normal, but deep down I was devastated.' Simon suffered somatically what he was later able to put into words, a 'wounded heart'. The 'wounded heart' stood for the sensation of hurt and loss which was particularly poignant as it was experienced as an unrequited love. Simon's pining was constant and, like a haemophiliac, he could not stop bleeding metaphorically: 'I am bleeding – I lost my love.' His wounded heart was also a bleeding heart. Simon in the somatic state was suffering from a profound reaction to loss intensified by his early experiences of maternal rejection.

As I shall show, the somatic can express emotion, meaning and a sense of loss. I find that Laplanche, despite putting forward somewhat binary thinking, describes how psychoanalysis can help us understand how body functions can and do fundamentally err from their 'proper' course, how such biological processes are not simply bound in an absolute and determined way to stereotypical expression and fixed limits.

Here another more viable model of biology emerges, in which there is an openness in the functions, so there is not another register superimposed on the first, or a fixed course for self-preservative functions, or a biologically determinate sexuality as opposed to the freedom of a drive-based sexuality. It is necessary to understand how the vital biological functions that are associated with a restricted physiology have this potential to err from a 'proper' course and to become confounded with emotion and meaning.

The problem with Laplanche's formulation is that he works so hard to clarify a point by creating an analytic distinction between the vital order and the field of a psychic sexuality that the conceptual division is made too concrete. In turn, binary thinking is proposed and ontological claims are established about two orders — the vital and the sexual-psychic domain of psychoanalysis. On the one hand, Laplanche does not want to exclude biology and body processes from the domain of the marginal effect and the emergent sexual register; on the other hand, biology cannot be engaged if ontological claims are confused with analytic distinctions. This is the case not only for Laplanche, but for the psychoanalytic community at large when confusions reign concerning the status of the somatic in relation to psyche, when there is not only a descriptive difference but a more fundamental body/mind divide.

Laplanche distinguishes between a biological hetero- and self-aggression and Freud's genuine formulation of masochism and sadism. So in clarifying Freud's distinction Laplanche notes a natural hetero-aggression which he states belongs to the level of the organism, its self-preservation function, an instrumental non-sexual aggression towards the outside world directed at anything or anyone who would obstruct the organism's life activities. Likewise, a primitive aggression towards the self takes place as a form of self-conquest to gain control over the limbs (Laplanche 1985: 97). Winnicott similarly observed that an early aggression is required for physical exertion and control.

Such 'sheer behaviour' is said to contrast with a process of an 'entirely different order from a real activity (of the muscles)' (Laplanche 1985: 97). What then emerges out of a complex manoeuvre implicating propping's marginal effect and its metonymic and metaphoric move is the 'internalization of the action on a psychical level' (97). The activity of self-preservation is displaced for the drive by what Laplanche describes as brushing back on the self. This is not a primitive attempt at self-domination but a replacement of the object attacked 'by a fantasy, an object reflected within the subject' (83). The activity is now said to be psychic, extending as a metaphor into a series of mental introjections of suffering.

Here Laplanche is also addressing what is termed the auto-erotic or auto-affective relation, where the 'self' turns back on itself. This involves Freud's discussion of narcissism (1914) and the auto-erotic relation. The problem I have with Laplanche's formulation is that a division again emerges between the organism as sheer behaviour and the psychical level as the realm of ideation. In this formulation the affective turn of the self is a psychical construct and has no relation to the somatic field.

In actuality the auto-erotic relation directly involves bodily experience and somatic expression and the complexity of relations therein, but in the first propping account outlined, the biology as bedrock model returns to keep the level of biology and the vital body processes outside the sphere of a nuanced auto-self/object imaginary which is, strictly speaking, for a psychic ideational sphere. Likewise a neat divide is created between physical and psychic trauma. Rather than a wound piercing the surface of the body which results in a violent shock, a breaking-in to the organism's envelope, there is instead what is to become 'an intrusion into the psyche of a group of ideational representatives' (Laplanche 1985: 134). Laplanche argues that the 'foreign body' becomes an 'intrusion of ideas into the psyche'; by placing the entire transposition of the experience of trauma onto the so-called psychic sphere, this formula effectively leaves the body out of the account.

Laplanche provides insight into a general trend in British-based Kleinian-influenced psychoanalysis, the moving of trauma into an understanding of the mind. So, for example, Garland (1998) in her development of psychic trauma via Bion shows that the breach is in the function of the mental container and that Freud's reference to the protoplasmic vesicle is not to do with the body or physicality, but instead is a metaphor for the workings of the psyche. The problem here is that the focus on trauma as a mental phenomenon fails to account adequately for the way trauma can live on somatically. As a reading of Freud, Laplanche and Garland's focus on the psyche and the mental does not allow for the way Freud's discussion could be furthered to understand the body–trauma relation (to be expanded in Part III), here what is being shown is how the problem gets set up and why there is a need for a shift in formulation.

Laplanche refers to 'the spine in the flesh' to describe metaphorically the psychic experience of the 'alien entity', or 'foreign body', as a way of addressing an intrusion of ideas into a psyche that cannot be assimilated.

However, Freud's reference to a breach in the surface of the vesicle, in 'Beyond the pleasure principle' (1920), refers to the skin boundary of the vesicle. Laplanche's account focuses on intrusion into the mental sphere, whereas I shall return to the idea that a body boundary is breached and look at this specifically in relation to the skin and body surface in Part III. The aim will be to transpose Freud's language of quantities of 'masses in motion' breaking into a surface with force, to a relational language, where, instead of a vesicle, what is in its place is the vulnerable, entirely exposed surface of the child's body perturbed by the premature entry of the environmental other.

Between Skins: The Alien Entity and the Flesh

The aim is to understand the phenomenon of 'the alien entity' that resides neither outside nor wholly inside, and exists like an uninvited intruder, not only as a group of invasive ideas inside a psyche but also as a feature of somatic symptoms involving organs and other bodily processes. In Part III, I shall focus on altering sensory states of the skin surface. These will be related to a fundamental breach in bodily integrity – not only a mental breach but a veritable breach in bodily being.

Let's say there is an inevitable breaching of the other into the body lived as a somatic state in the very senses of the flesh and not in the mind's eye alone, an inevitable intrusion felt in terms of somatic states. The premature entry of the other is understood in a number of ways in Laplanche's later writings (e.g. 1989), as the enigmatic signifier, as an incomprehensible adult sexuality intruding into the child, or in attachment as the disruption of affiliate bonds, which is so often a fundamental perturbation between attachment and sexuality, as in cases of sexual abuse or the instant of the violating other that lives on in visual and somatic flashbacks that occur in the aftermath of torture (post-trauma).

I shall attempt to address more adequately somatic phenomena as described by my American patient Daniel (see also Diamond 2003):

> Daniel had been abused by his adopted elder brother from the age of 5 to 10. I started working with him at 13. As he recalled the abuse he would intermittently recoil with pain in the genital and related areas. He explained that the sensation cut him open and was simultaneously painful and pleasurable. It was the most disturbing sensation. He felt that it was somehow not his but that the pain was being done to him, as if he were inhabited by someone else who left him breathless, gasping for air, with no space and at the same time sexually aroused.

This is 'the alien entity' not only mentally experienced but sensorial and lived. In his paper 'The uncanny' (1919) Freud describes a state of *Unheimlich* as the experience of estrangement in the familiar, not being at home at the hearth. In the above case, Daniel, in a state of anguish, said that the sensations in his genitals were weird: he felt strange in himself, as though he was being controlled by someone else.

Victor Tausk in 'On the origin of the "influencing machine" in schizophrenia' (1933 [1919]), refers to bodily estranged, uncanny states in schizophrenia, taking the form of visual perceptions. In this book I regard such states also as sensory, and often occurring as part of a somatic symptom, which are also present in the general population, although they are more marked in trauma cases. What is interesting is how the somatic symptom is described as a way of not feeling at home in one's own body and likened to bodily states of depersonalization and de-realization, a state of *Unheimlich*.

To Sum Up

In Laplanche's main propping account there is a real object for the fixed biological vital order but not for the psyche, where 'the object to be re-found is not the lost object, but its metonym' (Laplanche 1985: 102), for example, the symbolic breast, not the milk. There is an object for the vital physical functions but an absence registered only for the level of psychic activity, which relegates the complexity of the symbol, as based in absence, without an object, as existing for the psyche only. The vital bodily processes are left bound to the object of the need outside the order of symbol and meaning.

The distinction between biological need (tied to the actual object) on the one hand, and the psyche (as the field where the symbol resides and absence is registered) on the other, is widespread in psychoanalysis. This leaves the vital body order stuck in a preordained biology outside the domain of the symbol. I wish to explore how the biological vital order partakes in absence and sensory loss and can access significance, and how functional and sensory alterations relate to this dimension of experience.

6

The Problem of Dualism and the Division between the Vital and the Psychic Order

Propping fails as an explanation of the transformation of one register into another. Instead, it ends up asserting an unbridgeable division between two discrete orders. This does not only return to an old mind/body dualism but also highlights where the difficulty lies. It is in the assumption of a fixed vital body, so unchanged as an entity that it fails to provide any opening to a different order of being, so rooted in its proper place that propping results in a stasis rather than an account of a movement.

Propping in terms of its genesis assumes that there is a natural order at origin, a move from body to psyche. Laplanche overtly argues that his philosophical basis is Hegelian, noting that the derivation from vital terrain to the psychic order is the movement of the 'thing itself' (1985: 9), a truth which he notes Hegel made explicit (9), a derivation beyond an etymology, a semantics (10), a 'slippage of meaning' (50) which is 'happening parallel to a certain slippage in reality itself' in the 'domain of entities' (Laplanche 1985: 50).

However, the vital biological order so preordained and determined, so in-itself that it remains steadfast, no negation of identity from within to get it on its way. There can in fact be no derivation of the second order from the primary register: metonymy described as continuity and metaphor as resemblance, both of which are now in the failed logic, bound to the identity of the thing – the vital body, so much so that metonymy simply evokes a continuation of its first order to an adjacent field, while metaphor carries over an analogous likeness of the entity, a resemblance based on a similarity in structure and function.

What occurs is a simple carrying over of the vital order as itself, a continuity of the same; hence, in the displacement of the milk for fantasmatic breast,

Between Skins: The Body in Psychoanalysis – Contemporary Developments, First Edition. Nicola Diamond.

what occurs is a 'relation of essential continuity which leads us to slide almost indifferently from one to the other from the milk [to not milk] and then the breast as its symbol' (Laplanche 1985: 20). Because absence, that is negation of the object milk cannot in fact occur for the biological bodily function itself, grounded as it is in the object of the need, the 'almost indifferent sliding' becomes an absolute indifference to difference.

The vital biological order cannot leave its origin: either it passes over as the self-same or there is an abracadabra switch to the psychic register – the breast in its absence as symbol for the psychic ideational field alone. So Laplanche reverts to the language of psyche and the mental sphere. A rift is thus created between the vital order and ideation. The relational connection between sensory somatic states with the field of ideas cannot be conceived, nor can 'the turning around of the subject's own self' relate to the auto-erotic body; such 'reflexive' complexity is for the psychic field.

It remains a mystery as to how loss can ever be brought into the vital order. For loss is the registering of an absence as a lack and the vital order is described as being so present, so full of being, that there is no means to instil, no ability to register, a negation.

Propping cannot declare a process of becoming but is arrested: unable to budge, there are two stages as punctuated moments which, like the example of Zeno's paradox, cannot account for the movement from one point to the next. Instead one is left to play at jumping over an otherwise unbridgeable gulf, hence the sudden switch to the second order of register, the psychic field, an entirely distinct realm.

The creation of the psyche from that of the body involves a movement without motion, such a slight erring, requiring a miracle for a shift to take place from nature's ground into the domain of psychic being. Instead of a slippage there is simply an unexplained rupture which creates binary terrains (of body and psyche), thus returning to the very problem that propping was meant to overcome.

Thus derivation from within the thing itself – the fixed biological order – cannot take place. Being so much itself, the fixed and determinate order cannot open up to anything other than itself. By definition its being is indivisible; it cannot open up to negation and difference from within. So a binary ontology is a consequence: 'what realm of reality . . . the living organism . . . or a totally different level from that of biology?' (Laplanche 1985: 51). Propping in this account does not open up the vital processes to and onto something other but instead functions in a binary logic where two discrete registers are invented each pertaining to an identity closed in on itself.

On the one hand, there is the biological organism grounded in its mechanistic and material physicality, a matter of 'sheer behaviour and physiology' (Laplanche 1985: 97). On the other, there are the drives proper and their symbolism which for sexuality is psychical and ideational, 'the mental field of fantasms', 'the reflexive turning around on the self' (89) entails 'an internalization of the whole of the action on the psychical level, a process of an entirely different order from a real activity (i.e. of the muscles)' (97) – the reflexive turn for the psyche only and of an entirely different order from the physical domain where the body is located. The body remains stuck in its brute and dumb being. In this chapter the dualist ontology has been made explicit, this is not exclusive to this context. Such underpinnings also typify residual dualisms existing in the other psychoanalytic accounts discussed.

7

The Vital Revisited
Deconstructing the Vital Order from Within

The vital order fails to function as a life process.[1] What has been discovered is how biological life has come to resemble an inert state without momentum rather than being vital and life-giving. The main propping thesis has attributed a biological sufficiency to the functions, providing such a substantive blueprint that no space exists within the vital biological order for the deviation of source, aim and object. No such detour can take place, leaving the psychic register with no choice but to be a second register imposed on the first body order which in essence remains itself.

The Reversal and Implications: The Vital is Not the Prop but Now Requires Propping

I shall now explore a very different account of propping, based on an entirely other logic that shall be traced as a logic of the supplement[2] (Derrida 1976). The vital biological order in this logic will be revealed as more plastic and open, as in fact insubstantial in being and thus in need of supplementation. The prop is now needed in order to support the biological sphere where it is found lacking, and this is supplied by the other in the form of a communicative provision.[3] The (m)other is now required and acquired to provide a structure for the vital processes. What is described is nothing more than a scaffold-type construction derived from this (m)other. Now what will be observed is how models of life that construct the vital terrain are already underway in bodily processes directing the pathway to be taken.

Between Skins: The Body in Psychoanalysis – Contemporary Developments,
First Edition. Nicola Diamond.
© 2013 John Wiley & Sons, Ltd. Published 2013 by John Wiley & Sons, Ltd.

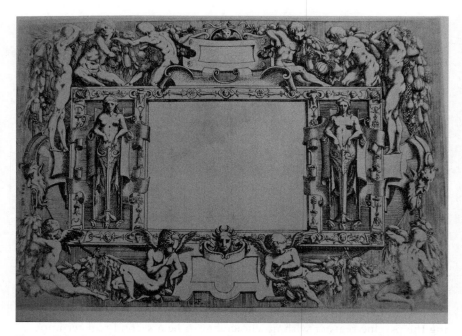

Figure 7.1 Derrida's parergon theory, illustrated in drawing by Antonio Fantuzzi (*c*.1544).

The *Oxford English Dictionary* describes a prop as like a scaffold that supports a building. At first sight and according to convention a scaffold can be described as framing a building, and as a frame it is not the building itself. According to Derrida's initial description of the parergon, there is a frame distinguished from that which it frames – the ergon, the work itself (Derrida 1987b). The parergon, which frames the work (ergon), is viewed as outside and external to the work; however, on closer inspection it appears to be undeniably and unalterably part of the work, just as a scaffold is an inherent part of a building's construction and structure (see Figure 7.1).

In the case of the vital biological order, it is found to require support; it is effectively propped and then becomes indistinguishable from the prop itself. The vital order is thus no longer substantiated by a given biological substratum, but instead is made out of a prop derived from the (m)other.

Instead of the propping concept acting as a bridging term between the body and the psychic order, it shows that models of life derived from the other are endemic to the vital order itself. This prop from the other within the vital sphere, propping up the biological processes, opens up the vital biological terrain, from the inside to the outside world.

In this more radical and, I would argue, viable account Laplanche notes: 'it is doubtful that we have the right to hypostatize [the] vital order in the human being as an earlier stage, an a priori or infrastructure, (1985: 47). This is a position that I embrace in this book. He continues to describe how the vital order lacks a definite structure and direction. For at first it is somehow 'feeble or immature' and thus requires the introduction of sexuality into the human child (47) before the child is ready:

> The very term 'genesis' evokes the notion of an emergence, the possibility of a linear understanding of what is later by what precedes it. But this perspective should be corrected by a reversal. On the one hand, the proposed genesis implies in fact what might be called a fundamental imperfection in the human being, a dehiscence. What is 'perverted' by sexuality is indeed the function which is somehow feeble or pre-mature. Therein lies the whole problem of the 'vital order' in man, and of the possibility, or rather the impossibility, of grasping it beneath what has come to cover it over. (Laplanche 1985: 25)

This definition of course completely eschews the linearity of the main propping thesis, the chronology of the vital order as a first state, the initial ground and bedrock for all to come is 'corrected by a reversal . . . of the idea of a prior state, which is then succeeded by another second order' (25). It needs also to be said that this fundamental eruption of the linear model of development is in keeping with contemporary models of the developmental process whereby a developmental line is rejected in favour of greater temporal complexity.

The recognition of how vital body processes are experience-dependent for development means that the environmental influence is a condition of what is to follow and there is a relational process, where the intervention of the other, required for any vital happening, brings a temporal delay, and fills the gap with a communicative response which can have effects retroactively. The absolute and determinate biological bedrock model is fundamentally at odds with the second model, that of the vital-natural order as lacking and incomplete and requiring a prop in order to prosper. In pinpointing the difference in this double claim, another model of the body emerges as the key focus, which proves to be much more helpful and viable and is not to be conflated with the immovable biological bedrock (and linear model). I shall draw out this second model and spell out and develop its radical implications.

Laplanche's crucial rereading of Freud continues to generate discussion and is not circumscribed or limited by intent at the time of writing. Laplanche was aware of the dual models of the biological at work. What he does *not* do is foreground the significance of the second model and its reframing of the vital biological (bio-logos) to a more open plastic model of bio-life. Nor does Laplanche explore how the alternative bio-life model can better help us understand the symptomatic somatic states that are encountered in the consulting room and in everyday life.

My aim in this book is to draw out and expand upon the second view of the vital order (as bio-life) and show how this model provides a way out of the dualistic impasse and reveals a fundamental relation between body and world. In *New Foundations for Psychoanalysis* Laplanche adds:

> The instinctual set ups are insufficient, and in any event they appear too late, with a gap: they are not there when one would expect, i.e. at birth. From birth onwards, insofar as this gap subsists, there occurs a kind of disqualification of the Instinct, the satisfaction of needs cannot pass through pre-established set ups, that will emerge only gradually, and according to the maturational rhythm of the central nervous system, but satisfaction must pass from the beginning through intersubjectivity, i.e. by way of another human, the mother. (1989: 60)

There is a lot to unpack here, but for now suffice it to point out that the relation of the biological functions to the drive and the developments therein no longer takes place in a vacuum, in an entirely interiorized and internal process. From the first, the biological processes have to go through intersubjective mediation and the other becomes inherent in the experience.

Given that the instinctual set-up is insufficient and has to pass through the field of the other before any established set-up is in place, the intersubjective field already intervenes and exerts its influence. The other is required to prop and thus support the biological processes which are insufficient in themselves. By the time of maturation, the field of the other and all the provision this brings has had its effects and has fundamentally altered forever the course that maturation takes. Take many of the body functions essential to life. At birth the digestive system cannot process solids and the baby often regurgitates food, the sphincter has no control over excretion, hence the need for nappies, and the baby's regulation of temperature is not stable, hence the need for environmental control.

The other's intervention arrives and already props up the function, influencing its course forever; maturation is incomplete and then arrives too late. The feeding relation directs the course that ingestion takes. The other's intervention provides a response and influences the style of taking in and of spitting out the food. Here it is interesting to think how the mode of intervention becomes inscribed in the body processes themselves. For example, in the development of sphincter performance is there a tendency towards greater withholding or releasing, and where does the pleasure lie? What are the associated mood memories accompanying these bodily activities? In my view, the relational developmental pathway can have profound effects on appetite, manner of eating, desire and its relation to food, bladder control or lack of control, bowel inhibition/expression and sensation, mood/pleasure/displeasure states and meaning. What types of meanings get established with the bodily acts, their frequency or a tendency towards abstinence? Cultural norms and rituals, attachment and loss, sexual desire and separation, I suggest, can alter the bodily processes themselves.

Motor coordination has not yet developed, hence the 'premature' entry of the mirror other and the reliance on image (Lacan 1977b) to provide an appearance of form when there is still muscular incoordination and neurological immaturity. What I argue specifically in this book, is that the development of the body ego relates to the lived body, which is lacking in form, the premise being that from the first, as my reading of Esther Bick (1968) emphasizes, the newborn does not come into the world with a body that is 'held together', which is reflected in chaotic body movement (see also Part III). The newborn who is placed supine on a fleece flays its arms and legs in all directions. There is a lack of motor control and coordination. Swaddling has historically been practiced, and can be described as a way 'to bind the baby in one piece'. This is what physical holding does – 'hold together in a unity' what is otherwise giving at the seams, where 'the centre cannot hold' (as Yeats puts it in 'The second coming'). I further suggest that motor control and coordination can be inhibited, agitated and styled into ways of comporting according to the relation with others and the affective–bodily meaningful exchanges that ensue. Likewise, the skin sensation – excessive irritability, sensitivity, or lack of it – are possible outcomes of the premature entry of the other and the ongoing developmental relations, the quality of sentient responses these interactions bring (see discussion with examples in Part III).

The response of the other can incite and excite and thereby open somatic states and sensory experience in divergent ways: there is regulation and deregulation. Laplanche refers to the 'marginal effect' that transgresses certain quantitative thresholds, which in experiential terms is related to a certain level of excitation and excess. It is clear that the body is involved in this effect, as Freud made clear in his writings and as Laplanche notes: zones are generalized and every cutaneous region and orifice can become subject to the marginal effect.

Reframing the Vital Order: The Lack of Preordained Limit and Excess

In his reference to feeding, Laplanche (1985) notes in Freudian style the taking in of milk and satisfaction by the object and the sucking at the breast, but more than this the 'lust for sucking' that Lindner has also identified (in Laplanche 1985: 18). Laplanche refers to the fundamental distinction between functional pleasure, the reduction of tension and the more radical principle once related to the death drive, of an increase in excitation that disrupts equilibrium. However, what can be witnessed in the marginal effect is the interruption of functional pleasure from very early on, with the possibility of increases in excitation, a potential that is already at the heart of the vital processes. Laplanche notes that once the linear genesis is eschewed *dehiscence* better describes the movement. In place of a fixed, immovable bedrock at the vital origin, what is found instead is *dehiscence* which is defined as 'a gaping' and 'divergence'. In botany, the term implies 'the bursting open of capsules, fruits, anthers, etc., in order to discharge their contents' (*Shorter Oxford English Dictionary*).

It is a common occurrence for a baby to take too much milk too often, so that it spills out of the corners of its mouth. A baby often wants to suck too long, and strives to find the nipple again, even though the (m)other may not think her child needs it. *That limits fail to act as such* in the infant's early struggle and enjoyment of nourishment, and the attendant impatience frequently shown by the child who wants to have the sensuous experience again, speak of excess as a condition for the force that motivates the striving for nourishment and its after-effects.

When the infant does not limit its intake of milk, it indicates that regulation has yet to be established, because the immaturity of the digestive system leaves biology open to the intervention of the other to facilitate regulation and structure, and also because excess and the sensuous lust for sucking are already being stimulated and are therefore part of the somatic process, in this instance of taking in nourishment. If the functions were cleanly fixed with preset limits, how would the experience of uncontrollable cravings even be a potential for hunger?

Merleau-Ponty, noting an overflow, observes an *exstasis* (to use Heidegger's term) as part of vital processes – 'forms of vital behaviour deviate from their pre-ordained direction, through a sort of leakage' (1962: 189) – beyond any preset threshold before the limits have been set. The functions are breached in their open nature to the marginal effect. So the erring in sensual striving does indeed take the biological rule with it. That is why the process and experience of the bodily functions for life can become profoundly confounded with the sensual and sexual, such as when the nourishment for life turns into a form of sensual pleasuring and excess demand.

Likewise, the intensity of sexual and sensuous stimulation is bodily. Freud in 'Instincts and their vicissitudes' (1915) and 'Three essays on sexuality' (1905) refers to 'polymorphous perversity' to describe a primary sensual openness and potential for divergent possible paths for somatic expression. Clinically it can be observed that in cases of early stimulation in 'precocious' sexuality and sexual abuse, the repetition of these experiences, where excitation is more excessive and a developmental pathway forms which results in an increased striving for stimulation, sexual hyper-arousal is common and can be the basis of an 'addictive' sexuality.

> John was sexually abused by an older cousin, and the course of his corporeal experience was activated in this process, as was the direction of his sexuality. For him, the slightest touch from another would cause an erection and he would complain of feeling what he called 'over-sexual' all the time.
>
> John began 'precocious' sexual relations with a boy from school, Bill. He described how Bill would stimulate him for hours. They had a rule: Bill could touch John, but it was one-way, Bill getting vicarious pleasure through John's pleasure. John said, 'I got double stimulation – for the both of us.' He found as an adult that he could lie in bed all night in a heightened state of continual arousal. He told me how even in a public setting it could feel so urgent that he had to seek out a toilet.

Appetite is open to excess and this can be expressed as an essential biological function, like eating, sleeping, excreting, secreting, or as a hyper-aroused, sensual sexuality. Any function can be highly sexualized, as Freud observes in *Studies on Hysteria* (Freud and Breuer 1893–5) and 'Three essays on sexuality' (1905). This may sound obvious, but the dominant trend has been to ignore the soma, which means that we have forgotten or lost sight of the obvious.

The vital field does not revolve around satisfaction and satiation alone. Freud notes that at the heart of instinctual processes there is a resistance to complete satisfaction:

> The reproach against the mother, which goes further, is that she gave the child too little milk (or too much), which is construed against her as a lack of love. Now there is some justification for this – but whatever the true state of affairs may have been, it is impossible that the child's approach can be justified as often as it is met with. It seems, rather, that the child's avidity for its earliest nourishment is altogether insatiable. (Freud 1932–6: 122)

And Laplanche describes how in a state of nursling dependency the bodily processes aiming for 'satisfaction' necessarily from the first have to pass through intersubjectivity and a gap subsists 'between immediate satisfaction and the signs which accompany every deferred, imperfect contingent and mediated satisfaction brought about by a fellow creature' (1985: 71).

The Other, Temporal Delay and Somatic Lack

The other's imperfect responses introduce a temporal delay and a deferral of satisfaction and the gap marks sensory experience for evermore. When 'maturation' is said to come into play, such a pathway has already been fundamentally disrupted and altered, for the somatic has already been opened to the marginal effect and deferral, a lack being introduced in the sensory field, the effect of the other on bio-vital experience.

Absence and separation come into being initially as a gap in the temporal delay and the fact of the imperfect response marking for ever the somatic striving. Whether the flow of milk falters or the breast is temporarily removed, wanting is experienced as a longing for what is not available and transforms into a somatic craving. In the ebb and flow of the other's goings and comings, the gap furrows a lack endemic in somatic life itself. Lacan's concept of need–demand–desire describes the shift of need into desire; clearly, what is emphasized here is the way the somatic lives this out.

Interestingly, Freud notes in 'The project for a scientific psychology' that it is not simply energy passing through the system, for the 'senses appropriate by a period of excitation' (1895: 310), inferring that a temporal delay spaces sensory experience and characterizes sensory receptivity. In the same work he states that the nursing infant is dependent on the other to have its essential bodily needs met, and in consequence 'the path of discharge acquires a secondary function of the highest importance, that of communication' (1895: 313–317).

The Vital Bodily Processes Open onto Memory

Freud could be interpreted as saying here that the path of discharge is concomitant with the function of communication. The caretaker introduces a response which conveys affect and meaning, which in turn indelibly colours somatic experience, giving rise to somatic–affective–evaluative states.

Now the somatic requires a prop support derived from the other, and the communication this brings. The intervention of the other and the sensory signs that accompany the response are already at work from very early on (prior to full maturation), facilitating specific pathways in the developmental process, reliant as the somatic processes are on a particular pattern of interaction between parent and infant.

As early as 'The project' (1895) Freud, as Laplanche comments, expresses all this in terms of neurons, facilitations or frayings: 'since the reproduction of a past experience is not a resurgence of qualitative elements, it is likened to the fact that energy will again pass through certain paths in the system' (Laplanche 1985: 60). Freud's reference to neurological processes and pathways could be viewed as relevant, in so far as the qualitative intervention derived from the (m)other impacts on brain and body processes, creating and forging neurological relations, setting up dynamic connections between sensory receptors and networks in the brain. This is done as the (m)other intervenes – touches and mirrors her infant – offering a communicative, sensorial-gestural and vocal response and intonation with every deferred act – a style patterning interactive experience.

In addressing memory in 'The project', Freud provides a hypothetical description of the physis and psyche neurons, where in the language of quantity, memory is understood as a cathexis of energy within the neuron. This enables the neuron to become impermeable to the impact of undifferentiated quantity and hence retain the forged pathway based on acquired memory. Freud here is referring to what he initially calls the psyche neurons and how differential neural pathways and connections are formed and retained by memory, as a portion of quantity is held back.

In 'Freud and the scene of writing' (1978) Derrida reworks Freud's language of quantity to show how Freud is struggling to think memory as the trace, the non-present remainder of the past that forges facilitations by resisting any onslaught of fresh stimuli, which would threaten to flood the neuron and thereby level out and lead to undifferentiation.

Freud at first makes a clear distinction between the physis and psyche neurons. The psyche neurons 'retain a cathexis'; in quantitative terminology this implies memory. In contrast, the physis neurons are described as fully permeable and divested of energy which implies no retention of cathexis and therefore no capacity for memory. However, later in the paper he notes that, owing to 'another circumstance' (1895: 257) this rule is broken. This other circumstance is very familiar to us, which is the demand to meet the 'exigencies of life' (the urgencies to survive – to eat, to shit, to sweat, to breath, to sleep and so on) and how this requires an increasing complexity of the organism, whereby to meet a biological function there is recourse to another who responds to the bodily functions – hunger, respiration, attachment – and in doing so:

> In consequence, the nervous system is obliged to abandon its initial trend to inertia [that is, to bringing the level (of) Qn to zero]. It must put up with (maintaining) a store of Qn sufficient to meet the demand for a specific action. (Freud 1895: 257)

This implies that the decisive distinction between the workings of psyche and physis neurons breaks down. For the physis neurons also have to retain a cathexis of energy (memory in quantitative language) in order to perform basic biological processes to sustain life.

This breakdown in distinction between physis and psyche neurons on the basis of memory implies that the function of memory is broadened and cuts across any division between psyche and physis neurons. By translating quantitative terminology into relational terms, it could be said that Freud describes how the mark left by others remains as a neural memory. The trace of past experience, envisaged as a breach by force which initially breaks open pathways. In relational thinking this would be the inevitable intrusion of the other that leaves their permanent mark as memory trace.

Freud states in 'The project' that 'the path of discharge acquires a secondary function of the highest importance, that of communication' (1895: 313–317). Thus when the other intervenes to complete the specific biological action, and that the physis neurons require a 'store of quantity' (cathexis) to meet the specific action (257). With this formulation there is a transformation of meaning regarding the vital functions. Whereas basic vital functions had been understood as automatic, an instinctual process, and likened to a reflex action, they now become a biological need expressed in a relationship where a memory is acquired and the 'pathway of discharge', the 'neuronal pathways', are forged from memory of past experience, from a communication that leaves its indelible mark.

A specific action changes its sense, from a simple instinctual response to a specific set-up that derives its structure importantly from the other's intervention, her communication and the memory henceforth laid down. The vital order is no longer based on pre-programmed processes but becomes the vital set-up (a point that will be elaborated later).

Contemporary developments in neuroscience like Ansermet and Magistretti's book *Biology of Freedom* (2007) argue for neural plasticity and memory. This opens neuroscience and psychoanalysis to a joint understanding of memory as trace, whereby experience leaves its mark upon us but at the same time such a memory is not biologically fixed once and for all but is open to change. Ansermet and Magistretti note:

> the concept of plasticity means that experience can be inscribed in the neuronal network, the event leaves a trace, and simultaneously time is embodied. But this trace can be reworked or put into play again in a different way by being associated with different traces. (2007: 13)

This complements Derrida's (1978) reading of 'The project', where he notes that Freud is struggling to regard memory as trace, which in the language of the project means trying to address memory as both a permanent alteration of the neuron and a memory open to change, capacity of the neurons to forge new facilitations.

Diamond and Marrone (2003) refer to the way memory is not immediately laid down, but is a process that neuroscientists recognize as temporal and psychoanalysis notes can involve deferred action, or *Nachträglichkeit*. This is when the significance of an event becomes elaborated after the fact and is revised retrospectively. Memory, both from a neuroscience standpoint and in lived experience, is in movement temporally and can change over the life span, with ongoing interactions bio-social relations.

Ansermet and Magistretti point out that 'plasticity is not exclusively a mental phenomenon but involves the body. For . . . traces left by experience are associated with somatic states' (2007: xvii). They draw upon Damasio's description of somatic markers, whereby memory is based in affective somatic states (Damasio *et al.* 1991). The neuroscience standpoint I adopt views interpersonal and intercorporeal relations as fundamental and primary. In the context of the Freud–Klein controversies of 1941–5, the counter-argument to Susan Isaacs' 1948 paper on phantasy was that bodily impulses do not internally give rise to rudimentary mental representatives sui generis, and, as Hayman (1994) notes, Edward Glover argues that the feeding relationship is already underway and the memory trace derived from it acts as the raw material, the daily residue, from which 'fantasy' can be build. In this respect any reference to 'internal' somatic states relating to the 'exigencies of life' are necessarily and always situated in a relationship which brings a response and a communication.

The memory trace, with every revivification of the somatic striving, is always a repetition which is never exactly the same each time. From this perspective the memory trace and somatic states coexist and revivification brings the mark left by others that live on as memory. As noted, in dealing with even the most basic definition of the exigencies of life (urgent biological functions) and the specific action (the process performed to meet the urges), there is no somatic need without some relation and context and there is no somatic state without the activation of the memory trace. The interpersonal world has already been introduced, with body sensations and strivings, as have the memories derived from it.

To sum up: the memory trace, a remembering, a certain non-presence with every future re-evocation of a somatic need, a temporal deferral and delay yields a gap and an absence of any object for somatic longing, giving rise to a potential symbolic dimension. Absence is in somatic life and is not relegated to an entirely other psychic plane.

Identity as Difference: The Vital Order as Vital Field

The vital biological order is no longer defined as a founding origin, sufficient in itself, in its own identity/being, for what has been shown is how a fixed bio-logos fails to prop, in terms of acting as indivisible ground, but instead requires propping from a field outside itself – in the other, from the first. The prop derived from the environmental other is not an addition superimposed from a pure outside, but becomes integral and endemic to the structure of the vital processes.

Ontologically speaking, Heidegger in *Identity and Difference* (1969) describes how the logic of identity fails to say what it means to say, for the premise begins that for A to be itself, A is A. However, the formula $A=A$ (A is equal to itself) already evokes two: $A+A$ in fact implies *a relation with* for A to be the same *as itself*. Any absolute claim to identity already has fission at origin: there is divisibility therein.

In *The Legend of Freud* Max Weber observes that for Freud to account for the origin of life he must depart from the logic of identity:

> To do this, he must partition the origin so that the walls of its Fort! are no longer impervious to an exteriority without which [vital] Life can never depart. For it is only as the effect of a double or split [vital] origin, an origin that is dislocated and disrupted by 'external' forces – influences and which leave their mark upon us. (Weber 1982: 139)

I have traced how identity attributed to the vital order is dislocated and already disrupted by external relations right from the first; the vital order is opened to the other from within, the interior is already outside itself, inside is outside, and the metaphor of Merleau-Ponty's glove turned outside-in demonstrates clearly the internal processes as indelibly marked by an exteriority which forever leaves its mark – an 'internal–external instance' where the other really lives 'deep' inside our skins – 'starting' at the heart of what can no longer be called the vital order but is now referred to as the vital field.

Notes

1   The vital order is another way of referring to the biological order, particularly the body functions that Freud describes as necessary for the 'exigencies of life', often seen as deriving from the body interior, which is internal to the organism. These include digestion, excretion, secretion, sexual urges and attachment needs. I use a broader definition and would include other visceral autonomic processes.

  For sake of clarity I refer to the 'vital biological order'. It is what I earlier referred to as the biological bedrock account, but the word 'vital' connects to Laplanche. As the chapter unravels the vital order begins to transform into the vital field or the vital set-up. This is because, through the reworking of the propping account, the vital is not simply biologically pre-programmed and with identity, but requires propping which is derived from the other and from the social field. Responses are from the other, as is the communication this brings; this sets up memory pathways/patterns and provides structural support and constructs for the vital or what I refer to as 'bio-life'. The vital becomes a set-up, a vital set-up. By opening onto an outside world and others, the vital order becomes a vital field.

  Likewise the meaning of 'specific action', which had been largely an automatic instinctual process describing the action of meeting the biological urges, becomes a specific set-up where the other, their communication and the memory this brings are the prop structure for the process.

2   Derrida, particularly in his earlier writings, has been seminal to this book. He is a key philosopher of the past century, particularly in post-phenomenological developments, and his concern with writing is not reducible to any text but has broader implications: the way the trace marks the flesh–nature–matter, affecting all living beings and our relation to artifacts, technology, communication media

and so on. Derrida's deconstructive strategy has not only led to a crucial reworking of key texts, but has been a means of addressing the nature of the body and
of biology itself.

3   'Communication' is a very general term to begin to signpost, referring as it does
to the understanding that emerges from the affective–semiotic exchange, the
birth of the symbol, the nature of language and the mark it leaves upon us. It
derives as a term from its use in everyday language; in my use of the term, I do
not assume that communication exists as an unproblematic communion between
persons.

8

Rebuilding the Vital Field

The Edifice: Intercorporeality

In the opening chapters of the book, I referred to the key players in the paradigmatic shift from a one-person-body psychology to a two-body and multi-personal approach. I also touched on the philosophical way of describing persons as intersubjective, and most pertinently bodies as intercorporeal, and the way these descriptions have been the basis for findings in developmental psychology, neuroscience and are evident in psychoanalysis.

Access to language, Trevarthen (1978, 1990, 1993) makes clear, starts with the intercorporeal embodied space whereby affect and sensory relations build a rudimentary and an ever more complex semiotics. However, there has been some misunderstanding in the debates. Daniel Stern (1977, 1985) has described how in reciprocal interactions shared meanings emerge. Stern refers to 'shared affective states' in infant–parent interchange. Here he describes a quality of empathic attunement. This, however, has resulted in some confusion concerning the meaning of 'intersubjectivity' and 'intercorporeality'.

In its original philosophical meaning, the *intersubjective* opening between persons or between bodies (intercorporeality) is inevitable and unavoidable, since what is implied is the fact of somatic interrelatedness as such, that in a fundamental way there are no discrete organisms but instead a direct altering and infiltration of one another is possible: the other body is in me and I am in them, and we have no control over this.

Intercorporeality describes a way of being affected that just is; it is a condition of existence, of social being. This does not presuppose any state of harmony, of being in union, of oneness or total attunement; on the contrary,

Between Skins: The Body in Psychoanalysis – Contemporary Developments,
First Edition. Nicola Diamond.
© 2013 John Wiley & Sons, Ltd. Published 2013 by John Wiley & Sons, Ltd.

the experience can be profoundly disquieting owing to the fact that intercorporeal states threaten the belief in the bodily I and the simple idea of body ownership and the majesty the egoistic self.

Therefore intersubjectivity and intercorporeality, as conditions of existence, are not predicated upon a well-attuned quality of relating but exist between us regardless. It is for this reason that 'negative' intersubjectivity or intercorporeality can and do equally affect us, get inside our skins and into the vital and visceral processes.

It seems that Lacan's later rejection of intersubjectivity relates to what has been identified as a qualitative definition, where harmony, unity and more imaginary and idealized ways of being with the other are presupposed. From my perspective here, a qualitative insight into types of intersubjectivity and intercorporeality is relevant only for understanding specific developmental trajectories and should not be confused with the ontological existence of an inevitable intercorporeal state of being. It is clear that from this perspective intercorporeality should not be confused with an undifferentiated symbiosis; it is a space that primarily is not organized around the ego (I); such a clean differentiation between bodily self and other comes later, as the outcome of specific relationships that facilitate such development.[1] The oceanic feeling Freud writes of, which may be nostalgically held up as bliss, is a product of the ego-I that desires to merge and make everything the same as itself.

When Laplanche refers to the vital processes passing inevitably through intersubjectivity he implies the inescapable fact of intersubjective-intercorporeal existence. As has been noted in previous chapters, intercorporeality implies that the other comes first. In 'The child's relation with others' Merleau-Ponty describes how the child finds its body in the other's body (1964: 146), that is, the infant finds the body in the gesture of the other. There is a relation between Trevarthen's (1978) work on proto-conversation and intersubjectivity as defined in phenomenology. Meltzoff and Moore (1977), who refer to 'innate intercorporeality' (which can be likened to Trevarthen's 'innate sociality') likewise observe adult–infant interaction. They show the way a baby mirrors or mimics the other's gesture. Forty-six minutes after birth a baby can stick out its tongue from observing an adult doing the same, but this is before it knows where its body is and where the tongue is located. Merleau-Ponty describes how the infant primarily feels and finds its body in the other and from there derives an experience of its own, while Heidegger believes that this kind of spatial situation is not based in geometric space which locates bodies as discrete entities.

Later thinkers argue that there is a neurobiological basis for intercorporeal existence. The discovery of mirror neurons is one basis for such bodily claims. Mirror neurons simulate the other's actions in neuronal activity. Mirror neurons in a monkey's premotor area F5 fire not only when the monkey performs a certain class of action but also when it observes another monkey or the experimenter performing a similar action. Human emotional learning through mirroring the gestures of others based in the simulative capacity of the mirror neurons has been regarded as implying that our neural systems are in contact with the other and that their actions resonate in us (Rizzolatti *et al*. 1996; Diamond and Marrone 2003: 134–135). Such findings also claim to account for the neurobiological process that underlies identification as described by Freud.

There has been a proliferation of papers in research on mirror neurons, in particular exploring their relation to empathy. Recent publications suggest that dysfunction of the mirror neurons can be found in cases of autism (Iacoboni and Dapretto 2006). Gallese and colleagues (2004) focus on touch and the way the touch of another is simultaneously neuronally mapped. An example is taken from an adult watching a James Bond film in which a tarantula crawls on Bond's chest and how this makes the viewer literally shiver – as if the spider were crawling on their own chest (Gallese *et al*. 2004).

A visual-tactile direct mapping of the other's body on our own neuronal system is advocated. The mapping of touch is considered in relation to the homunculus, the brain–body map of the primary somatosensory cortex (postcentral gyrus), and the adjacent secondary somatosensory cortex (lower parietal lobe). It was found that the secondary somatosensory cortex associated with integrating, and more complex cortical processing became specifically activated in the observation of this visual-tactile mirroring system (Gallese *et al*. 2004).

> Jessie, one of my patients in a group workshop, described how she was sitting opposite Adam, a man with whom she was profoundly infatuated. As she watched him on the other sofa, he began to stroke the shoulder of his girlfriend, who was lying next to him. Jessie had the sensation that it was her shoulder that was being stroked: a 'shiver went down her spine' and she felt sexually aroused in her genitals. It was like a wave, quite overpowering. She hoped no one would notice what she felt, as she feared she might be showing some outer sign of what she was feeling.

Schore (1994, 2003a, 2003b) argues against explaining empathy too readily by reference to mirror neurons. He argues that locating a neurobiological process as such does not account for the developmental and relational experience that is the context in which the capacity of empathy emerges. In other words, empathy is the outcome of a complex qualitative body–other interaction and cannot be understood as a neurological feat alone. Schore examines the intercorporeal somatic as the basis of the attachment relationship which affectively and biologically regulates and/or dysregulates all the main bodily functions – Freud's 'exigencies of life' and the autonomic nervous system function, hormone production, effects neural cell growth, brain development, immune system. This view extends the profundity of the other's influence on body process and function. These intercorporeal body processes are in play as the semantic articulations develop in the gestural and sensory patterns derived from the adult world.

Sensory Semiotic Vital Set-Ups

Laplanche describes how the 'signs' which accompany the imperfect response henceforth take on 'a value of arrangement of differential elements at first limited to several barely elaborated elements' (1985: 60). He describes what he refers to as a simple fantasy set-up from the adult world. For example, there are the signs accompanying pleasure (the breast accompanying the milk, the smile of the mother, the exposure of the breast, 'a mouth, a movement of a mouth seizing a breast' (60), one spoon for love and so forth – in other words, a series of gestures, facial and bodily, that will henceforth signify some rudimentary meaning, arranged as differential elements forming a pattern of sense, in other words a series of gestures, facial and bodily, organized into a gestural style. Appetite is potentially open in nature, in the lust for sucking and to the marginal affect and yet requires sustaining by the other. Why does one so often have to encourage children to eat, to offer them 'one spoon for daddy and one spoon for mummy's love' (48) – were it not that appetite also has to be supplemented by the other's demand.

Somatic excitation in the sensory exchange takes place as does a demand in relation to the other – one spoon for love. Thus the child is fed meaning and, as Lacan points out, desires to fulfill the other's demand; yet this is already at work in the sensory gesticulatory articulation patterns forming rudimentary fantasy set-ups which are imparted from the adult world of meaning.

In foregrounding, the vital field (not a fixed vital order but a bio-other and environmental set-up), fantasy is not reified as pure ideation but is expressed as gestural signs, communicated in embodied interaction. Furthermore, it is via the gestural set-up propping vital processes, the structure derived from the other that provides organization and is no longer distinguishable as prop, that the structure helps build the vital set-up. For model(s) of life derived from the other are now required to support insufficiencies at the vital origin. Biology does not function as the blueprint for all to come but is found lacking as it requires a sensory-semiotic scaffold.

The vital processes, simply fixed by a preset nature, but rather how the vital excess produced by the marginal effect is bound into a gesture-based fantasy scenario, relatively contained by a series of gestural signs. I will term this the second and radical propping account and it is this that moves the analysis towards a signifying set-up which creates a syntax that organizes different sensory elements into a scene.

According to the *Oxford English Dictionary* syntax is: (1) an arrangement of parts or elements, (2) constitution of a body. The syntax can be said to assemble a body; indeed, a body assemblage is made out of sensory relations derived from the adult world supplementing some lack in structure and function at vital origin.

On the Way to Language

Laplanche's reference to gestural differential elements is suggestive and can be linked to Saussure's structural theory of signs, whereby in linguistic expression meaning is created by elements in a system being set up in differential relation to each other and thus patterns of sense are created. I suggest the same principle applies to a gestural exchange, which thus becomes a semiotic play of differential elements in relation.

Building on what was noted in the early chapters, I return to Merleau-Ponty's chapter 'The body as speech' in *The Phenomenology of Perception*, where he argues that just as speech or the word is not mere clothing for thought that lies elsewhere (1962: 182), so is gesture the means of expression that in the act brings the expressed into being and makes significance possible. This fundamentally challenges Platonic thought. For Merleau-Ponty thought does not exist as 'pure idea', in a non-empirical realm, but is created in the act of expression and in the lived world. The gesture, just like words or speech, enacts meaning. There is, he explains, a composition of elements into a gesture of significance, the way the 'joins link the nose, the lips, the flash of the eyes, which only together create a smile' (1962: 132), producing an articulation and a style.[2]

Gallagher (2005: 125–129) refers to the body in gesture and, after considering counter-arguments, experimental research and evolutionary thinking, concludes that gesture can be considered generative of meaning. He agrees with Merleau-Ponty's analysis that significance is created in the expressive gestural act which in turn is the outcome of a social process founded on an intercorporeal reality. As Merleau-Ponty states, 'It is no more natural and no less conventional to shout in anger or to kiss in love . . . Feelings and passional conduct are invented like words' (1962: 189), thus noting the importance of cultural specificity and context:

> The fact is that the behaviour associated with anger or love is not the same in the Japanese and an occidental . . . The angry Japanese smiles and the Westerner goes red and stamps his foot or else goes pale and hisses his words. (1962: 139)

Merleau-Ponty avidly opposes a debased sense of the non-verbal sign and questions whether the body is bound to a natural order of things. He opposes an exclusive linguistic definition of signification and language, and departs as much from Desmond Morris as from Lacan. He rebukes the idea that there is a fixed 'anatomical organisation of our body' which would produce 'a correspondence between specific gestures and "given states of mind"' (1962: 139). Instead, he refers to gesture as *contingent* and notes: 'The psycho-physiological equipment leaves a great variety of possibilities open, and there is no more here than in instinct a human nature finally and immutably given' (139).

In addition to the gesture, Merleau-Ponty also refers to tactility and the field of vision, implying the other senses too. This sensory language not only creates significance but affective states organized into complex social emotion; cultural differences in gesture produce differences in the emotions themselves, social use and manner transforming affective being and meaning.

As Alphonso Lingis observes:

> Merleau-Ponty describes the sensorial field . . . articulated not so much into terms as into differences. With its oppositional contrasts, its synchronic relieves and diachronic recurrences, the conjunctive tissue of the sensible field is described as a text incarnating . . . The silent world is already structured like a language. (1985: 161)

Lingis makes it clear that Saussure's differences between terms is transformed and yet applicable to the sensorial field. Gestural and sensory elements figure in differential relations to one another.

Developmental research supports Merleau-Ponty's view. The proto-conversation is described by Trevarthen as a semiotic affective-sensory exchange between infant and others, expressed in gesture, touch and mirroring, and potentially including smell, taste and of course vocalization. With regards to vocalization, what is implied is intonation and 'quality of voice', what Barthes terms 'the grain of the voice' and speech therapists refer to, more concretely, as the the super-segmental pitch, stress or juncture pattern – but most importantly the basis of sensory language is musicality – a rhythmic spacing (Trevarthen 1978, 1993). Trevarthen foregrounds musicality, beat and pacing, the language of affect, the melody and staccato, observing the basis of musical tempo in a premature baby and father who sustain a four-second stanza beat in a vocal exchange: the baby cocooned in the father's arms coos in turn with him, in four-second timed intervals (Trevarthen, in privately circulated video compilation entitled 'Primary Intersubjectivity').

For Trevarthen 'innate' musicality prepares the infant for sociality, a nature open to and orientated towards sociality. He argues that mimicry in gestural expression anticipates meaning in linguistic development and turn-taking, that rhythmic spacing in melodic tempo is the forerunner of syntax in speech and writing.[3] Trevarthen (1990, 1993, 1994) fundamentally questions earlier linguists such as Peirce and thinkers like Piaget who proposed that language is based in intellectual development and the acquisition of logical thinking, which are associated with left brain functioning. Cognitive psychologists likewise take similar views in respect to logical learning and language acquisition. Trevarthen, in contrast, relates language to early affective emotional learning in the sensory semiotic exchange; this not only anticipates linguistic acquisition but provides the basis for what is to come. Schore (1994) refers to the emotional right brain in early development and, like Trevarthen, emphasizes the importance of the non-verbal affective-bodily exchange.

The process of semiotic and linguistic development is not simple and linear. While the embodied gestural form of communication is dominant from the first, the infant's comprehension of speech is already underway, well before the articulation of words; in that sense the non-verbal and the coming forth of speech are coterminous. The sensory and linguistic modes become developmentally interwoven as they coexist; the sensory mode infuses the linguistic with, for example, the language of sensual and affectionate intimacy, rhythm and melody, rendering, for instance, poetry powerfully evocative of affective states.

Although the linguistic field builds and refigures in more precise and definite ways, it does so with what is already in play, restructuring the sensory field. The power of linguistic structure is acknowledged, but somewhat reframed to redress the balance, so as not to focus exclusively on the linguistic speech aspect of language. In formulating the relation of the sensory field and language, the emphasis is on sensory discrimination, thereby introducing the world of nuanced differences. This is not a debased sense of the 'sign' in relation to the somatic field, because of the fact that temporal deferral in the others coming and going introduces a gap in somatic experience where urge becomes a longing precisely for what is not there and in that space memory leaves its trace.

A gestural articulation involving sensory elements in differential relation to one another, producing significance in affect-sense, can be compared with Saussure's structural description of how meaning is constructed in the linguistic context. The sensory field cannot be reduced to a field of simple plenitude and immediate pleasures, for there is the temporal pacing, the way the 'sense organs register stimuli via an appropriation of period' (Freud 1895: 310). There is rhythmic transmission, but in the musicality of the sensory dance there are missteps marking temporal delay.

Alexithymia from the View of the Proto-Conversation as the Basis for Linguistic Access

Earlier it was pointed out that the 'psychosomatic' state alexithymia (having no words for emotions) had been understood by McDougall (influenced by the French school of psychosomatics, Pierre Marty and others). McDougall proposed that alexithymia was the result of a developmental deficit, where affective states that should have matured into mental thought and contained therein, instead bypassed an underdeveloped psyche and became directly discharged into the body. Somatic states in her view thus fail to become 'psychically elaborated' (McDougall 1986). The theory assumes that affective states in psychic development are 'normally' bound by a mentalizing process, forming thoughts with the use of symbols and ideas. In contrast, in the alexithymic case affective states remain beta somatic states, where all feeling is physical and is expressed bodily. The influence from Bion can be seen here and in McDougall's account the psychoanalytic emphasis is on developing what in neuroscience terms would be referred to as higher cortical processing.

The problem with the mentalizing account is the implicit denigration of beta elements as brute soma on the one hand and the implication, on the other hand, that alpha function exists in a pure ideational realm. This all comes about because any symbolic capacity by definition has to knock the body out of the picture. The somatic in the presupposed binary is reduced to raw affective unprocessed experience, at best a 'primitive' type of thinking that leaves all higher-order functioning to mental processing and the ideational capacity.

Instead of assuming and thereby endorsing the dualist split mind and body, Allan Schore gives an account of the development of the relation between right brain and body. He argues that somatic affective states have to develop relationally in their own right and we cannot jump to left brain processing to explain the basis of affective body processing. For Schore it all starts with the body and relational development. From my perspective what needs to take place is the connection of feeling and body states with semiotic relational sense.

It appears that the problem in alexithymia is a difficulty of integration. What appears to occur is that the soma is not brought into an affective relation with the field of others. There are developmental trajectories where the early embodied communication goes askew. In such a case alexithymia is understood as a disturbance in somatic-affective-relational development, what Schore refers to as disturbance in right brain development, a difficulty in beta somatic processing, rather than being rooted chiefly in a failure of alpha functioning (that is, a failure to mentalize).

Although a baby is in an intercorporeal space with (m)other, it does not receive adequate empathic engagement from the other. This is where Stern's 'affective attunement' enters the picture, or Winnicott's 'maternal preoccupation', or Bowlby's 'sensitive responsiveness' or Bion's 'maternal revelry'. Failed revelry results in a barring where the affective expressive meaning connection with the other falls short. The hooking up of bodily affect and empathic connection with the other is impaired. There is a primary cut-off state in the affective gesturing, not even a 'disassociation' in that an adequate affective empathic association has not been brought into play in the first place.

So when the initial attunement (Stern) between infant and caretaker fundamentally fails to get established, or the relationship is bereft of maternal revelry (Bion), the link between gestural affect and meaningful contact with a receiving and responsive other does not develop. In consequence, when linguistic expression is accessed, as the infant starts to understand speech and learns to vocalize words, a disturbance in the linguistic use becomes apparent. The words will be uttered but be empty, lacking affective passion and emotional significance. An affective failure in the sensory proto-conversation leads to an inability to integrate affect with expression and linguistic sense. This indicates a problem with the integration of right and left hemispheres in later development.

Using words without affective cathexis is a form of alexithymia: words lack affective sensibility, and somatic expression lacks semiotic and symbolic significance. Alexithymic patients not only fail to make an affective connection with words, but their bodily expression also remains limited, lacking affective elaboration and semiotic significance.

Typically, in the early accounts the Pierre Marty school described operational thinking and concretization in terms of somatic symptom expression.

A woman with chronic ulcers was asked about a fatal road accident. She had run over a boy with her car, and described what had happened in a very matter-of-fact way. She showed no sign of feeling but would mention her painful ulcer. Whenever the interviewer tried to explore a possible emotional significance or meaning the conversation would go nowhere, and the woman returned to complaining about her physical discomfort.

Kevin came to see me saying he had difficulties in his marriage. He also complained of irritable bowel syndrome. It turned out it was his wife who had sent him to therapy and it was she who thought they had difficulties in the marriage, not him. But when I tried to explore the problems in the marriage with this somewhat hen-pecked man, he could see no difficulty. What he really wanted to talk about was his bowels and the distress they caused him.

Kevin described how his wife complained that he lacked emotional engagement, and that included his performance in bed, in which he engaged without interest. Kevin explained that sex for him was a physical thing and he could feel nothing more about it. In looking at his childhood history he considered that he lacked closeness to either parent. He described his father as a drinker who was in the pub all the time, and his mother as someone who kept her head above water in terms of practical needs and life but otherwise showed little affection. He knew that his mother had come from a large Irish family; she was the sixth of eight siblings.

Kevin suffered from a problem with his attachments, and as I heard more about the family history it seemed to run across the generations. It appeared that in his early relationship with his mother affective-empathic links failed to be established, and his relationship with his father did nothing to compensate for this. The result was a lack of empathic connectedness which left him with profoundly impoverished affective and sensual relations.

What is noted is the early developmental failure underlying alexithymia; however, the failure is not chiefly related to ideational processing of affect into 'mental' thought but to a more fundamental deficit in initial linking of the soma-affective sphere with relational semiotic communication. The empathic failure of (m)other to infant impairs the quality of the relationship (in Stern's sense) and the infant's affective bodily states never adequately find semantic expression. This is a disturbance in the affective-semiotic proto-conversation which is to be associated with an impoverished affective-relational expression in the development of a procedural bodily know-how.

Notes

1   Intercorporeality as a basis for the existence for affective bodily and neurobiologi-cal relations provides a general description of bodily existence. There are certain developmental trajectories that result in avoidance and withdrawal or involve such extreme forms of relational failure (privation) or excess (s(m)othering) that funda-mental disturbances in intercorporeal being can arise, at worst foreclosure where interaction with a field of others is effectively blocked. In such cases there is clear disturbance in the differentiation between the body-ego and the other, leading to alteration in skin experience, boundary self/other relationality and so on.

   Philosophically phenomenology describes human existence in its generality, while Heidegger refers to the ontic and the ontological. The ontological is the basic and general structure of existence, the ontical is the actual existence in its specificity as it is lived. My point is that in actual bodily relations different developmental trajectories can arise. Merleau-Ponty (1964) was aware of development and of how it can impact on ways of being-in-the-world. Derrida is radical in his critique of Heidegger and suggests that the ontological as a general structure of existence can never remain pure. As Andrew Mitchell, in discussing Derrida, states: 'the ontological cannot be spirited away from the ontic: the two necessarily come into contact and intermingle with a resulting ontic contamination' (Mitchell 2008: 133).

For now, the point I wish to make is that the ontic context matters and the way bodily being is lived in relational developmental situations can perturb and disturb, and even bring about radical alterations in intercorporeal experience of being bodily in a world.

2   The form the gesture takes and the style of emotion conveyed vary from culture to culture and depends on context. A Turkish mother with her baby (as shown by Trevarthen in a privately circulated video compilation entitled 'Primary Intersubjectivity') is bold in her movements and persistent in her responsiveness, to an extent that makes English audiences frown and sigh. They describe the mother's behaviour as intrusive and over-stimulating, whereas other groups of viewers (from East Africa, and from Morocco) did not make any comment in respect to this episode. On being questioned, they remarked on the clip where the father takes the active role rather than the mother and baby sequence. In other words, gestural styles and 'sensitive responsiveness' (to use Bowlby's term) are culturally specific. Attachment research requires greater awareness of cultural differences in affective rearing style and in Western developmental studies we need to be very careful when exploring infant–parent interaction, in order to avoid ethnocentric bias.

3   Schore and Siegal (1999, 2012) have developed a form of therapy based on interpersonal neurobiology, where developing facilitating interactions and positive affective states give rise to the development of new neuronal networks and ways of experiencing embodied self and world.

9

Body Memory and Know-How

Reference has been made to body memory as the somatic trace left by sensory relations with others, which is rooted in the adult world of fantasy, a memory trace as the mark left by others' lives within the body of the infant as a social-semiotic articulation, a somatically linked memory brought about in the gap created by the deferral of satisfaction and revivified in every reactivation of a biorelational impetus.

In terms of neuroscience and the trace, there is neuroplasticity (Ansermet and Magistretti 2007) and brain–body memory-making. A brain–body relation implies that body memory cannot be simply located in the brain as opposed to the body, but exists throughout the brain–body dynamic more diffusely in so far as body memory can be activated by sensation, in sensory states, in and as enactment. In regard to body memory, I suggest that there are memories rooted in the sensory and somatic which are bound to semiotic meaning derived from gestural-sensory relations with others and their after-trace.

Koch and colleagues have proposed 'body memory' as the generic term to cover a variety of different ways of typifying memory. They refer to procedural, intercorporeal, incorporative, painful and traumatic memory, as well as situational memory (Koch *et al.* 2012: 9; on situational memory see Casey 1993, 2000). Koch's specific contribution refers to embodied dispositional responses relating to body memory (in Koch *et al.* 2012: 4).

Recent developments from cognitive neuroscience to phenomenology have focused on understanding bodily memory and research on this is in progress. My interest is in foregrounding the somatic component in memory, both sensation-based and sensory memories. Proust is well

Between Skins: The Body in Psychoanalysis – Contemporary Developments,
First Edition. Nicola Diamond.
© 2013 John Wiley & Sons, Ltd. Published 2013 by John Wiley & Sons, Ltd.

known for having referred to the memory of smell as evocative of mood, whereas Koch refers to atmospheric association in the context of body memory. Distinctions between memories, such as implicit and explicit, or episodic and semantic (Tulving 1972, which Bowlby made use of) are considered by Sheets-Johnson (2012: 44) as an Aristotelian dichotomy of types. Sheets-Johnson suggests that such clean distinctions encourage thinking in false binaries (I have noted how confusions can arise when a logical conceptual clarification is taken too literally). If such 'logical' conceptual clarifications can take us away from the phenomenon as it presents itself in its complexity, and can be mistakenly equated with ontological claims, a type of unhelpful reification can occur. I wish to avoid such a mechanistic description and prefer a more multifaceted description of the body situation.

Putting In Question an A Priori Unity to Body Experience

When reference is made to body memory and body constructs in 'normal' circumstances (that is, when brain and neurological damage or abnormalities are not part of the picture), a gestalt figure, a unity and a functional integration, is generally presupposed. This is so when Gallagher and Cole (1998 [1995]) refer to body image or when kinaesthetic body memory and procedural habit body memory are discussed (see Koch *et al.* 2012) and when the brain–body map is addressed by various researchers.

From the psychoanalytic perspective, the ideal of unity is not always assumed and functional integration does not dominate all understanding. There is greater awareness of the potential for more fragmentary and disconnected body states, as there is an understanding of how readily these disjointed states can enter the body construct and exist as kinds of body memory. For Freud the body ego is not simply innately given, but is a formation that has to be developed. I wish to look at the way this psychoanalytic observation is not exclusive to a mental body image. There can be an awkward and real seepage of such states into lived body experience, somatic sensation, and even affective disturbances in neurological and motor functionality. Lacan's stress on the inevitable return of the fragmentary body and somatic states is embraced and there is no easy delegation of such a fragmentary state of affairs to the domain of mental image.

Functional habit-based somatic and motor activity can and does break down in affective disturbances and this can be meaning-related. To address this question I want to consider how there can be a relationship between body memory and body meaning and alteration that can affect image and the action-based body. There is a lot of hard work that goes into keeping things together and there can also be strivings that work against this.

Procedural Body Memory Know-How
and Anti-Knowledge

Merleau-Ponty describes how body memory is formed in the doing. It is not a matter of contemplation but of doing. Dancing, running, riding a bicycle, playing the piano or making love are all bodily activities. I suggest that developing a body know-how produces a body style which cannot be predicted beforehand but is brought into being in the enactment. This body know-how can involve doing that is skilled, or that is more spontaneous and context-bound (for example rocking to the rhythm of the free dance moves or getting into a choreography of specific body stances). It is also emotionally learned and developmentally acquired as body experience is formed in interaction with others in the early years and throughout the life span.

One can refer to motor skills and learning Piaget-style or, according to Merleau-Ponty's understanding, as body know-how which is affective, where feeling is expressed as rhythmic resonance which reminds us of Trevarthen's observation of the blind baby conducting with its arms, in vibrant and rhythmic motion in tune with the mother's melodious voice, the grain in her voice (Barthes 1985). What Merleau-Ponty points out is that when we drive a car or dance we are using a pre-reflective know-how, not consciously contemplated, which is part of our body habit. The movements and body coordination have become automatic, so no conscious reflection is required; a certain patterned style has been formed and it just comes out a certain way.

The discussion of a know-how doing memory could relate to Gallagher and Cole's (1998 [1995]) body schema. However the model put forward here is more expansive and heuristic, and is informed by a fundamentally relational and affective understanding, with a more psychoanalytic take on the unconscious and its propensity to fragmentary body states. The definition of body image used also differs and there is no clear-cut divide between body-ego image and lived motility in the emotionally driven somatic states examined in this book. (As stated, rather than deploying Gallagher and Cole's body image/body schema distinction, I employ a different frame of reference, linking the sensorimotor cortex strip, understood as brain–body mapping, to body-ego formation derived from Freud.)

Cohen and Squire (1980) refer to implicit and explicit memory, as procedural and declarative memory. Procedural memory is long-term; it is a form of body memory and relates to unconscious body know-how, and is closest to Merleau-Ponty's description. Declarative memory is associated with chronological memory and is understood as more factual (remembering of dates sequencing and events) and related more to conscious recall and functioning. Procedural or implicit memory is action body-based memory. This type of memory is based on doing, bodily movement, gesture, dance. We do it with our bodies, and that is the way we remember how to do it. Procedural memory is implicit know-how as to the way of doing something; it is pre-reflective. Procedural body-based memory acquisition continues throughout our lives.

Procedural memory has been rooted in habitual and emotional learning. The body learns sensorimotor tasks through repetition, during which neurological pathways get established and form patterns that are then recalled without any conscious premeditated intervention. Procedural memory has been related to the limbic system as well as neuroplasticity. Complex dynamic brain–body relations and feedback loops characterize procedural memory. In terms of brain processing, the dorsolateral striatum is associated with the acquisition of habits, and links to the basal ganglia circuit and the limbic cortex; the main looping circuit involved in the motor skill part of procedural memory is referred to as the cortico-basal ganglia–thalamocortical loop.

A more mechanistic reading of habit-acquiring tasks is the mainstream reading of procedural memory, but developmental and attachment research has foregrounded the emotional aspect of this kind of body memory and expanded the definition of body know-how that is acquired. In this context procedural memory is related to a relational intercorporeal know-how acquired in the sensory-gestural body in the early relationship with others but also in ongoing relations in later life.

From this perspective procedural memory relates to the affective bodily sensory interaction that Trevarthen (1978) describes as the proto-conversation. In Lyons-Ruth and colleagues' (1998) research on infants, implicit knowing has been understood as a form of emotional body know-how. Fonagy and Target (1997) have related emotional embodied know-how to the quality of reflective function and higher cortical integrated modes of self-organization. In line with this book Schore (1994, 2003a, 2003b) places most emphasis on procedural memory as rooted in right brain body development, and Bowlby's early working models of body–other relations derive from sensory–semiotic interactive experience (see also Diamond and Marrone 2003).

Schore (2003a, 2003b) argues that autobiographical memory is not solely related to declarative conscious chronological memory but is also partly based in unconscious procedural states. In this hypothetical model of procedural body know-how I have identified both the affective–sensory proto-conversation and the semantic non-verbal signifiers of the fantasy set-up. The hypothesis to be developed is that this implicit intercorporeally based knowledge, where the legacy of early relational dynamics leave their mark in patterning emotional behaviour, can underlie procedural acting out, the compulsion to repeat.

Know-how as a procedural knowledge can be a negative embodied know-how, where fundamental missteps in the dance (attachment), in which perturbing relations (sensual) and developmental deficits are lived out somatically as re-enactments. Likewise there can be a bodily relational know-how, engaged with the difference of others (otherness) and emotional learning, that develops from a qualitative relational environment, where there is empathy and engagement with difference (see also Schore 2011).

The focus in certain developments of thinking has been on mentalization and the emphasis on the transformation of beta into alpha functioning, whereas my focus in this book is not on a reified contemplative mode alone, but on the importance of the procedural level of reworking know-how: how shifts in enactment are required for any affective change to occur.

From the affective neuroscience and developmental research perspective, Perry and colleagues (1995) argue that embodied affective patterns can be difficult to shift when they are more hard-wired, as in cases of long-term chronic emotional trauma or extreme relational adversity in childhood. However, there is the possibility, with later therapeutic or other positive forms of intervention, and in less adverse cases, for neural plasticity to allow for the development of new neural networks, sensory associations and patterns of relating, based in different relational interactions which potentially allow for different ways of reorganizing procedural experience.

For affective somatic and relational change, in terms of seeking help through therapy or co-construction dialogue with other(s), a creative reworking of memory needs to take place (see Freud 1937). Mentalizing, I would argue, is not enough, as what is necessary is a focus on shifting the pre-reflective and implicit body know-how (see Schore 2011), the style and quality of body know-how.[1]

Sheets-Johnson (2012) praises the descriptions and style of the neuroscientist Luria for addressing procedural know-how and for moving away from the tendencies of a 'motor behaviourism' towards a more kinaesthetically informed language which can in some way also capture kinetic melodies and the complexity of movement. This is in keeping with Trevarthen's (1978, 1994) emphasis on the musicality of the non-verbal proto-conversation, and on rhythmic pacing and temporal spacing.

Trauma and Body Memory

In relation to the duration of body memory and its potential alterability, reference has been made to neural hard-wiring in the context of repetitive traumatic experience over an extended period. Perry and colleagues (1995) refer to the way states can become traits, as neurobiology is use-dependent; that is, frequency of use and neural structuring go hand in hand. Neural pathways repetitively activated in traumatic childhood situations involving abusive experiences are relived again and again. This is more devastating when other possible experiences and innovative new neural developments and connections are limited or foreclosed.

The post-trauma literature documents how body memory in the context of extreme trauma has specific features: the overriding of Broca's speech area and declarative conscious event recall memory, resulting in what Kolk and colleagues (1996) refer to as 'speechless terror'. LeDoux (1996) empha-sizes the activation of the amygdala, registering fear, the suggestion being that when a traumatized person starts to relive the traumatic experience a bodily state of fear is reactivated. A traumatized person in a state of reacti-vation of fear is hyper-aroused. The sympathetic nervous system is activated and cortisol is produced. Sweating occurs and hyper-vigilance as a hyper alert state is common, with impoverished memory recall. LeDoux notes how affect is remembered but not the event.

Procedural memory is vividly activated in so far as it repeats as a mode of visual or somatic sensory re-enactment; this also often involves behaviour and the creation of trauma situations, with the embodied compulsion to repeat. In trauma-based memory, a sense of agency is annulled. The sensory-based memory dictates the subject, and the person feels subjected to the power of the memory; he or she feels no control over the experience and is overwhelmed by it.

'Situational' body memory is where smell and atmosphere can be relived in sensory ways. There are specific flashbulb memories, and visual sensation body memories, which are lived as hyper-vivid and real. The body memory speaks the subject: this means that the memory is overpowering as a force. In relived memory the person is always placed in a helpless, passive position while things are done *to* them. The person re-experiences being traumatized, the scene takes over, there is imposed enactment and temporal flow is altered or arrested as the happening re-occurs. Whereas in traumatic memory play and flexibility cease, this contrasts with everyday situations and memory, where there is an active temporal process and a potential for memory to be proactively taken up.

Body Memory and Deferred Action Reconfigurations

In a very real sense life is traumatizing. The encounter with the other, lack, loss, abandonment, rejection, exclusion, frustration, thwarted desires, acceptance and giving up, hopelessness, helplessness, apathy, being a desir-ing subject – the list is endless – these are all experiences we cannot control or fully understand. They can overwhelm and overpower us, resulting in perturbing somatic states, and can fundamentally destabilize any sense of bodily integrity. Body memory is not only habitual and familiarizing, but it can disturb and disorientate, open an unknown in the somatic field.

There are different kinds of trauma. Sexuality itself can be considered traumatic. For example, the enigmatic impact of the adult world of sexuality on the child (Laplanche 1989) both structures and perturbs; sexuality can be experienced as intrusive, stirring up the child's body before it is ready or can assimilate it. This kind of sexuality differs from the child's early sensuality; adult sexuality can remain shocking and strange, contributing to excess agitation and excitation. Sexual body memory and its activation can give rise to perturbing effects throughout life, for example in long-term marriages sexuality commonly joins the familiar and everyday so that the experience loses its edge. We can often search out excitement by bringing out the Oedipal forbidden and the 'naughty' but this may turn into what cannot be controlled and end up being unmanageable and traumatic.

Recent findings regarding the complexity of memory note that they

> are not automatically laid down, imprinted as an accurate recording, for there is a temporal period where hormone and protein changes take place. It is also during a period that it is likely that . . . perceptions [other memory traces] intervene, altering the memory as it is laid down . . . memory traces . . . become labile again when they are reactivated. (Diamond and Marrone 2003: 162–163)

I have looked at the deferral of satisfaction and the belated return of the other with a substitute for her presence in the form of a semiotic sensory response which leaves behind a memory trace. This is sensory communication transmitted through music and rhythm transmission; there is temporal spacing 'between beats' and 'appropriation by period' (Freud 1895: 310). Body memory can be seen as a process subject to temporal delay; the deferral movement is memory being formed.

Freud introduces the notion of *Nachträglichkeit* ('deferred action'), which refers to the temporal movement in memory-making whereby:

> The concept of deferred action refers to the restructuring power of later reactivation of memories in relation to earlier experience. We could describe this as a retrospective activation that gives fresh meaning to an earlier memory. See, for example, Freud's discussion in the *Project for a Scientific Psychology* (1895) of the pubescent girl who reacted with intense anxiety on entering a shop without apparent cause, until Freud identifies the earlier memory of entering a sweet shop and being fondled by a shop keeper. The first memory had not appeared troubling to the girl at the time, but had been activated by the later event in adolescence with its corresponding genital sexual awakening. (Diamond and Marrone 2003: 163)

> In Freud's framework, the concept of deferred action refers more specifically to the way the full effect of a potential traumatic event is not (necessarily) experienced . . . at the time of its occurrence or immediately after it. The traumatic significance and effect of the event remain latent. Yet a later event which has some symbolic resemblance with the first scene is capable of reactivating memories of the earlier event, this time with its traumatic effects and symptomatology. This relies on both surviving remains from the past and potential significance, although at the time the event was not conceived overtly as traumatic, and a later experience that provides significance to the situation and retrospectively reposes the experience. (Diamond and Marrone 2003: 169)

This memory has been understood by Laplanche as strictly ideational, a group of incubated ideas that return to invade the psyche; however, there are bodily enactments.

There is Daniel, the sexually abused American adolescent I worked with who had been abused by his elder brother from the age of 5 to 10 (see also Chapter 5 and Diamond 2003). The body memory had been deferred, like that of Freud's adolescent girl who entered the sweet shop. It was only years after the abuse, when he was 13, that seeing a programme on TV triggered an associated memory about what had happened to him. Thereafter he no longer suffered an amnesia. Like Freud's adolescent girl, he was an adolescent experiencing a burgeoning sexual awareness.

His symptoms were not so much a group of ideas intruding psychically but a series of somatic symptoms. He remembered in terms of his body – sensations that repeated in his genitals and related areas – what could not at first be put into words or even thought. The body enacted and showed a negative body know-how in the compulsion it was repeating; in a form of sensory body memory, he experienced spontaneous overwhelming sensations in his body. They were sensations that were both sexually stimulating and repelling at the same time, and above all traumatizing. He felt terrified, threatened and overwhelmed with their sudden and intrusive onset. They spontaneously recurred without warning, taking him unawares. This relay of somatic states was humiliating for him, hitting him to the core in his belief of who he was and in his masculinity.

Note

1   Schore's (2011) and Siegal's (1999) work on interpersonal neurobiology and the formation of a therapeutic approach which optimizes affective-relational brain development and integration of hemispheric functions. While I am sympathetic to the thinking I also place emphasis on psychoanalytic ways of addressing negative affective states and ways of working in the analytic relationship.

10

Attachment and Sexuality
Regulation versus Deregulation

In his writing on sexuality and its emergence Laplanche refers to a rudimentary fantasy set-up. This, I have suggested, binds and creates the vital set-up in terms of simple fantasy structures. Here I mean that non-verbal sensory expressions from the adult world are patterned into a form of communication which helps to bind the infant's biological processes to meaning. Earlier I referred to the infant taking in nourishment which is conveyed in an affective gesture as the parent feeds the infant – one spoon for mummy's love, one spoon for daddy's. The quality of the gestural exchange, the visual mirroring, the style of touch and the sensation of taking in, ingestion, are coloured by the relational sense that the interaction brings. In this little exchange the significance of the demand of love becomes installed as part of the biological process of taking in nourishment.

There are two tendencies that typify the vital set-up. The first is derived from the adult world of fantasy and is more open and fluid in meaning. The second vital set-up is organized around more habitual behaviour and the biological processes serving the specific action, where 'norms' of regulation take precedence. In the latter case, it appears that attachment-based affective–biological interactions play a more prominent role. In this chapter I shall reframe the self-preservation system and move it away from the natural vital order to show how it is a vital body set-up derived from the other who regulates the biological processes through attachment and cultural habit. I shall also identify how the relation with the other, and therefore also a vital set-up, can result in deregulation which is both sexual and related to trauma.

Between Skins: The Body in Psychoanalysis – Contemporary Developments,
First Edition. Nicola Diamond.
© 2013 John Wiley & Sons, Ltd. Published 2013 by John Wiley & Sons, Ltd.

The Relationship between Attachment and Sexuality

Somatic excess requires regulation by the vital set-up; this involves cultural normalization via rearing practices, habit and custom, which all play a crucial role, as do rituals and attachment forms of affective bio-regulation. In this formulation, even for the specific action there is a semiotic and binding vital set-up, derived from the (m)other, which emerges coterminously with the formation of the fantasy semantic set-up, derived from the adult world of sexuality. The latter is also somewhat binding but more labile and open to play, potentially more free-roaming and readily open to greater destabilization and protean phantasmagoria which can be experienced in sensorial states – an exaggerated and deformed vital geography. As noted, there are different tendencies in the vital relational set-up: towards regulation and, in the other, towards deregulation.

Whereas the later Laplanche (2002) acknowledges attachment, he aligns it with self-preservation (as belonging to a fixed biological order) and opposes to it the field of sexuality (psychic and open to variation). Such a sharp divide falls short when habitual and 'normalized' bodily functions are readily confounded with sensual-sexual strivings and significance, when for example appetite for food is sexualized or 'shitting' is sensuous and laden with sexual meaning. In this regard the fantasy vital set-ups described by Laplanche can become intertwined with attachment regulatory tendencies required for the specific action. Thus there is an open potential interplay between the two tendencies and no clear-cut dividing line between them.

Schore (1994) has described how affective regulation of the bodily pro-cesses, which modulate activation of the nervous system, hormones and homeostasis, are set up and organized in secure enough interactions. These interactions affectively regulate biological processes in the context of the semiotic proto-conversation. As argued, in the contemporary neuroscience field associated with attachment, there has been a recognition of greater plasticity in the biological processes and the crucial role that early rearing plays in regulation, most pertinently the regulation of biological states through interaction with the key caretaker.

In the attachment neuroscience field Schore (1994, 2003a, 2003b) fore-grounds how the embodied exchange between infant and caretaker stimu-lates neural production and connections in the baby's brain, arouses and inhibits the sympathetic and parasympathetic nervous system, and activates hormonal secretions and regulation in somatic infantile experience. The adult's body is also directly affected in this process, and although the other is a strong formative influence on the biological processes of the human infant, this biological–affective interchange and mutual alteration goes on in interactions with others throughout our life span.

Schore describes how the non-verbal bodily and facial articulations regulate the baby's affective-somatic states, bodily processes including modulating arousal, regulating the nervous system, hormones, temperature, metabolism, the body processes essential for life. Although the infant–caretaker relation is the focus here, the affective intercorporeal changes continue in later life and ongoing intimate relationships throughout life.

A biological attachment 'norm' for the vital set-up can be shifted by a more labile fantasy-orientated set-up. There are the more open and fluid sexual and fantasy tendencies in contrast to the more exacting regulating tendencies of attachment relations. The 'rearing practices', customs and rituals socially style the regulating set-ups and support attachment relations in establishing functional stability and bounded meaning.

Unbound sexuality has a tendency, as Fonagy (2007) notes, to increase excitation and to destabilize. Whereas attachment affective bio-regulation leans towards binding and fixture, though not immutably so, fantasy vital set-ups derived from the adult world offer some containment but are less stable and are able to 'pervert' the biological 'norm' from its habitual course. Where there is a freeing up of meaning, there is a greater potential for play, in so far as meaning becomes fluid and more open to shifting in sense.

The vital, sensuous set-up could be related to Kristeva's description of the maternal semiotic field, which sets up a more fluid play of differences, opening up a 'poetic' musicality with different tempos which characterize the working of the preverbal.

In the history of the debates, attachment and sexuality have been placed in competition for primacy, Bowlby versus Freud and Klein. In *Attachment and Intersubjectivity* (Diamond and Marrone 2003) we suggest that attachment and sexuality are developmentally linked. Emergent sexuality develops in the context of the attachment relationship and necessarily exists in a two- and multi-person relationship. The emotional quality of the interaction will alter the direction sexuality will take relationally, that is whether sexuality is cut off from affective engagement with or open to an appreciation of the other's 'otherness', or organized around part objects. It is, however, also acknowledged that once sexual desire is on its way, depending on the developmental trajectory, it can eschew any taming, and there can be a fundamental clash between attachment regulation and sexual striving for excitement and fantasy rather than realistic possibilities.

From an affective neuroscience perspective, filial imprinting and sexual bonding are neurochemically related (Panksepp 1998: 255). Current neurochemical findings show how opioids are released both in sexual intimacy and gratification in social bonding, particularly in the case of maternal reunion. Social comfort is also produced by the same brain chemistries that help mediate maternal and sexual behaviours (see Panksepp 1998). Furthermore, urges to care for offspring probably relate to a set of subcortical systems that initially governed female sexual urges (Diamond and Marrone 2003: 195). The biological interdependence of bonding and sexual urges is particularly striking (Panksepp 1998: 249). The point here is that the attachment bonding can have an impact on sexual bonding and the style of relating that develops.

Jaak Panksepp identifies a number of distinct emotive-motivational systems with specific neural substrates, including the panic-separation system (attachment) and the pleasure-lust system (sexuality). Panksepp describes how the neural pathways necessarily intersect and interrelate according to the developmental trajectory and eventually integrate in terms of the brain in neocortex functioning. In other words, such pathways are experience-dependent and develop in the interpersonal social and relational context, so our stress on the potential intertwining of the sexual vital set-up with the specific habituated functions has a potential interconnection.

The quality of interaction and the developmental context will affect the type of interdependence of attachment and sexuality. In *Attachment and Intersubjectivity* (Diamond and Marrone 2003) we noted a number of trajectories including how sexuality can be divorced from attachment in a number of cases, like the serial lover who has no understanding of emotional intimacy. In such an example attachment and sexuality have failed to integrate, because of developmental history and context.

From my perspective, attachment strivings and sexual pathways can and do become confounded. On entering a sexual relationship in which one becomes attached, attachment issues raise their head with great intensity. For example, the relation to attachment loss could be dominated by abandonment issues; alternatively, at the other extreme, impingement, as the core attachment style, could inform the response to separation and connection to a lover.

Alternatively, looking for love as an attachment tendency could become highly eroticized and hyper-sexualized. Or, in contrast, divergent pathways could form, resulting in a split between, on the one hand, the anaclitic marriage partner who continues to facilitate habitual regulation, and associated safety and security, while in another compartmentalized sphere seeking out high levels of sexual excitation, risk and possibly 'part-object' multiple partners (see Diamond and Marrone 2003).

Eagle (2007) argues that attachment and sexual strivings are fundamentally incompatible, sexuality striving for excitation, risk and the unfamiliar, and attachment settling for stability, the familiar and safe. This is an important observation on the contrasting tendency of sexuality and attachment. However, I do not agree with Eagle's decontextualized and deterministic bio-evolutionary model; I place much greater emphasis on the relational developmental context and how this influences the specific way sexuality and attachment interrelate, how pathways cross and whether they eventually integrate, segregate or become disorganized.

Social ways of ascribing gender and corresponding outlets for sexual expression play a role in organizing sexuality and attachment. In my practice I have increasingly seen men who are in 'stable' marriages in which they are attached and feel safe; all their vital processes are habitually regulated – meal times, routines of sleep and work – and there is little or no sexual relations in the marriage. In contrast, these men have a ravenous appetite for sex on the Internet, pornography, call girls and the like, where high excitement and risk prevail, fantasy scenarios dominate usually in the style of porn stereotypes in which they can become both virtual and actual protagonists – short-lived and 'sweet'. There is narcissistic affirmation of their body in the virtual world of the image; however, the end result is either a feeling of emptiness and/or the compulsion to move on to the next sexy-looking number.

Culture plays a key role in this: consumer dating and sex bait desire – all you want sold as the field of the possible at a flick of a button. Heterosexual asymmetrical constructs abound, where woman as 'object', or better as 'part-object', can be had like sweets in a sweet shop, playing on phallic omnipotence and control: he can play at being the phallus in the seduction and possess the phallic woman precisely because she is like a twinkling jewel dangled in front of him, temporary, without commitment and soon to fade, but promising a great deal at the time – all fantasy, a ruse and short-lived. This is something that women in the phallocentric economy also buy into when they too find narcissistic reward in being the temporary idealized object of desire.

Attachment and sexuality are both forms of vital set-up that can affect one another, for both are constituted in the inevitable trauma of separation and loss. The compulsion to repeat painful negative states which Freud explores in 'Beyond the pleasure principle' (1920) could also relate to re-enactment of traumatic attachment failure, and not just the compulsion to repeat in the field of sexuality. Likewise, Panksepp's (1998) panic-separation and lust-pleasure systems, which are neurobiologically described, can become intertwined in development.

Sexual Arousal and Loss

Sensual response, the somatic sensation of arousal and climax, can relate to sexuality and attachment issues. The example below relates to a developmental scenario where separation in the attachment sphere has been stifled by 'cotton wool' parenting, where there has been a prolongation of mothering and a denial of loss and separation, which impacts on sexual desire in the relational sphere. The parental fantasy is that the 'little' girl is the 'plug' that stops up all gaps; in being idealized, she becomes the phallic object in the fantasy – she has it all.

Mary came for couple therapy with her boyfriend, Paul. Her complaint was that she had no desire for sex. Mary had everything, or so it seemed: a 21-year-old doting boyfriend, beauty and money. She still lived with her parents and her every want was catered for.

I asked Mary how she viewed Paul. 'Oh, he is like a friend, a soul mate.' 'Is he a bit like a brother or close friend?' I asked. 'Yes,' she said, 'absolutely.' It turned out that the same pattern had structured all her relationships. For the first few months she was sexually engaged and could become aroused and achieve orgasm, but after a matter of months she lost all interest. It turned out that the only thing that could turn her on easily with Paul was watching porn with him. She was particularly aroused by the idea of having Paul and another man attending to her, and also where two men were with one woman.

Juliet Hopkins, in her paper 'The dangers and deprivations of too-good mothering' (1996), explores the detrimental effects of mothering which is too well adapted to an infant's needs. Hopkins describes 'too good' mothering pursued beyond the baby's earliest months, and how this can lead to the child remaining in a state of arrested development, 'merged with her'. What she describes is an attachment where the mother evades separation from her child, and in avoiding her own pain of loss, prohibits the child from experiencing frustration and working through loss. Mother attempts to stop up all gaps with the too perfect environmental provision.

In the case of Mary, the all-encompassing parental provision, on top of early developmental 'too good' parenting (attachment to mother's constant milking nipple) and her idealization of all available boyfriends, secured a plug into the hole too well! 'The problem is,' I said, 'you have it all. Everyone is there for you. All your whims are catered for. You have never left home, and never quite grown up into a woman. There is no experience of a threat, of separation, for you to feel a longing or to endure a yearning for your lover.'

Paul is like a friend or brother to Mary, and dogged attachment to her does not help in this context. He is not experienced as separate and different from Mary in herself; the sense of his otherness is not there. Like everyone else around her, he feels like an extension of her and of everything else. However, this happens to all men whom Mary encounters and within just a matter of months. It is only when the sense of difference and otherness enters the picture that sensuous sexual longing is activated. This occurs for Mary only when the man is a completely unknown quantity, effectively a stranger, and has not yet been incorporated into her undifferentiated system. Mary finds porn exciting because it functions as the other, unlike the over-familiar, and it is not surprising that she is turned on only when a new man enters the scene.

In this example Mary's bodily sensuality and orgasm is not a simple biological response but is predicated on and in her capacity for separation in the overlapping vital set-ups of attachment and sexual relations.

In the 20 years Joan had lived with her husband, she had repudiated sex and thought of herself as having a very low sex drive. About a year ago she discovered her husband was in love with another woman and having an affair. She fought to get him back and ever since has had intensely pleasurable orgasms and wants sex almost every day.

Joan had always had a sense of abandonment, dating back to her childhood and her insecure attachment history. Her mother had been a child of the Holocaust and emotionally unavailable, and had worked full-time when Joan was a baby, employing a series of nannies to look after her.

Even before her husband's affair, Joan had suffered from separation panic attacks, experienced as emotional and physical states of anxiety. These attacks could occur if her husband did not phone her when he had said he would or turned up late for dinner, which happened regularly. However, the realization that she could lose her husband to another awakened her desire. It was a desire for the unobtainable, which aroused the inevitable 'perversity' of a sensuous sexuality circulating around the 'irretrievable object', as expounded by Lacan – the relation of sexuality to lack, the way pleasure and the impossibility of desire are lived out in the sensual body, whereby attachment loss and sexuality are conjoined.

When her husband went to Australia for 12 days, the longest they had ever been apart, they made love the night before he left. She experienced two orgasms, which had previously been unknown. It was the most intense vaginal pleasure she had ever felt, and she had burst into tears after the second climax.

Loss and the awakening of the capacity of the symbol are expressed in the sensory field of the soma and not relegated to the ideational mind. In my clinical work as a staff psychotherapist at the Women's Therapy Centre, as a consultant psychotherapist at the Helen Bamber Foundation and in private work as a psychoanalytic psychotherapist, the exploration of sensual pleasuring and separation/loss in the context of a developmental history has been a focus and the subject of continuing research, in particular, the experience of orgasmic pleasure.

Gender and the binaries of sexual difference play a key role in women's experience of orgasm. Lacan refers specifically to *jouissance* and the feminine undecidable position in a phallocentric economy, where sexual pleasuring can operate without such rigid boundaries and has the potential to become more unbounded. My focus is on somatic being in the context of a relational history and the impact of interpersonal and cultural experiences, particularly how loss contributes to the orgasmic experience. The somatic itself is altered in function and sensation; absence transforms the somatic and leaves a trace in sexual pleasuring.

Body-Based Trauma and Deregulation

Deregulation is linked to trauma – being overwhelmed, for example, by excitation, affective perturbation. This can take the form of a roaming anxiety that is somatically experienced. In trauma the meaning of one's life can break down and this can lead to less bound states. These states can lead to associated phantasmagoria including somatic-sensory types of symptoms and fragmentary body experiences. Deregulation and trauma can affect both the spheres of attachment and of sexuality; both attachment and sexual trauma relate to the experience of loss.

The movement of somatic states towards unbinding is not simply viewed in terms of excitation and its reduction; it relates to somatic plasticity that takes place in the sensory-semantic field, opening the chain of significance into unbounded association and potentially to non-meaning. In this movement, which threatens somatic coherency and everything that is familiar, preservation of a bounded body falls short and disorganized somatic states prevail.

There is always some relationship between binding and unbinding. When Freud refers to binding and unbinding in terms of secondary and primary process, he describes how some binding is necessary for the movement of unbinding. I would say that a certain binding – fixing in the habitual body set-up – is necessary, as is relative binding in the fantasy vital set-up; indeed this is required for the movement of unbinding. When binding is dominant somatic limits are more in place and there is some fixture of semiotic meaning; when there is a tendency to radical unbinding there is more of a breakdown in somatic closure and 'leakage' as boundaries fail, and alterations in affective-sensory states occur.

Heidegger states 'the point is to experience the unbinding, bond within the web of language', that 'there is a bond running through the web that remains strange, unbinds and delivers language into its own' (1982: 113).

Merleau-Ponty makes reference to somatic 'extasis' and situates Heidegger's explorations in the corporeal space.

In relation to trauma and the body, a radical unbinding movement could be either exhilarating or on the negative axis of trauma – devastating. When people respond by accepting and affirming the movement from the familiar to the radically other and unknown, this can make the experience more playful and even joyous, but fearing and evading the experience can create greater distress. The problem is that, if the concern is to create a unity in body experience and to feel safe, it makes matters worse, whereas if one can let go and go along with it, one is not fighting against what cannot be controlled anyway.

There are somatic symptoms that relate to trauma and deregulation which cannot be explained by an organic aetiology or causation alone and that live on creating discomfort, inexplicable pain or amplified sensation, including functional disturbances in body functions. Pontalis notes how the body symptom 'blurs the frontiers, it distorts a body geography', 'revealing an unknown land' (1981: 199), this breach of boundaries and the production of pain is described by Freud 'as an excess of excitation [which] hinders binding activity' (1895: 296). Pontalis describes how in this state 'sense can slip from grasp' (1981: 199–200), leading to sense that borders on nonsense.

In such circumstances, there can be a compulsive focus, prereflective in that the obsessive attending is not within the person's conscious control. Rather than the sensory state remaining bound and localized, it can be experienced as expanding – intensified and increasing in circumference. The somatic symptom as an attempt to create some containment and organization soon opens onto a more unbounded state where phantasmagoria and the like more freely abound, anxiety simply escalating. In opening up some unknown territory, the somatic state is experienced as ego-dystonic, alien, other, unfamiliar, strange and estranging; there is the urge to rid oneself of it, but there is no escape from a sensory state of alterity since it exists as part of the somatic situation, as endemic to the body.

Introduction to the Uncanny in the Somatic Sphere

The interest in the sensorial experience of the alien and other in somatic states has already been mentioned, developing the theme further. I relate this to Freud's (1919) discussion of 'the uncanny' (German *Unheimlich*). *Unheimlich* has many associated meanings including estrangement in the homely, a state where one feels not at home in the safe and familiar. A state of *Unheimlich* is associated with foreboding, the unfamiliar, alien and other – and even includes the black arts. *Heimlich*, the implied opposite, refers to the homely, familiar and tame. A state of *Unheimlich* can be interpreted as a state of feeling not at home in the hearth of the home; it is used in this discussion of the somatic symptom to suggest feeling radically estranged on somatic sensory states and in one's own body, bringing otherness, which is at the heart of somatic being, to the fore. Here, in the context of the uncanny, it means feeling uncomfortable and strange in one's own body. In such a context the patient may complain of troubling sensations and of pain leading to discomfort. The *Unheimlich* body state has similarities with states of depersonalization or de-realization.

In the tradition of psychoanalysis, the idea here is that in the most extreme states of distress some truths about the normal and the everyday of human experience can be discovered. In working as a clinician with 'survivors' of the worst adversities and atrocities – from torture to multiple abuse and rape, chronic loss, radical attachment trauma and disturbance in the field of sexuality, living after the Holocaust – we find the extremities of somatic upheaval.

The tendency towards unbinding can be an entirely overwhelming and what is starkly exposed is the hole in the symbolic and semiotic fibre, resulting in massive upheaval in the somatic field. In this context the Humpty-Dumpty that falls cannot be put together again as the ideal of somatic integrity threatens to finally collapse in vital function once and for all. In such encounters the failure of meaning and containment of any kind in the vital habitual set-up is evoked. The vacuum in the experience threatens to consume, so that the person falls through the somatic matrix, slipping into no sense and sliding into a radical derailing and unbinding. Phantasmagoria can proliferate, with every perturbing sensation and the soma runs amok; 'the object [entirely] ceases to function as a possible surety' (Pontalis 1981: 196) there is an enduring confrontation with the unrepresentable experience, an encounter with the real (Lacan) and with Bion's 'nameless dread'.

'The spine in the flesh', the alien entity that Laplanche (1985: 24) refers to, is no longer simply a metaphor for an intrusive group of ideas that breaks into consciousness and fails to be integrated into the mental ego, but describes a sensory state of *Unheimlich* that lives on in sensations and somatic dysfunction, indicative of something alien unknown and other in our own body.

Part III

Exteriority
The Body Surface

11

The Skin
An Introduction

In this section of the book I focus on the skin, the outer surface of the body, and its senses. Whereas the vital order becomes a vital field of relations, where the outside world becomes inherent in the vital terrain, the skin, touch and the relational field are also integral to what has been referred to as the skin or body-ego. In this chapter I shall introduce the alternative framework to provide a context for a new understanding.

There will be a reworking of Anzieu's *Skin Ego* (1989), which uses the propping hypothesis to describe the emergence of the skin ego from the skin surface. As with Laplanche's *Life and Death in Psychoanalysis* (1985), I shall work through traditional impasses to allow for a new model of the vital set-up to emerge. My aim is to develop through the discussion a more comprehensive analysis of the skin surface ego.

As with Laplanche, the problem with an analysis which begins from a biological bedrock model is that it ends up with a fixed biological order, in this instance the skin sac. This is ultimately of a different order from the psychic-ideational skin ego. An implausible divide between the material world and mental life is created. The skin is the organ thought of as first and foremost an individualized entity bound by itself, set apart from other discrete bodies bound by its own sac. Like Laplanche, Anzieu does not intend to fall into dualistic impasses; however, the traditional frameworks that dictate understanding have a profound influence and circumscribe possibilities in thinking.

Anzieu adopts the main propping account from Laplanche. Laplanche explains that propping results in a metonymic slide whereby the living organism is transposed to a different site, to 'a differentiated organ of the psyche: here the ego as a metonymy of the organism' (1985: 9). There is a continuation from

Between Skins: The Body in Psychoanalysis – Contemporary Developments,
First Edition. Nicola Diamond.
© 2013 John Wiley & Sons, Ltd. Published 2013 by John Wiley & Sons, Ltd.

one field to another, the mental ego retaining its former form, in being defined in relation to the rest of the psyche by a limit, a gestalt (Laplanche 1985: 63), which circumscribes a region in which energy circulates at a constant level.

The metaphorical shift replaces the model of the living being by its 'intra-psychical precipitate in the image of the individual' (Laplanche 1985: 33) 'a mental projection of the surface of the body' (131). The body image(s) becomes a libidinal object, capable of passing itself off as subject. Here Laplanche is addressing the formation of the body ego, which Anzieu will develop as the skin ego, a psychic derivative originally modelled on the skin and intact body form.

The problem with the propping formulation in both Laplanche and Anzieu is that there is no account of how the mental body or skin ego, with its versatility in changing shapes, qualities and meanings, directly affects skin experience as such, actual body form and function. As noted, what remain are two domains, the shifting field of the imaginary ideational body/skin ego and the actual body form and skin fixed outside in the external world. This results in an inadequate formulation, as no relation can be established between the physical and the mental field.

Anzieu repeatedly observes how skin experience can be affected by relations with others and by meaning, can alter in sensation and in function, even for changes in the manifestation of body form. Examples will be given of alteration in gait and motility, the argument being that it is inadequate to formulate such phenomena in terms of mental/psychic perceptions or projections. What needs to be accounted for is how shifts in affective states and changes in meaning and ideation directly alter sensory and somatic states themselves, bringing about different kinds of bodily phenomena.

Freud's idea of the body ego that has to be developed and constructed is my starting point. The body ego cannot be reduced to an intra-psychic experience, divorced from the sensory-somatic body or from environmental context. In this part I revisit and further develop the opening chapters of the book, in which I began to address neuroscience findings and psychoanalytic insights that helped challenge the claim that the body image exists as pure idea inside a psyche, and/or and intra-psychically.

Perhaps even more fundamentally, my aim is to show how the constructed body ego cannot be set apart ontologically or otherwise from the form of the living organism. This will involve the questioning of an a priori body form that is simply given by nature, presupposed as some kind of inalterable ground which gives rise for all to follow.

The Skin Surface

The biological bedrock model assumes a skin surface as given in natural form and function, from the prototype model is derived, which results in a fixed, static and unchangeable physical order. Yet the body form is not an a priori biological given, in so far as structure and function are unformed in the new-born, who is premature at birth. Esther Bick (1968) describes how the baby is like an astronaut catapulted into space without a suit; the skin is at first unable to function as a containing sac to hold together the body as a coherent form. She notes how the naked new-born, placed supine on a fleece, flays its legs and arms in all directions screaming. The body at this point has no bounded unity, is motor uncoordinated and neurologically underdeveloped.

In earlier historical periods and according to custom and culture, the practice of swaddling was not uncommon. As already observed, swaddling can be seen as a way of holding the baby all in one piece, arguably offering the skin a support, a prop, to supplement the skin originally found to be lacking. Swaddling is an age-old practice which involved wrapping infants in cloth, blankets or similar materials so that movement of limbs are restricted; swaddling bands were often used to further tighten the restriction. Swaddling fell out of favour in the seventeenth century, but has returned in various guises both across cultures and in more contemporary times. An intact form, I suggest, is more the outcome of a developmental achievement and today it is a culturally driven ideal.

According to Lacan, the intact body image is the result of a gestalt effect, when the baby encounter's the mirror image. Later English analysts such as Winnicott (1971) refer to the style in which the baby is mirrored and held, the emotional quality of experience, while Bion (1962) refers to a more complex containing process, as does Bick (1968), but unlike Bick or Bion I avoid jumping too soon into a mental sphere, and shall stay with the skin phenomenon.

'Holding' has to develop and is derived from the field of others via visual and affective experiences like mirroring, touching, being held. A binding of the body surface through early sensory communication, as Anzieu describes, can build a skin matrix, the (m)other playing a key role early on. My emphasis is on the intervention of the other prior to completion of maturation and how this implies that the other is already there, influencing the way the body composes and comports itself. The premature entry of the other while the biological system is more open affects the course of development for evermore.

A mirroring that is simultaneously exteriorizing, to which Lacan and the discovery of mirror neurons testify, relates fundamentally to surfaces out there, mirrored from a space derived from without. The body appears from the field of others, in the surfaces they deflect and construe.

The skin as a surface always relates to other surfaces from sensory-mirroring surfaces derived from others, to social surfaces such as media surface projections, billboard advertising surfaces; from glossy magazine surfaces to screen surfaces, the skin surface is never fully owned. This is one way of understanding and developing Freud's reference to the skin ego as not only based in being a surface entity but in fact existing as a surface projection.

Freud states in *The Ego and the Id* that 'The ego is first and foremost a bodily ego; it is not merely a surface entity, but is itself a projection of a surface' (1974 [1923]: 16).[1] One of my aims will be to develop the meaning of the body ego as 'not merely a surface entity but itself a projection of a surface' (16), and how the skin surface is a surface that is bound to others and to a social field. This body ego – a projection of a surface – originally derives from sensations arising from that body surface. Tactility is of key importance, not only the visual field, as Freud points out:

> A person's own body and above all its surface, is a place from which both external and internal perceptions may spring. It is *seen* like any object, but to the *touch* it yields two kinds of sensations, one of which may be equivalent to an internal perception. (1974 [1923]: 15)

However, in contrast to Freud's simple description of the skin surface as yielding two types of sensations which, like the main propping model, assumes the doubling in tactile sensation is simply inherent, in build, to the biological bedrock, I shall attempt to go further. I suggest that sensations that come from within and those that come from without are experientially and relationally dependent. I argue that the differentiation in tactility is more complex and is testimony to the development of a relational biology, to how the other enters somatic experience. The double aspect in skin sensation is not reducible to a derivation from a fixed biological substratum.

Merleau-Ponty describes the experience of the body being mirrored and touched. I shall explore and further develop this in Chapter 13. I shall show how from the first, as soon as the baby comes into the world, it is touched and held by the other, and that even before the infant begins to touch itself, it has already been exposed to the gaze and touch of others. The infant's body thereby becomes an object and an other for itself. It is never a pure subjectivity, for while the infant as the subject is doing the touching and feeling, it is simultaneously exposed as object touched and felt. The internally felt perception is thus never untainted and wholly my own. The other from the outside is there already inside, arising and inseparable from the sensory experience of being touched. I shall explore this somatic auto-relationship to show that Freud's discussion on narcissism (1914) is necessarily embodied and implies that in normal development secondary narcissism (where there is a relation with the other) is already at work in order for a primary narcissism (self-relation) to operate.

Here when I refer to the other, I imply a structure, where alterity, from the field without, is never quite assimilated as pure 'ownness' and remains as a 'spine in the flesh'. This inevitable alterity is to be distinguished from a quality of relatedness (Stern 1985). The latter is the outcome of a specific quality of relating in certain interactions, whereas the fundamental installation of otherness in sensory experience is a condition of an affective relation. That is, whether we are related to well or badly is not the point; all of us, in being in the world bodily with others, will inevitably encounter a sense of the alien within, my skin as somehow not fully my own, as there for another (appropriated by the look or touch) derived from without.

Taking this idea of a relational skin surface and revisiting Freud's vesicle in *Beyond the Pleasure Principle* (1920) one can observe how Freud in this paper describes an exposed exteriorized surface, which like the skin, is rendered vulnerable not simply to 'overwhelming stimuli' (masses in motion) but in a more interpersonal language to the unavoidable entry of the other which forever leaves an inalterable mark. This lives on as a sensory perturbation, 'the alien entity' as 'the spine in the flesh' no longer only a psychological metaphor but a veritable state directly affecting skin experience.

Although a somatic state of the skin as alien and not owned is something we all experience at some point in our lives, such states are more intensely disturbing and disruptive when the skin has been exposed to very adverse relational environmental conditions. These can range from negative and fundamental disturbances in quality of relating, to foundational disruptions in affiliate bonds, radical traumatic loss and separation, abuse and torture. In such cases the breach of the other can bring about radical and extreme states of *Unheimlich* (of not being at home in one's own skin).

What will be looked at is the way somatic memory is relived in the symptom well after the fact, living on as a breach in skin integrity, which can be compared to estranged and depersonalized bodily states and, as already noted, what Victor Tausk (1933) describes as the anxiety of 'the influencing machine'. But whereas Tausk refers in his study to cases of 'full-blown' schizophrenia, my exploration here is more inclusive: I believe that states of sensory alterity and skin experience are a potential for us all.

My purpose is to readdress the relation of trauma to the body and to challenge and rebalance the trend in certain strands of British psychoanalysis to move trauma away from the body entirely and towards solely an understanding of the mind and its reified being – whether in terms of Laplanche's entire transposition of trauma into the psyche, the 'foreign body' becoming nothing other than a 'group of ideational representatives intruding into the psyche' (1985: 134), or as in post-Kleinian thinking where there is reference to a breach in the mental container (see Garland 1998). These developments knock any adequate understanding of the 'somatic foreign body' out of the account.

Brain–Body Maps

What has been repeatedly identified throughout is the dominant tendency in Anglo-American psychoanalysis to reduce the complexity of the body ego to a mental phenomenon. This reduction comes in a number of forms, for example, the body ego has been interpreted as a mental representation per se, or as a mental body image and no more, or it has been reduced to the superficies of the mental apparatus, either the surface of the brain or the perception-consciousness system as described in Freud or as developed in post-Kleinian thinking as the mental container function, following the developments of Bion (Garland 1998). These psychoanalytic accounts have something important to offer, but when psychoanalysis treats mind or psyche as an autonomous sphere, divisions between body and mind, materiality and non-materiality, mind/psyche and the world, resurface, and the necessary link between mind and body, the effect of others, their bodies and the wider social field are lost.

So how can Freud's reference to the body ego not only as related to a surface projection, but also as 'a mental projection of the surface of the body . . . representing the superficies of the mental apparatus' (1974 [1923]: 16) be understood, without resorting to a split between body and mind? In an earlier discussion the relation between body ego and *mental projection* has been related to the sensorimotor cortex strip (including the primary and secondary somatosensory cortex), the brain–body map. Indeed Freud states:

> if we wish to find an anatomical analogy for [the body ego] we can best iden-tify the 'cortical homunculus' of the anatomists, which stands on its head in the cortex, sticks up its heels, faces backwards and, as we know, has its speech area on the left-hand side. (1974: 364–365)

Damasio (1994, 2000) likewise relates the sensorimotor strip to the body ego. So, as noted in Chapter 1, the notion of the body form in the psyche (Laplanche's psychic gestalt) as the basis for the body ego is related to the sensorimotor cortex strip, the body maps in the brain, or the brain–body map(s). However, I have been at pains to note that the brain –body map(s) cannot be reduced to the mental body image, in so far as the primary somatic sensorimotor cortex is rooted in somatic body processes and is directly con-nected to different parts of the body and susceptible to environmental influence. Already there is an inevitable relation of brain and body as well as no presupposed or irresolvable divide between soma and world.

Evidently the primary sensorimotor cortex is the skin surface in the brain and exists on the superficies of the brain apparatus, and the brain–body map is intricately wired up to receive sensory and motor information, the senses being directly plugged into the world. In normal circumstances, the sensory neural and motor pathways develop in interaction with the environ-ment; sensory information is not simply raw data picked up by the senses but gets arranged in semiotic patterns of sense derived from interpersonal and social communication systems and brain–body map processing.[2] Anzieu's *Skin Ego* helps to describe the sensory formation of a semiotic skin matrix (or matrices), derived from others, which helps to filter and pattern sensory information and, I suggest, informs brain–body mapping.

When thinking of sensations arising from the skin, Ramachandran and Blakeslee note, we usually think of touch: 'But in fact neural pathways that mediate sensations of warmth, cold and pain also originate on the skin surface' (1999: 33). These neural pathways can become interlaced in highly complex ways that are dependent on neuroplasticity and mapping.

The skin can indicate affective arousal through conductance. This is known as galvanic skin response (GSR), and can be measured as electrical currents as the level of moisture alters. Patterns of perspiration link the skin surface expression to the nervous system – sympathetic and parasympathetic changes. Sensory body experience relating to skin periphery states can alter and shift and are affectively charged. The role of the skin in sensory and somatic body feedback loops affects the brain–body states.

Corporeal and visual communications derived from others, the interpersonal and social construction of body image, the historical formation of somatic memories (including procedural memory) and cortical remapping all alter and inform brain–body maps (which are never singular). Indeed, as noted much earlier, the discovery of neuroplasticity and brain–body map formation in recent neuroscience research has been the challenge to an over-reductionist reading of a determining and fixed genetic body map – a neuromatrix as defined by Melzack (1999).

I am expanding on what was introduced in Chapter 1 as the brain–body map. I shall look in a bit more detail at the neuroscience literature which suggests that the body map(s), as part and parcel of sensory and lived body experience, involve model building and cannot be reduced to a fixed genetic body map.

On the contrary, body maps are seen to have some plasticity and protean potential. Ramachandran and Blakeslee (1999) argue that the more that is known about brain–body processes, the greater the challenge to the view of the intact body/self as simply singular, coherently unified and experienced as 'owned'. Likewise psychoanalysts has observed that the coherency and unity of the body ego is more transient and illusory than actual and constant. Ramachandran and Blakeslee further note that sensory bodily states or motor activity need not express a simple ownership of one's own body but can show up something inexplicable and uncanny, that there is some kind of other – the alien or the zombie – lurking within, a state of alterity inhabiting the body or parts of the body. Ramachandran and Blakeslee suggest that body ownership is a temporary state of affairs and should not be assumed as a neurological given.

Bodily memories live on in the creation of brain–body maps. These can be based on past sensory experience but creatively and painfully so. The research on phantom limb phenomena is fascinating:

> soldiers who have grenades blow up in their hands often report that their phantom hand is in a fixed position, clenching the grenade . . . the pain is

excruciating – the same they felt the instant the grenade exploded . . . a woman . . . had experienced chilblains . . . in childhood . . . now has a vivid phantom thumb and experiences chilblains in it every time the weather turns cold. (Ramachandran and Blakeslee 1999: 51)

The brain–body map has been shown to be more fluid and open, and influenced by developmental experience. Price (2006) argues that body image is derived developmentally from others and influences the brain–body map. In examining how body image is developmentally accrued, experientially learned even interuterine and certainly from birth onwards, he describes how the body image is created by a mirroring derived from the field of others and the role of the mirror neurons in this process. It is because of developmental experiential learning, Price argues, that a limb experience can be derived from comparison with others, and mirror neurons simulate visual and affective states, based on the observation of others. The suggestion is that body image and its construction through mirroring via others can influence body memory and brain–body mapping.

Price questions the genetically hard-wired neuromatrix hypothesis (Melzack 1999) as the explanation for the existence of phantom limb phenomena among congenital amputees. He argues that Melzack's position is simply assumptive: if congenital amputees are born without a limb but experience a phantom limb in its place, this is not evidence for a hard-wired intact body form or image. Given that it is impossible to study amputees' experience of their bodies before experiential learning and developmental acquisition, it would seem perfectly possible that amputees don't simply derive the image of the body from internal sources but from mirroring and sensing others who have limbs, and simulating this so it becomes part of their own body experience.

One of my patients born congenitally deaf and into a deaf family had no problem with her deafness in so far as hearing had always been missing and therefore had not been experienced as a loss of something once experienced. However, from early on from interacting with her peer group she discovered that others experienced her differently – as lacking something – and she sensed their capacities in comparison to hers and inadvertently the stigma attributed to her condition. This fundamentally affected her experience of her body and identity and left her focused and preoccupied with her 'hearing'.

Ramachandran and Blakeslee (1999) detail how visual information through mirroring constructs can alter body image and sensory experience. The famous mirror box experiments with amputees and painful phantom limb phenomena are an example of this. Experiments with the mirror box, whereby a healthy moving limb is shown in the mirror (where in reality there is no limb) can provide visual feedback that 'corrects' the distortion and the experience of pain, the visual mirroring informing brain–body mapping resulting in changes in bodily sensation.

Robert, a man with a fixated fist clench which characterized his phantom limb and who suffered terrible phantom pain,

> looked at the [mirror] box, positioned his good hand to superimpose its reflection over his phantom hand and after making a fist with the normal hand, tried to unclench both hands simultaneously. The first time he did this Robert exclaimed that he could feel the phantom fist open along with his good fist, simply as a result of the visual feedback. Better yet, the pain disappeared. (Ramachandran and Blakeslee 1999: 53–54)

Ramachandran and Blakeslee point out that the phantom limb experiments can have more general implications: they show that body image and sensation can alter in a matter of minutes, indicating the labile nature of brain–body maps where there is neuroplasticity. This point is very interesting and deserves to be singled out. It suggests that we can change protean configurations of somatic sensation and visual gestalt virtually in minutes.

From this neuroscience angle the labile and mobile shifts in sensory and brain–body representation are impressive. I would like to connect this to the psychoanalytic observation that there are shifting sensory states in somatic symptom formation, and these are not only visual but also sensory. It is recognized both in neuroscience and in psychoanalysis that there is a body–other relation and a developmental role in the formation of body representation (the formation of the skin ego for psychoanalysis and brain–body map for neuroscience) and there is the possibility of protean movement therein.

It is now very evident that neuroplasticity plays a key role in the formation of brain–body maps and the extended inference is that the body form is in fact a kind of phantom construct. For Ramachandran and Blakeslee, 'there is a deeper message here – *Your own body is a phantom*' (1999: 58). They have devised a number of experiments which show how a person can experience sensations from a dummy hand or as if arising from the table or other objects. It is as if the body periphery has become extended in space and sensation is emitted from this exteriorized point:

> Construct a two foot by two foot cardboard 'wall' and place it on a table in front of you. Put your right hand behind the cardboard so that you cannot see it and put the dummy hand in front of the cardboard so you can see it clearly. Next have your friend stroke identical locations on both your hand and the dummy hand synchronously while you look at the dummy hand. Within seconds you will experience the stroking sensation as arising from the dummy hand. The experience is uncanny. (Ramachandran and Blakeslee 1999: 61)

Ramachandran and Blakeslee show that there is a galvanic skin response: by threatening to hit the table or the dummy hand they elicit a high galvanic response. This displacing of sensation onto external objects, they note, can be likened to out-of-body experiences, voodoo dolls and the like, and can extend even to objects that have no affiliation to the human form. Ramachandran and Blakeslee relate these body phenomena to the experience of the uncanny.

What this suggests is that the skin surface can be experienced as a shifting and changing border which is not fixed or constant. It is an observation that Merleau-Ponty documents when he describes how we feel ourselves in the other's body and in a relational field and how this is a reality of skin experience. This theme in Merleau-Ponty's work in relation to the skin surface will be further discussed and developed later.

The skin border is potentially more amoeba-like (Freud's protoplasmic vesicle or Lacan's *(h)omelette*), and indeed this protean skin border can become confounded with other bodies or with an environmental field. Where does my body begin in relation to others and the outside world? These demarcations are somewhat precarious and this has important implications for the discussion of the skin surface as ego.

Gallese and colleagues (2004), in advancing the mirror neuron hypothesis, refer to the tactile–visual simulation system, emphasizing tactility and the intercorporeal basis of the experience. The example mentioned of a James Bond film when a tarantula crawls on Bond's chest, describes how this makes the watcher experience the crawling spider on their chest. Touch can be simulated by observing the action of another.

Contemporary neuroscience describes intermodal relations established between the senses: for Ramachandran and Blakeslee the inter-modal relation of vision and tactility in the creation of overlapping intersecting neural pathways in brain–body maps; for Gallesse and colleagues, visual–tactile simulation made possible by mirror neuron activity. Ramachandran and Blakeslee refer to moisture temperature and pain as sensory somatic states linking the skin to brain–body mapping.

Mirroring the Body Surface: From Neuroscience to Psychoanalysis

Relating the neuroscience mirror experiments and phantom limb experience to psychoanalysis, one notes that the amputee who 'mistakes' the able hand for what is in fact the absent limb is demonstrating a 'misrecognition', whereby the mirror image derived from without is taken for his or her own body. It is this context that allows for the 'corrective' visual feedback.

As Lacan observes, the skin surface can be constructed through mirroring, and this is supported by neuroscience findings. Lacan is well known for pointing out how the idealized body in the mirror image, intact in form, the outcome of a 'gestalt effect', produces the body ego phenomenon and how this belies the actual motor incoordination and neurological incoherency in the immature infant. Ramachandran and Blakeslee suggest that for us all what is 'mistaken' for our own body can actually relate to a phantom body; in this respect Lacan and Ramachandran are in agreement.

The skin surface mirroring and the role of the other are intimately intertwined; neurologically, the mirror neurons would support this. I emphasize the mirroring from the field of others, via proximal and wider social relations, from the mirror in the hall, the mother's look, the father's judgement, the peer's response, to the billboard Lord Kitchener-style of interpellations and the filmic play of images across screen surfaces.

After Winnicott, Bowlby and others, analysis (including Kohut 1971) has looked at the relation between disturbances in mirroring and in the sense of self. There has been exploration in attachment studies of the 'annihilating' style of mirroring in disorganized attachment patterns and the like, which either forecloses or fundamentally disrupts any idealizing imaginary. This can result in far from an idealized gestalt; there is the possible development of an affectively charged deranged form, from impaired to grotesque, a repudiated body, a body dysmorphia indeed. How does this impact on body map processing?

The dominance of fragmented body states or the consistency in body gestalt experience can vary. From a relational and developmental perspective, the experience of some bodily continuity will be greater in cases where the infant receives consistent responsiveness from a caretaker (security in quality of attachment and sensitive responsiveness) and in other ongoing relations, whereas early radical disruption and inconsistency in affiliate bonds and highly ambivalent, avoidant and specifically disorganized attachments will result in more pervasive fragmentary disturbances. Ongoing or later violation, abusive relations, from war trauma to torture, will likewise create greater bodily disarray and in some cases call into question any ability to maintain illusory body cohesiveness. *With regard to the skin surface, this is related to the skin sensation of a skin boundary, a sense of the quality of the skin border, experience of pain/pleasure, temperature and moisture. Disorganization of the body gestalt can alter comportment and motor coordination* (a point which will be elaborated later).

Fragmentary body experiences, however, can present as visual, spatial, sensory states as well as affecting motor ability, comportment and coordination. These experiences are pre-reflective: the body does things; the person suddenly becomes clumsy in his or her gait; a sensory state becomes exaggerated and intensifies apparently of its own accord; things look different visually and spatially – a person who had appeared tall and elegant, on second meeting, looks shrunken and less of a presence.

A Broad Definition of Body Image

A number of my case examples will show how the body enacts fragmentary body states in motility and movement, the language of gesture and in sensation, but there may be no cognition, or conscious sense, awareness or understanding, of the situation. In this respect, the body image cannot be defined as conscious as opposed to unconscious; image and action can come together and therefore are not rigidly separated in lived experience.

Herta Flor (2002), picking up on the important role of developmental acquisition, further suggests that what is involved in phantom limb pain is a form of unconscious learning similar to motor reflexes and perception skills, procedural in type. Françoise Dolto (1984), from a psychoanalytic stance, takes up Lacan's findings to propose how unconscious learning constructs body image through interpersonal development. This can be related to Price's emphasis on mirroring and the role of others but with a psychoanalytic input that accounts for the unconscious formation of body image. Although there is no clear relation with neuroscience and psychoanalytic understanding in terms of the different use of concepts and framework, the possible connections and inferences are of great interest and invite informed debate and research in the intersecting fields.

A psychoanalytic understanding of unconscious acquisition moves away from an over-cognitive and rationalist approach to learning; although the language of affect is not favoured by Lacan, it is mainstream to British psychoanalysis and contemporary developmental understanding. I favour the language of affect and emotion here, as the acquisition of body image and the protean transformation of body image are affectively charged. In my approach I look at how fragmented and disfiguring experiences of the body can in fact underlie any illusory states of unity. The imaging of the body in a spatial and visual sense (including the fact that blind and partially sighted people can develop spatial mapping of the body) is considered conscious and unconscious. In my understanding this is in no way contradictory. One can have a conscious awareness of the body while simultaneously experiencing fears and anxieties of fragmentary body states. Disconcerting images of the body can show up for fleeting moments and break through into conscious awareness and then be met with denial or stronger defences. Or disturbed body states may simply underlie what goes on more consciously. I have also referred to the pre-reflective know-how, whereby the body acts without conscious focus and awareness.

States of unawareness or awareness are processes in which there is some fluidity and the possibility of certain relations. I do not view states of unconscious and consciousness as static and fixed, or as, in any way, ontologically opposed, with an absolute and unbridgeable divide between them. Whereas consciousness used to be considered primary, it is now realized not only by psychoanalysts but also in contemporary neuroscience that the unconscious and pre-reflective body processes are central, rendering consciousness more the tip of the iceberg.

Brain–Body Maps and the Skin Ego

It is evident that mirroring is not only visual but tactile, and potentially involves all the senses. In referring to the sensorimotor cortex strip as the brain–body map, consideration has to be given to complex brain–body processes more generally, and to dynamic brain processes, the role of the limbic system and the parietal lobe which Ramachandran relates to the body image.

The brain–body maps effect sensory-somatic experience. I argue that this shifts how the ideational component of the maps is understood. It is to be noted that even in Freud's (1893) hysterical paralysis of a limb, the idea of the arm is sensory and lived. Although where the arm begins and ends is based on the appearance of the arm in the mirror image, not on the areas actually affected in a typical organic paralysis, there is nevertheless sensory alteration of the limb. It is anaesthetized and desensitized – stick needles in it and it will not flinch. The immobile arm is rendered functionally useless, hence motor function is affected. It as if the body symptom is saying, 'focusing attention on the arm where nothing can be felt is a way of not feeling any feelings.'

The model I propose shows how brain–body maps are affected by mirroring (and thus image) and also by sensory information from motor activity that can bring about changes in the brain–body maps. In turn the brain–body maps are rooted in both the sensory and the action body. Motility and motor activity, as well as mirroring and thus body imaging, are considered to be influences on the brain–body maps. In this model the body-skin ego is considered in relation to brain–body mapping and the skin as an external surface in a world is part of this package. In the proposed schema the body map is tied to skin surface and the relational field.

I revisit Schilder, Gallagher and Cole's work to extend and clarify the argument. Schilder (1950 [1935]) does not separate body image from kinaesthetic sensitivity and lived motility. As noted in Chapter 1, Head (1920) refers to a postural schema, while Gallagher (1986, 2005) and Gallagher and Cole (1998 [1995]) offer an initial account of what they refer to as a body schema which is based in motility and in non-conscious processes. Gallagher and Cole stress that body schema is not to be confused with body image. They question Schilder's slippage of terms which confounds body image and schema and suggest that this is not only unhelpful but has led to continuing confusion in the field. They point out that although body image and body schema intersect in lived experience, they are nevertheless separable and the conceptual distinction finds some empirical support in cases where the subject has an intact body image but a dysfunctional body schema and vice versa, as found in cases of double dissociation and unilateral neglect. However, I have explored how alterations of the body gestalt can influence motility and, of course, posture; the suggestion is that changes in motility can have an effect on body image. So it would seem that even if a definitional distinction were upheld between image and schema, it should not endorse a rigid opposition between them.

To revisit Gallagher and Cole: the body schema is for them

> a system of motor capacities, abilities, and habits that enable movement and the maintenance of posture. The body schema is not a perception, a belief, or an attitude. Rather, it is a system of motor and postural functions that operate below the level of self-referential intentionality, although such functions can enter into and support intentional activity. The preconscious, sub-personal processes carried out by the body-schema system are tacitly keyed into the environment and play a dynamic role in governing posture and movement. Although the body-schema system can have specific effects on cognitive experience . . . it does not have the status of a conscious representation or belief. (Gallagher and Cole 1998 [1995]: 372)

In contrast,

> The *body image* consists of a complex set of intentional states-perceptions, mental representations, beliefs, and attitudes – in which the intentional object of such states is one's own body. Thus the body image involves a reflective intentionality. Three modalities of this reflective intentionality are often distinguished in studies involving body image: (a) the subject's *perceptual* experience of his/her own body; (b) the subject's *conceptual* understanding (including mythical, cultural, and/or scientific knowledge) of the body in general; and (c) the subject's *emotional* attitude toward his/her own body. (Gallagher and Cole 1998 [1995]: 371)

The definitional terms become more complex and potentially less clear-cut as they become elaborated. So although Gallagher states 'the body image, as a reflective intentional system, normally represents the body *as my own body*, as a personal body that belongs to me' (2005: 28), in pathological states like unilateral neglect this is not the case. Also, 'ownership' as a general norm of body image is implicitly made less straightforward by Gallagher's acknowledgement of intercorporeality as a basis of human development. Furthermore there is recognition of different modes of consciousness and body image.

For Gallagher (2005) other thinkers have confused body image and schema and come up with incoherent notions like the body image as a non-conscious representation and a conscious image. As far as Gallagher is concerned, the first statement cancels out the possibility of the second because for him the body image cannot be both a conscious phenomena and an unconscious representation unbeknown to the subject at the time.

In the perspective I adopt, and from a psychoanalytically informed position, the idea that the body image can be conscious and also unconscious is not implausible and impossible. One could say that the body image is in part both unconscious and conscious; the states are not static but in relation and process. Gallagher and Cole's particular framework is one of cognitive psychology and this becomes a master discourse, combined with an intentional phenomenology. What gets presupposed is a more rationalist emphasis on cognitive development and capacities; in contrast, the focus in this book is on the pre-reflective and unconscious, on our *inevitable* tie with others and alterity (foundational, not an additional afterthought), on the power of affect in shaping experience and I emphasize a more fluid way of thinking according to which binary-type definitions are seen to create more problems than solutions. Instead of cognitive psychology and intentional phenomenology, I favour poststructural and relational psychoanalysis and post-phenomenological developments. As Merleau-Ponty intuited long ago, psychoanalysis and phenomenological enquiry can be bedfellows.

So, it is agreed that when there is no neuropathology the body schema is automatic and subconscious, governed by habit for posture and movement. But what is of interest here is how body motility is influenced by affective states including unconscious ones like a mood that can take one unawares, how habit profoundly involves the influence of others and cultural organization in the creation of styles of comportment (see Young 1990).

My focus is on the way the body image exists not statically as a reified concept or idea but as bodily experienced and lived. Perhaps most importantly, body image is informed by body ego formation which is built through sensory means of communication and relates to body motility, where gestalt effects can be more precarious and affect movement as well. Bodily ownership is considered problematic rather than given, and the unconscious derivations of the formation of body image are seen as influential. Centrality is without doubt given to relations with others and our sociality, the latter profoundly affecting coherent gestalts of body image and motility function, which are fragile and vulnerable to change.

Owing to the critical address of a reduced, 'mentalist' psychoanalytic model, my framing of body image as more than an idea or belief differs starkly from Gallagher and Cole's more restricted definition. In my formulation, meaning and non-verbal sensory communication are bodily acts, involve movement and gesture and are not reified as a concept. The formation of body ego is not simply a state of consciousness, intentional or otherwise, and is affectively lived in sensory and somatic states.

Thus Gallagher and Cole's framework is in some ways so fundamentally different that their assumptions and underlying terms are as distinctive as are our agendas. Their terminology is respected and viewed as somewhat different in focus, which is why I have preferred not to use their definitions but instead to refer to the brain–body maps and their intricate link with body ego formation and the skin.

The brain–body map, as I have shown, is not singular but can involve maps. I suggest the brain–body maps can be related to body ego formation. They are sensory related and have somatic roots in the body. Brain–body mapping is developmentally informed and is related to the skin as a surface, which in turn is inscribed in an environmental interpersonal and social field.

Notes

1   This section devoted to discussing Freud's body ego as a surface projection pursues a theme taken up by Lafrance (2009), Manning (2009) and Pile (2011). All three question the idea of an innately given skin integrity, and examine the connections between the skin and a social and environmental field. My work applies the developments in thinking, particularly to clinical somatic symptom formation, and broadens the interdisciplinary discussion.

2   When considering more complex processing and integration of somatic and sensory states with memory and semiotic relations, it is important to refer to the primary and secondary somatosensory cortex: the primary cortex, represented by the homunculus, is associated with direct sensory and somatic input, while the adjacent somatosensory cortex is related to integration, involving more complex processes such as memory and language.

12

Didier Anzieu and *The Skin Ego*

The Laplanche–Anzieu Propping Connection

Didier Anzieu's *The Skin Ego*, published in French in 1985 and in English in 1989, is a key text, which has been influential in developing Freud's understanding of the body ego, in its theoretical rigour and advancement, and in offering an understanding of body symptoms and its clinical application. Following Laplanche's understanding of anaclisis (or propping), Anzieu works towards a more comprehensive account of what he terms the skin ego, where the body is not left out of the picture, nor relations with others. However, despite this intent, various problems arise due to the use of the anaclitic propping model.

> Jean Laplanche . . . recommends the concept of anaclisis be reserved for the sexual drives to find support in the organic functions of self-preservation, but I want to give it a broader interpretation. The psychical apparatus develops through successive stages of breaking with its biological basis, breaks which on the one hand make it possible to escape from biological laws, and on the other make it necessary to look for an anaclitic relationship of every psychical to a bodily function . . . For psychoanalysts like myself, the skin is of crucial importance, providing the psychical apparatus with representations both of the nature of the ego and its principal functions . . . no longer concerned with satisfaction of vital needs of self-preservation (food, breathing, sleep) on which the sexual and aggressive drives will come to constitute themselves anaclitically, but with communication, pre-verbal and infra-linguistic, on which linguistic exchange will, in due course, come to be supported . . . tactile, visual, auditory, and olfactory communication . . . the original form of communication, both in reality and even more intensely in fantasy, is direct, unmediated from skin to skin. (Anzieu 1989: 96–97)

Between Skins: The Body in Psychoanalysis – Contemporary Developments,
First Edition. Nicola Diamond.
© 2013 John Wiley & Sons, Ltd. Published 2013 by John Wiley & Sons, Ltd.

By taking Laplanche's reading of propping as his basis, Anzieu unwittingly takes on a legacy.

Life and Death in Psychoanalysis argues that the psychic model of the ego derives from the living form given to the body. Anzieu adopts Laplanche's main propping thesis and uses it to develop the idea of the skin as biological envelope and its formation via the representation of the ego. Anzieu's understanding has not been challenged since; yet, despite his very rich and fruitful contribution, flaws and impasses do exist and are similar to those found in Laplanche's first propping account.

Anzieu follows Laplanche's account in its claim to create a link between psychoanalysis, biology and theories of representation. He adopts what I have termed the biological bedrock model. He views the skin as a biological substratum and tries to relate this to the emergence of the psychic skin ego. Anzieu was a psychoanalyst in France, and in his earlier thinking was influenced by the French analytic tradition of Jacques Lacan. But, like Laplanche, Anzieu makes a connection with Anglo-American psychoanalysis and readings of Freud, and returns to Freud in a way that is accessible to Anglo-American psychoanalytic understanding. For that reason his work has been powerfully influential in the English-speaking world.

Laplanche, in clarifying Freud, argues in his first propping account that there is a non-technical definition of the ego relating to the living being, the veritable entity in contrast to the ego as a mental agency: 'it is the psychical level that is the centre of our Interest' (1985: 52). He argues for the slippage in meaning and the metonymic and metaphoric derivation, the representation initially propped on the body as physical counterpart and preconstituted actuality and then radically deviating from it.

Laplanche questions Lacan for defining the body image as a mere lure or ruse, and refers to the sheer gravity of the body image. This is an interesting comment, but the first propping account creates a total split between the body form as a veritable entity and the mental phenomenon. The first propping account is founded on physical being: the organism as defined by a logos in nature, an entity given in form, fixed in identity – it cannot budge and as such has to remain outside the order of the psychic ego.

The ego in this model is thus relegated to an agency of the mental apparatus, a psychic representation, while the body image figures as a mental phenomenon alone. The ego as a psychic phenomena relates to narcissism and libidinal cathexis of the mental body image. In this schema alterity in respect to the experience of the body is for the mental body image alone, set apart as it is from the veritable being. This problem in argument is to be seen to occur again in Anzieu's work. Suffice it for now that in my view body form is not a simple a priori biological given and the body image ego cannot be studied as a psychic experience, divorced from the sensory-somatic body or from environmental context.

The Skin Ego sets out to explain how the biological skin of Laplanche's non-technical definition of the ego, the living individual, takes on a symbolic function in the formation of the ego. For Anzieu the skin ego is both bodily and psychic, and its formation is dependent on early infant–mother interaction, skin contact being the primary means of communication between mother and child. Successful development of a skin ego provides what Anzieu calls an interface for the child, which allows the latter to differentiate between inner and outer reality. Anzieu tries to overcome the body/psyche division, to help us think our way out of the impasse, 'to escape biological laws' and to take real skins, so to speak, into the symbolic terrain; yet by adopting the first propping thesis he ends up stating that (1) the skin surface is based on the biological bedrock model and the skin ego is propped up by this; (2) that the surface yields internal and external sensations (whereas it is the psychic reflexive mode of the skin ego as ambiguously subject and object that is derived from the biological substratum the skin, but in its more complex form, exists as mental phenomenon); and (3) that communication which eventually develops into a semiotics derives from direct skin-to-skin contact. This direct skin-to-skin contact leads to an impasse.

Summary of *The Skin Ego*

Anzieu begins with Freud's *The Ego and the Id* (1974 [1923]):

> A person's own body and above all its surface is a place from which both external and internal perceptions may spring. It is seen like any other object, but to touch it yields two kinds of sensations, one of which may be equivalent to an internal perception. (1989: 34)

The body is visualized as an object, and the tactile senses provide both an 'internal and an external perception', indicating the nature of 'bodily experience upon which the ego is anaclitally constituted' (85):

> [the] child begins actively to explore this two way nature of touch for himself touching parts of his body with his finger or putting his thumb or big toe in his mouth, thus simultaneously testing out the complementary positions of subject and object. (35)

Thus

> It seems likely that the doubling that is inherent in tactile sensations prepares the ground for the reflexive doubling of the conscious ego, once again basing itself anaclitally upon tactile experience. (85)

To support the argument, Anzieu quotes Freud's famous lines 'the ego is first and foremost a bodily ego'; '[the ego is] not merely a surface entity but itself a projection of a surface'. Freud describes how ego derives from body sensations springing from the surface of the body and can thus be regarded as a mental projection of the surface of the body (35).

The skin ego as an internalized psychic perception derives initially from the body sensations. The skin ego is a product of the metaphor–metonymy oscillation (6) which is ultimately founded on an 'inherent anaclisis of the ego' based 'upon the experiences and functions of the skin (96–7). These experiences not only involve tactility and visibility, but also temperature, smell, taste and respiratory as well as vocal motor sensations (which do not just begin in specific sounds) 'produced by coughing and by alimentary and digestive activities which turn the body into a resonant cavern' (163), the vibration of the vocal cords emitting the cry and eventual articulation of words. The body is the 'pre-sexual and irreducible datum, the anaclitic grounding of all the psychical functions' (21). One has to comment here on the richness of the Anzieu's description of the body and the senses; in so many ways he is spot on! (The problem is in the imported use of the propping concept.)

So 'the psychical envelope derives anaclitically from the bodily envelope' (34). The skin ego, as Laplanche's (and Bion's) mental container holding the thought (contents) together, emerges from the skin's structural function of holding the insides of the body together. The skin ego as a psychological container keeps the internal world in relational contact with the outside world. This interface, connecting inner and external reality, derives from the envelope's biological substratum. This consists of two layers: an outer and an inner layer, 'the two sided envelope' (31). Anzieu notes that, in 'Beyond the pleasure principle', this envelope was made out of a protective shield, a baked-through crust, and a second, deeper, receptive cortical layer, where the sense organs lie. Anzieu describes this actual dual structure of the skin surface:

> The two layers fit together, an external layer (screen against quantity, the cellulose membrane of plants and the hide cf. the sense organs of the epidermis or the cortex). The internal layer is protected against exogenous but not against endogenous quantities. (79)

So one layer is directed towards the external world, and a deeper lower layer is turned inwards, facing the interior of the body, an interface, as Anzieu calls it. This resembles Nicolas Abraham and Torok's shell and kernel (and outer shell and inner core, a container–containing relation), as well as Freud's mystic writing pad. Like the mystic writing pad, 'the skin's double structure has a protective shield (*Reizschütz*) and the receptive under-layer the surface of Inscription' (Abraham and Torok 1994: 10).

Anzieu then sets out to account for how the skin in structure and function is the basis of preverbal communication. He notes its ability to react to different stimuli 'the alphabet has been transformed into electronic impulses on the skin and taught to the blind' and goes on to mention Laura Bridgman and Helen Keller's achievements. Helen Keller, who was blind, deaf and dumb, demonstrates the possibility of primary communication by means of skin contact (Anzieu 1989: 19). In the same vein, Anzieu adds:

> The infant experiences the maternal gestures, first as sensory stimulus, then as communication. The massage becomes a message the novel and the film Jonny got his gun he argues shows this well. A seriously wounded soldier has lost his sight, hearing and movement, a nurse manages to establish contact with him by drawing letters with her hand on the injured man's chest and abdomen. (39)

He accounts for how the massage becomes the sensory message by describing the skin as a 'site and a primary means of communicating with others, of establishing signifying relations', as an 'inscribing surface for the marks left by those of others' (40). Anzieu focuses not only on the anaclitic biological basis of the skin ego, but also on the way the skin ego has to develop to be formed within a relationship between mother and infant.

A Relational Turn in Anzieu's Thinking

Here Anzieu takes on the meaning of anaclisis as a leaning on the mother, which Laplanche questions as an adequate reading in *Life and Death in Psychoanalysis* (1985). However, Anzieu does something interesting by developing Bion's container–contained relation to understand the formation of the skin envelope. This in fact also marks a turn in Anzieu's thinking away from an anaclitic account based on a biological bedrock model and towards a relational perspective.

He argues that the formation of the ego occurs through a dual anaclitic process: this is based on 'the container–content relation which the mother brings into play in her relation to the infant' (85). The mother initially acts as the container for the child: 'the mother acts as the baby's original protective shield against aggression from the outside world' (43). The skin ego emerges from the 'interplay between the mother's body and the child's as well as the responses the mother makes to the baby's sensations and emotions' (101). The skin, at first 'part of mother particularly her hands, has been interiorized' (98), maintaining the psyche in a functional state.

Mother's holding of her child forms a shield for the child which is interiorized through the interplay between infant and the parent, while the responses of the mother are internalized by the child. They come to function as a thought container for the child's psyche. Anzieu refers to Bion, who argues that the child's exogenous excitations are contained by the mother binding them via her responses to her child. Anzieu notes that the child is initially stimulated 'no doubt by its own mother', and only then does it derive experience 'from its own skin' (85). The mother not only contains but initiates a stimulation for the child. It is only when this function is taken on by the child's own skin and internalized that the child forms a skin ego.

W. R. Bion (1962) has shown that the transition from non-thinking to thinking, or from beta to alpha elements, is based on a capacity of which the infant must have some experience if he or she is to develop psychically. This is the capacity of the mother's breast to contain in a defined psychical space sensations (particularly cenesthesic and kinaesthetic), affects and memory traces (or mental images) which are then imprinted on the new-born psyche. The container breast halts the retrospective projection of expelled and scattered bits of the self and offers them the possibility of representation, binding and introjection (157).

Thinking develops by the mother helping her child contain multiple sensations; she aids their articulation by interpreting and differentiating between experiences. Mother binds the sensory experiences so that the child can take them back in a digestible form. Anzieu cites Winnicott who describes the way the mother holds and handles her child. If the mother provides a container for her child, then the experience of endlessly falling can be prevented; the infant can be caught and this will act as the block on which a self can be built. The building blocks handed over to the child via maternal gestures are touch, mirroring, soothing sounds, a bath of words, 'a rhythm, melody, inflexion' (157), all of which add up to an envelope container containing the contents. This is the maternal environment because it surrounds the baby with an external envelope 'made up of messages' (62), and because it extends to include

> the family group which takes over from her, of signals including smiles, gentleness of contact, physical warmth of embrace, diversity of sounds, solidity with which the child is carried, how it is rocked. (97)

The skin performs 'a primary means of communicating with others, of establishing signifying relations an inscribing surface for the marks left by others' (40) by being an 'original parchment which preserves like a Palimpsest, the erased, scratched out, written over first outline of an original pre-verbal writing made up of traces upon the skin' (105). A registering of tactile sensory traces 'that Pier Castoriadis-Aulagnier in *La Violence de l' interpretation* (1975) sees as a pictogramme function and what F. Pasche in "Le Bouclier de Persee" (1971) describes as the shield of Perseus which sends back a mirror of reality' (105).

Anzieu notes that in 'The project for a scientific psychology' (1895) Freud explains how the second cortical layer of the bodily envelope has sense organs; at their nerve endings lie screens which function like contact barriers. Anzieu quotes Freud: 'Q screens through which only quotients of exogenous quantity will pass it' (77), pointing out that contact barriers resist quantity and are capable of qualitative differentiation, facilitation and memory by the physis neurons, which become further complicated by the psyche neurons. He mentions that sensory information is picked up by 'period' via the sense organs. Anzieu relates this temporal movement to the 'institution of the role of resonance and of rhythmic dissonance in the constitution of the skin ego or in the development of rifts in it' (80); 'the network of contact barriers constitute then what I propose to call a surface of inscription' (31). A shield is formed that prevents quantity passing through, thus allowing the sense organs to receive a bearable quantity of stimuli. The contact barriers can then be left with the function of dealing with quality: this is what constitutes their 'filtering function' (80), for the 'contact barriers serve to separate quantity from quality and to bring to consciousness the perception of sensory qualities' (31).

The argument here is very innovative. However, there are areas of the formulation that fall short. For now suffice it to say that an impenetrable biological substratum cannot be receptive to the trace left as the signifying mark, indifferent as it is to relational differences. Yet Anzieu argues that this protective shield and the receptive surface can be likened to Freud's mystic writing pad, that the celluloid sheet is related to the skin shield surface, the cortical layer acting as the surface on which traces are inscribed. My question is how inscribed?

Anzieu then returns to a relational language and states that the mother needs to deal with 'the paradox of signifying contacts' (44). The mother who responds appropriately to her child can then help him or her form a narcissistic cathected skin ego, by supporting the illusion

> that a being attached to the other side, the outer face of the envelope, will react immediately and in a complementary, symmetrical fashion to inner signals. (This is the reassuring illusion of having an omniscient double at one's permanent disposal.) (44)

In other words, the maternal envelope as the external layer of the two-sided skin ego can protect the child by being narcissistically appropriated as the child's own skin. In contrast, the skin ego can become irritated. Anzieu argues that a mother, 'through the libidinal quality and intensity of bodily care and attention' (44), can produce such an excess of excitation that a secondary masochistic skin can be formed which experiences pleasure only at the most extreme limit of pain, an envelope of suffering and excitation.

Clinical Cases Charting Skin Ego Disturbances

Anzieu gives case examples of alterations in skin ego formation and notes a corresponding disturbance in physiological function. In a case of asthma changes take place in respiration, relating to how fullness and emptiness are experienced: 'Respiratory interaction with the physical environment is dependent on tactile interaction with the human milieu' (115). The respiratory system is 'stimulated by sucking and physical contact with mother' (115). A failure of the interaction results in rifts within the skin ego. The desire to retain air in the lungs can become associated with the fear of being emptied. In this woman's case, she was born with a cord wrapped round her neck and received insufficient maternal stimulation. Her asthma related to her battle for space with the internalized mother: either she felt empty or all was mother, which led to suffocation and no 'me'. Another case involved fluctuations of temperature. A girl's sadistic parents forced her to have boiling baths and freezing showers, disregarding her feelings. Later she became confused over how she felt and when she failed to articulate her feelings to the therapist or herself, she would suffer sudden changes in body temperature.

Another illustration is that of the olfactory envelope. In this case perspiration becomes symbolically overdetermined. The analysand presented with foul smells. Through analysis, Anzieu discovered that these odours were stronger when the man became sexually excited and/or in need of comfort. The smell was a combination of profuse perspiring and sexual stimulation producing genital odour. The excessive perspiration with the odour disappeared through analytic work. It had turned out that he had been delivered by forceps, which left his skin cut and bleeding. He would cuddle up to a woman he called his godmother, and it was said that this had saved his life. Lying close to the godmother turned out to carry with it a primal fantasy of fusion with mother. His broken, bleeding skin became sealed up in the fantasy of merging with the godmother's body. The godmother, Anzieu was told, was a peasant woman who rarely washed her body; she had become the man's protective shield to make up for his insufficient skin at birth. When he was in a state of anxiety and in need of comfort, he would erect this shield. His anxiety sweating would mingle with his body odours and this would result in the pungent olfactory envelope. Anzieu calls this body envelope a colander skin ego.

Anzieu also refers to Esther Bick's famous paper 'The experience of the skin in early object relations' (1968). Bick argues that the skin's primal function of binding together the personality is dependent upon the skin being contained by the skin of the mother, who maintains the child's body through her warmth, her voice, 'her familiar smell' (Anzieu 1989: 193). 'The containing object is experienced concretely as a skin', which becomes 'introjected, so the baby acquires a space within' the self (193). The experience of the mother's nipple contained in the infant's mouth and the mother containing the child allows for the perception to become the child's own. A failing of this function, which for Bick is not only to do with the mother but also with the child's degree of aggressivity, will affect the formation of what Anzieu has called the skin ego. Anzieu draws out the relevance of Bick's work for the formation of the skin ego. Here I shall reiterate her findings to signpost how Anzieu relates Bick's case studies to his notion of the development of the skin container. Baby Alice, reported by Bick, began to build a 'skin container' (Bick 1968: 24), initially by tolerating greater proximity to her child while simultaneously reducing the intensity of tactile stimulation.

This helped Alice shift from an unintegrated body state, which she expressed in chaotic jerky movements and trembling, and in uncontrolled sneezing, to a calmer, more balanced state, revealing the child's own containing skin function. After a move to a new house, the mother became neglectful and inconsistent, feeding her baby without physical contact and allowing her to scream all night. At the same time, she encouraged a pseudo-independence, which the child exhibited in outward aggressive behaviour. Her mother mistook it for a sign of her little girl's liveliness. The child's hyperactive movements and exaggerated responses functioned as a second muscular skin, a rhino skin, which, in Anzieu's view, supplemented the lack of the first skin ego to take on an adequate self-containing function.

Bick's patient Mary, the schizophrenic girl who failed to cope adequately with separation anxiety, would demand immediate physical contact from her analyst. Without this contact she would revert to an unintegrated body state, which was shown in her 'hunched, stiff jointed, grotesque' posture, resembling a 'sack of potatoes' (Bick 1968: 194), a sack which looked in constant danger of 'spilling out its contents' (195). Anzieu also refers to Frances Tustin's work with autistic children. Tustin (1981) identifies a primary, autistic, amoeboid ego which lacks support and any containing function, and a crustacean ego, in which a rigid shell cuts the child's body off from the world.

Anzieu notes that for a skin to form, a differentiation between the skin of the mother skin and that of the child has to develop, which allows the envelope to form two leaves and to be taken on by the child as his or hers. Without this, the common skin remains. The external layer sticks so closely to the child's skin that the development of his or her ego is suffocated; he or she is invaded by one of the egos in the environment: this is one of the techniques for driving others mad pointed out by H. Searles (Anzieu 1989: 62).

It would appear that Anzieu suggests a skin ego can form an interface only if there is a space created in between mother as shield and an inner surface and a difference between them. If there is no gap, then the sides stick together, as in the example of the psychotic body envelope. Federn (1953) notes the way psychotics often experience no body periphery ego feeling.

In contrast, the 'borderline' patient has a skin ego, but it is fundamentally impaired; the two leaves also form a single face but in this case the surface has become twisted. The borderline person suffers, unsure of the frontiers between his or her own body and those of others.

Challenges to the Main Account

The clinical examples show there is a relation between the skin ego and alterations in somatic states; however, there are some difficulties with Anzieu's deployment of the first propping account that prevent an understanding of ego–soma relation. What I shall propose to help us through this impasse is a counter-argument where, instead, the biological bedrock is not in itself intact. The relation with the other and the world already intervenes, providing environmental support for the skin, propping up the biological structure that now appears to have been lacking from the start. Furthermore, the reflexive turn cannot be conceived as simply inherent to tactility but is instead already a developmental, relational achievement which exists in a bodily, sensory way.

So rather than assuming an inbuilt discriminatory differentiation between the internal and external experiences of touch, I shall show how this differentiation is relationally acquired and that the reflexive mode on oneself as subject and object involves the body. I shall relate the doubling in innate tactility to the relational touching–touched experience, which does not and cannot derive from unmediated skin-to-skin contact, which in itself does not yield relation, but rather forecloses a semiotics of communication. My exploration will instead show that the meeting of skin and skin can make contact and establish communicative links only by mediation through a relationship. This alternative analysis will forge the brain–body–world model to reveal how the skin and touch are relationally inscribed.

I argue it is not the biological bedrock that provides the basis for the development that follows, but the relational and environmental set-up that props the body that is found to be lacking. It is the second, radical propping movement in Anzieu that I shall draw out, with its full implications. The first anaclitic account gets turned on its head to reveal a relational biology and body, a viable model for understanding not only the internal vital processes, but the exposed skin surface – and the nature of touch. It is not the initial propping account that resolves dualism but a second, less obvious, model which reveals a more open biology, the primacy of otherness embodied and the necessity of the sensory signifying mark. My purpose is to draw out the radical shifts in the second account that reveal a more viable model for the skin surface.

13

Permeable Skin

I have given a full account of Anzieu's *Skin Ego* in Chapter 12. A fascinating and creative exploration of the subject, it is very convincing in many ways, and Anzieu's use of more contemporary developments in psychoanalysis is very helpful in the context of this book. However, his relational account is at odds with his anaclitic genesis. It is also evident from many of his examples of skin ego experiences that he describes alterations in actual sensory skin states and in skin function and structure.

Anzieu addresses not only a mental body image, but the body as well. As noted, his examples of skin ego experiences describe alterations in actual sensory skin states and in skin function. His cases demonstrate how representation is an experience also of the flesh (the senses) and of the skin, allowing for a variety of configurations, that is, thermal, olfactory, muscular, tactile and so on. These examples of skin alteration will be further explored in conjunction with additional clinical examples. However Anzieu's use of the first propping account creates an impasse, where he cannot explain the complex somatic phenomena he observes. I shall address in detail the pitfalls in his thinking and try to come up with an alternative and more viable model of the soma.

Anzieu's attempt to create a connection between metaphorical relations – Freud's mystic writing pad – and the layers of the actual skin do not yield much. Since a fixed biological substratum is impermeable to a relational field of semantic differences, metaphor thus gets turned to stone. For Anzieu the skin as such is defined in its organic identity, its function as a boundary, and as fixed in form, with innate internal and external sensations. How can a skin which is so grounded in its physiological identity ever open to the other, or how could a writing of differences penetrate a skin membrane with

---

Between Skins: The Body in Psychoanalysis – Contemporary Developments,
First Edition. Nicola Diamond.
© 2013 John Wiley & Sons, Ltd. Published 2013 by John Wiley & Sons, Ltd.

signifying marks, when it is, as physical matter, indifferent to such differences?

In so far as Anzieu works with the propping account, which provides the initial form – skin structure and function – for the psychic skin ego, he has difficulty in accounting for the way in which the skin or touch can be affected by the varied experience of the psychic skin ego. However, it is clear from his examples of skin ego experiences that these can be lived out in the flesh – thermal, olfactory, respiratory, and the like.

Doubling in Tactile Sensation and the Auto-Affective Turn

Taking from Freud (1974 [1923]) the idea that the ego derives from skin sensations and from internal and external sensations arising from the skin surface, Anzieu proposes that: (1) differentiated internal and external sensations and perceptions are innate, built into skin experience; and (2) the reflexive turn, whereby the subject reflects on the self as both subject and object, is a psychic act. There is a split between the actual soma and the more complex elaborations attributed to the mental, ideational terrain.

In examining Freud's description of the two types of sensations emanating from tactile experience, Anzieu states the 'child begins actively to explore this two-way nature of touch for himself . . . touching parts of his body with his finger or putting his thumb or big toe in his mouth, thus simultaneously testing out the complementary positions of subject and object (1989: 85). He argues that the reflexive ego is anaclitically constituted on the doubling inherent in tactile experience. However, this anaclitic part of the account is couched in terms of one person-body psychology. It describes the child exploring the body like a lone traveller. Anzieu does note that Freud alludes 'to the fact that I feel the object touching my skin at the same time as I feel my skin touched by the object' (Anzieu 1989: 85). Anzieu's account also explores the two-way nature of touch between mother and baby but does not draw out the full implications of the more relational model.

In contrast, my aim is to show how the other is there from the first in the auto-skin experience. From the first the infant is in a state of nursling dependency; others mirror and touch his or her body, and he or she has to be held and physically responded to for any basic function (let alone the affectionate caress). This fundamental fact makes the doubling in sensation in auto-affective exploration take on a different significance. The other's touch and mirroring are already there: the body surface, the skin, directly exposed to a world, to the look, to the touch. Derrida comments:

> When I see, either because I gaze upon a limited region of my body, or because it is reflected in a mirror, what is outside the sphere of my own has already entered this field of auto-affection, with the result that it is no longer pure. In

the experience of touching and being touched, the same thing happens. In both cases, the surface of my body as something external must begin by being exposed in a world. (1976: 73)

Here the auto-affective experience of the skin is already open to otherness, exposed as it is to a world outside itself, from where others image and handle the skin as a surface. The breach of the surface by the premature entry of the other, where bio-life is already in the field of the other, *the doubling in sensation, is not inherent to a self-enclosed biology, for as soon as the body is perceived as an object and the touch derives from without, this implies otherness in the sense of touch.*

The body can be in an auto-affective relation only because it has already been taken outside the sphere of ownness – as an external surface to be looked at, to be touched – a specular and tactile dispossession. The reflexive turn in this model does not just exist as a higher order of development for some reflexive mental process, whether a conscious ego or psychical act, but is already emerging in bodily sensation and bodily relation. The implication is that the perception of an outside to the body and of the body as an object, as a distinguishable experience, is predicated on the other already entering the picture. The demarcation of external (the object without) from internal (the subject receiving) is in fact the outcome of a relational development and not inherent to tactility as such.

Merleau-Ponty refers to a respectable touching of hands, but of course hands can be used for other purposes, such as masturbation and the rubbing of surfaces, hence the implications for the auto-erotic relation:

If my left hand is touching my right hand, and if I should suddenly wish to apprehend with my right hand, the work of the left hand as it touches, this reflection of the body upon itself always miscarries at the last moment: the moment I feel my left hand with my right hand I correspondingly cease touching my right hand with my left hand. (1962: 9)

Merleau-Ponty further describes the sensory experience:

perceiving my skin as a glove through which I can touch myself and find myself present to myself in the contact, I find I can touch myself only by escaping myself. (1962: 9)

There is no fully present contact with my body as one, for what is encountered is 'where self – affection and reflexive conversion miscarry' (Gasche 1986: 135). The sensation is not unified but divided between touching and touched. The meeting of touching and touched fails and sensation fissures.

In his phenomenological description of the touching–touched relation Merleau-Ponty reveals how the doubling in sensation involves a reflexive process, how a perturbed turning around upon the subject's own self is at the heart of a bodily relation. The look and the exposed skin surface are the effect of the same reflexive ambiguity. He makes clear how it is the world of others which enters the experience, and there is no pure auto-relation without others: 'Because my outer appearance is derived from a "perspective for others"', 'I must be the exterior present to others' (Merleau-Ponty 1962: xii). This means that my 'personal perspective does not return to the self':

> As I discover the possibility: of an outside spectator . . . at the . . . extremity of reflection – I fall short of the ultimate density which would place me outside time, and that I discover within myself a kind of internal weakness standing in the way of being totally individualized: a weakness which exposes me to the gaze of others. (xii)

In *The Phenomenology of Perception* (1962) Merleau-Ponty presents the touching auto-relation as an isolated adult out of context. In 'The child's relations with others' (1964), however, he is quite clear that the touching–mirroring experience emerges in relation to others. He recognized how the universalizing tendencies of phenomenology had to be corrected by culture and context, and the crucial role of child development. In this sense Merleau-Ponty's generalized phenomenological descriptions of the touching–touched relation describe an auto-affective experience based in the relation the child already has with the other, for the skin surface in his example is already in the world, experienced as an object to be looked at and touched.

Derrida makes it more blatantly clear that this fundamental division in tactility relates to the way the skin surface is exposed to the other's touch and look, and becomes the way the subject experiences the body as object, as other in the auto-affective turn. In conclusion, the external–internal skin experience is relational and does not exist simply as an a priori binary. Laplanche's description of 'the spine in the flesh' captures this sense of other that is endemic in the skin experience – simultaneously both actual and metaphorical, a veritable 'spine in the flesh'.

Freud emphasizes that the body ego has to be formed and that developmental trajectories vary. I suggest that the degree of relational sensitivity of skin experience is dependent on the particular developmental history of the individual. Anzieu refers to Tustin's observations about skin experience in psychogenetic autism. Tustin (1981) argues that a relationship with others is so emotionally threatening to children who have autism that they cut themselves off to and from others. Sensation, she notes, is affected despite the fact that their physiological apparatus remains intact. Tactile sense is altered in such cases: it is more flat and one-dimensional – the child shows no tactile awareness of objects with insides (Tustin 1984: 20), or of their own body surface having an inside and an outside. Evidence of this can be found in the autistic use of objects or shapes, or in the way the child bumps into other individuals and objects as if they do not exist. Fingers are used to create clenched fists, the pressure marks assuring themselves a presence against the skin, where touch is used to affirm the proximity of skin to itself, without distance, foreclosing relational sensibility.

I refer here to Tustin's observations to support my claim that the doubling in sensorial skin experience is a relational inscription whereby the experience of the other permits a differentiation in skin surface perception. In contrast, where there are fundamental perturbations in relational development, sensory states and skin experience are likewise affected. When a differentiated skin experience is not present, the sense of a relationship with the other is likewise impaired (a point that I shall develop).

In this context, it has been claimed in mirror neuron research that there is impairment of mirror neuron function in cases of autism (Iacoboni and Dapretto 2006), though this is not unchallenged (Callaway 2010). What is interesting is that in autistic individuals the processing of visual sensory information is slower. Discussion continues as to the neural 'cause' of difficulty in processing experience relating to social skill. If it does not lie in the mirror neurons, perhaps it does in synapse transmission, and so the arguments continue (see also Trevarthen *et al.* 1998).

I think what is important here is Iacoboni's point that there are complex neurobiological and social developmental factors involved when there are disturbances in social relations. As noted earlier, Schore warns against viewing mirror neurons in isolation. Interactional development that dictates the quality of relating is crucial for the type of attachment and, as Tustin points out, the traumatic experience of separation is key in addressing psychogenic factors.

It appears that to experience discrimination in tactility requires an embodied and relational sense of the body surface. Federn (1953) gives an example of psychotic patients who lack sensory and skin sensitivity and how this involves a lack of a skin cathexis. Psychotic functioning is associated with fundamental disturbances in relating to a sense of the other. It would appear that it is necessary for the skin to act as a relative relational limit for any differentiation between inner and outer sensory states. In the case of the psychotic skin described above there is no sense of a border, a lack of sensory as well as affective differentiation. In the case of autism the autistic shape or object is used to block the other and to ensure a continuity of presence, which again results in a lack of sensory discrimination.

A Revision of Narcissism and the Body: A Relational and Multi-Personal Perspective

In this section, I challenge the idea of a pure primary state of narcissism which is said to typify the earliest auto-affective experience. Despite possible intentions otherwise, Anzieu's description of the lone child in bodily exploration in fact posits the existence of a primary state of auto-enclosed narcissism. I contend that a relation with the other, understood as part of the secondary stage of narcissism, has to be already underway in the primary narcissistic state if there is to be any possibility of an auto-erotic relationship.

The state of primary narcissism has thus always already been affected by a secondary narcissism, for to take my body as an object is to 'cathect' my body as other to myself, an object in the world for myself. I touch and look as another, towards my own body. The skin as an exteriorized surface – to be looked at, to be touched, cannot be escaped and is part of the most intimate body experience. Otherness is a condition for a sphere of 'ownness'. Never pure, a primary narcissism is already tainted by the secondary narcissistic process whereby investing in others is turned back upon one's own body, as both other and me. There is an intercorporeality already at work there, which does not figure as a harmonious intersubjective state, but is always somewhat discordant. The degree of this will depend on the developmental trajectory, in the context of the environmental provision derived from relations with others.

Other contemporary developments, such as those put forward by Thomas Ogden (1992), argue for a primary auto-state, more primitive and prior even to the schizoid-paranoid state proposed by Klein, where auto-stimulation can dominate. I prefer to consider such states as rooted in foundational perturbations in early developmental experience, which result in cut-off states and withdrawal. In later development these can appear as disassociation or as an extreme form of dismissive avoidance.

In my baby observation, I observed how a baby, born congenitally deaf, would at times rub her lips together repetitively and adopt a vacant expression. The mother and I observed this behaviour together and concluded that this was Emily's way of coping; it was an auto-withdrawal from an environment which at times was experienced as overwhelming and incomprehensible. I prefer to understand this auto-stimulation as a disengaged response, as a state temporarily retracted into after which the infant then returns to the world. Only in more extreme forms of environmental failure such as privation, where there is an absence of environmental provision, could such states be more profound and share similarities with certain autisms. The case of Genie is a good example of this. She was strapped to a potty as a baby and left in isolation. In response, she would masturbate compulsively. This was repetitive auto-stimulation as a way of creating continuity in sensation. It maintained the most basic state of aliveness.

In the model I propose, narcissism implies some bodily relation already involving the other at the heart of sensorial 'ownness'. As Heidegger notes in *Identity and Difference* (1969), any logic of identity fails from within, revealing divisibility at origin. The other is there, always already touching and mirroring the body, and when I take myself as an object, I am taking myself as other – I am already divided in relation to my own body. The body can be taken as an auto- erotic object only because it is already outside the sphere of 'ownness'.

To Conclude

In contrast to the skin being the fixed substratum and the psychic ego being where the reflexive turn occurs, I suggest that tactile sensations develop a state of otherness from the first; by deriving support from the other, otherness structures sensory experience itself.

14

The Emergence of Skin as a Support Matrix

It is not helpful when Anzieu describes the double-leaf structure of the skin envelope as anaclitically based in the two-layered structure of the epidermis and the deeper cortical layer of the skin, in so far as the organic substratum implies a fixed location in a permanent place, inhabiting, as Heidegger put it, Euclidean or geometric space. It is located in physical space as discrete layers, with a measurable distance between them.

In such a formulation it is impossible to see how these two static layers can function as either a mobile mystic writing pad or a palimpsest, for there is no way in which the epidermis can inscribe signifying traces onto the cortical layer. As noted, in being grounded in its organic being, the epidermis would simply act as an impenetrable membrane to signifying marks, indifferent to meaning and differences. At best the marks left by others as marks on the skin would eventually so cover the surface that it would be trampled down, leading to Freud's (1920) dried-up crust – the first formula of the vesicle overwhelmed by stimuli.

Work has to be done to show how the skin structure is open to relation and signifying differences. The answer lies not in the anaclitic model, based in the bio-logos, but in a different model of bio-life, where the skin is not sufficient in itself to provide a fully constituted structure. In order for a skin structure to function in relation to interaction with others, what Anzieu in fact describes is an environment envelope derived from the other which informs the skin-enveloping structure and the senses. It would appear that the construction of a skin ego within a relationship is required for the skin to create its structural and functional basis, to have relational sensitivity and affective sensibility, to be able to function in the relational field and to withstand interpersonal and environmental relations, as well as shift with them.

Between Skins: The Body in Psychoanalysis – Contemporary Developments,
First Edition. Nicola Diamond.
© 2013 John Wiley & Sons, Ltd. Published 2013 by John Wiley & Sons, Ltd.

The other meaning of propping, the more popular and the one I prefer but less liked by Laplanche, refers to a leaning on the (m)other which is read in this context as a bio-other relation. What this relationship brings with it is a prop for a skin. This prop helps form an affective shield that can act as a boundary, while it remains relationally open to others and the environment and eventually functions to transmit sense information as signifying sense.

I shall now reread Anzieu, to bring out the more radical and viable model. In this model, it is not the child's own body which forms the prop, but another's. The other comes first. Anzieu explains how the 'mother functions as the baby's original protective shield' (1989: 25) and her stimulation enables the child to feel life in its own skin: the child, 'initially stimulated no doubt by its mother, [then] derives its experience from its own skin, (25). The child's sensory awakening is stimulated by another, brought to life by the other's touch which touches. The Latin verb *tangere*, like the French verb *toucher* and the English *to touch*, means to 'put the hand or finger upon' or 'to affect with feeling and emotion'. For touch to be touching, it has to affect us, which implies a relation with otherness.

In the second and more radical propping account, Anzieu describes how from the start the child's own skin is insufficient to act as a protective shield or as a source of its own stimulus because it already requires the intervention of another to act as a prop, a prop that is not so much the mother's skin as such, but the 'environment . . . made up of messages' (1989: 62), from the mother but also from the family group and the varied world of others. Messages in this context are gestural and tactile, affective, multisensory and accompanied by others mirroring the child's body.

This provision of a scaffold sensory syntax structure is the matrix which acts as a protective shield by binding the child's diffuse sensations into a discriminating pattern of sensory sense. Anzieu's reference to what Freud says – that the 'sense organs register stimuli via an appropriation of period' (Freud 1895: 310) – suggests that the reception of stimuli is paced. Anzieu also suggests that the sensory responses from the other bind and help organize the infant's sensations. Whereas in the first propping account, which was based on the biological bedrock model, Anzieu had attributed a sieve function to the cortical layer where the sense organs lie, he now makes it clear in his relational account that it is the maternal skin matrix that supports the infant's sensory experience, and it is this that functions as the discriminatory filter. A filter which helps to transform the sense data into tactile messages. A model of the skin derived from the other is required for the skin to hold off undifferentiated stimuli by discrimination and differentiation, in other words, it performs a filter function. A protective shield props by supplementing, replacing, substituting for the skin function – supplanting the skin function where it has already been found to be lacking.

In my view Anzieu proposes that the transformation by the mother of beta elements into alpha functioning is primarily a form of somatic-sensory processing which forges a matrix –a scaffold – and thereby acts as a skin support. I would argue that the skin matrix exists as sensory *and remains so*, organizing sense information, acting as a structure and as a type of filter. I would emphasize a sensory semiotics derived from the environmental other, which structures and creates sense. Processing is not something that is simply instigated in the brain sui generis, but involves environmental patterning. I believe that brain–body mapping can be influenced by environmental patterning.

Trevarthen's proto-conversation is a multisensory semiotics where in the gestural-visual-vocal-sensory dance of (m)other with baby the discriminatory patterns of sense through timing and rhythm and musicality begin to be created, the syntax of the sensory field. Broadly, the varied world of performance and mirroring, which is cultural, is necessarily and simultaneously in play, deriving from the wider social context of imaging and ways of social conduct. This likewise patterns construes and organizes the body surface as construct. The body surface is discovered in this other field.

Dennis came to the session as he usually did, after a gym session and in his workout clothes. He was not a tall man, five foot six inches, and had suffered obesity up to late adolescence. He began the session saying 'I feel masculine but I worry about how feminine I can be.' He told me how many people throughout his life had assumed that he was gay. He described how people, both women and men, would come up to him and treat him like a woman, saying 'I wish I had a girlfriend like you', or hugging him tightly. This would happen in pubs, in public places and even among friends. Dennis had a congenital condition: he was born with a club foot. His case was not severe, but it added to the uninvited projections onto his body.

All Dennis wanted to be, he told me, was an attractive, desirable man – 'normal'. He identified himself as heterosexual and yet all his life his appearance had received projections from others that marked his skin surface in a way that now left him confused as to who he was. From early on his mother's low sexual esteem had been a burden to him, as he had been used by her as a confidante in place of her husband, who was not interested. She let his hair grow and curled it as if he were a girl. This had confused people as to whether he was a girl or a boy. His mother expressed her desire for him to be her little girl. She was a perfectionist. He always fell short of her body ideal and she would criticize and correct him, projecting her own self-attacks onto him. Later his clubbed foot set him further apart, it became defined as a lack and a deformity by secret and stolen looks. The later mirroring gestural-tactile responses concerning his appearance and sexual ambiguity were actually mapped onto earlier configurations, and therefore compounded and affectively intensified them.

In this case it is clear that, in the context of complex developmental and social influences, the exteriorized skin surface figures as a faulty protective shield and as a screen projected upon by others where visual images are played out.

Anzieu's Clinical Examples and Additions

Clearly Anzieu in fact moves away from the idea of a simple preconstituted bedrock and instead describes how the sense organs are affected by interaction and how more complex interrelational elaborations of body experience come about. Anzieu illustrates with many examples how the interpersonal formation of the skin ego has a direct impact on somatic and sensory skin states. Indeed he notes that if the interaction does not adequately facilitate the formation of a skin as ego, it is not just the psychic skin ego that is affected but the skin itself, in its surface-tactile sensitivity, in the way it holds together and comports itself and in the manner of appropriating sense.

Anzieu cites the example of a patient (in a case mentioned in Chapter 12) who emitted a terrible smell, whose odour eventually dissipated after working through in the analysis. In the analytic reconstruction of his life, the developmental interpersonal production of the 'olfactory skin' was discovered and named. As an adolescent, this man had been neglected by his mother and would stay at his beloved godmother's house and sleep in her bed, snuggling up to her for protection. A country woman, she did not maintain high standards of hygiene. As the boy grew older he would become genitally aroused as he continued to sleep in the same bed with her.

In the analysis it was suggested that he had taken on the godmother's body as a comfort blanket, with the familiar smell acting as a protective skin. He was recreating her presence by producing a skin odour like hers. A mixture of genital and sebaceous secretions were produced, and anxiety would worsen the problem. Whereas Freud explores similar phenomena (Dora's catarrh, for example) as an outcome of identification, Anzieu suggests that in this case the odour is related to the man's specific skin ego formation. Body memory and history play a part in habitual development of body function, and in this context there is an affectively charged and relationally based meaning-laden skin that shifts with the analytic process. The olfactory envelope forms in a developmental interpersonal-corporeal context and this effects somatic expression.

Anzieu also refers to the thermal envelope, whereby a patient suffers somatic fluctuations in temperature. In this case the patient suffered a failure of a nurturing environment where the father, in his sadistic cruelty, subjected his child's skin to immersion in freezing and boiling water. This suggests that a biological homeostasis that is assumed as a given can be fundamentally altered by developmental experience and relationship dynamics.

Referring to Bick's (1968) clinical studies, Anzieu describes how Mary, the schizophrenic girl, had a skin that functioned like a colander, which failed to contain and failed as a skin boundary, her actual posture and stance resembling a sack of potatoes (see also Chapter 12). She stood hunched and lacked motor coordination. It was not simply an alteration of a mental body image, but a disruptive skin set-up, a failing skin matrix that lacked key support functions. When, in terms of relations, there are fundamental disturbances in the holding ability of the skin matrix, and where developmentally there have been more severe failures to establish an adequate ego, this will show in the skin boundary effect. Citing Federn's (1953) work, Anzieu describes how sensation itself is affected. Federn observed in his patients no skin periphery feeling and a lack of a skin cathexis and noted how ego boundary disturbances can manifest themselves in skin sensation.

Melanie Klein (1987 [1930]) observed in the case of little Dick how profound disturbances in ego function were shown in Dick's indifference to the world around him – his expression 'lacking in interest' – and also in relation to his body – 'when he hurt himself, he displayed considerable insensitivity to pain' and would move without coordination (99). Klein identified this boy as schizophrenic, although Juliet Mitchell notes that today he would resemble the autistic child.

Anzieu refers to psychogenetic autism and Tustin's work where perturbation in the skin boundary is apparent, Tustin describes similarly to Klein how these children show little awareness of others and express this in bodily ways, bumping into other people or walking as if through them, as though they have no awareness of skin borders and little skin periphery feeling. Tustin (1981) describes autistic patients who create an indentation in the palm of the hand by clenching their fists very tightly in an attempt to reassure themselves of proximity and presence. In Klein's as well as Federn's examples, and in severer cases of psychogenic autism, there is such a deficit that the matrix has not been established, and because of this the skin experience lacks a form of representation and the symbol function is in question. This goes hand in hand with the fundamental disturbances in separation and the problems with registering absence in tactile experience.

Psychoanalytically there is a disturbance and/or failure of symbolization in such cases. Anzieu argues that symbolic structures and their relation to bodily experience are destroyed in psychosis. In a related way, this is also the case in psychogenetic autism. From a relational perspective – and clearly Anzieu can be seen as taking up such a position – the relation with others can damage, change, interfere or foreclose skin ego formation. These consequences do not affect a reified ego, but fundamentally alter the formation of the structure of a skin border, the relational function of sensitivity and sensation itself.

From this radical reframing of the genesis of the skin, what gets propped is the biological structure and function of the skin, where the environmental skin matrix can support the skin developmentally and influences the form and expression of the skin boundary. Such a skin support, it appears, is required for a skin periphery feeling and sensitivity. The skin as a boundary and in its sensorial being is more protean in nature and varying in sensation than the notion of a fixed, given biological state of affairs would permit.

A Skin Surface Projection

I have claimed that the biological skin is supplemented from the start by another. Freud states that the body ego is 'not merely a surface entity' but is 'itself a projection of a surface' (1974: 16). I shall now address the skin surface as a projected surface.

As I have noted from the first, the surface is derived from without. For the purposes of clarity and of drawing perspectives together, and at risk of repeating myself, I refer to Merleau-Ponty's description of how the infant discovers the body surface in another by living in the other's gestures, which anticipated Meltzoff and Moore's later observations and the discovery of the mirror neurons. Meltzoff and Moore (1977) observe how at 42 minutes after birth, the baby simulates the other's gesture of sticking out the tongue and thereby discovers the tongue before realizing its own tongue and where it is located, 'because the child . . . feels [it] is in the other's body' (Merleau-Ponty 1964: 133), an intercorporeal space is where the surface is experienced. The mirroring sensory neurons affectively simulate other bodies and have furthered understanding of the mirror image.

The surface is derived from without in the mirror image – from the mirroring smile of the mother (Winnicott 1971), from the touch of the other – in the way the skin matrix is derived from the other. As 'misrecognition' occurs with the mirror image, so the same occurs with images from the big screen, billboards, magazines and the like. Similarly, configurations of the body are produced by many social sites, not solely image-led, but also action-based, from gyms and workouts, to textual ideals for health from medical, legal and other discourses which regulate, refigure, incite and style the body.

Merleau-Ponty (1962) identifies the amoeba-like potential of the body boundary, which can be extended in the case of the blind man who feels with the end of his stick or the woman who touches with the tip of the feather at the top of her hat. Furthermore Merleau-Ponty (1962, 1968) notes that the body, by being an object in the world, can coincide with and exist alongside other objects and become in a sense one of them. Lacan cites observations from Charlotte Bühler's contributions to the field of psychology, in particular her work on the phenomenon of transitivism; for example, two children are running alongside one another; one falls down, but the other starts to cry as if he had been the one who fell. This is similar to Freud's example of a group of girls in a boarding school, where all follow suit to display a physical and somatized fit of hysterics. Freud refers to identification and projection and notes what can happen in transference and what is now known as counter-transference. Merleau-Ponty (1964), however, argues that these phenomena are based in affective-intercorporeal space, which is most obvious in infancy but exists throughout the life cycle. I agree with Merleau-Ponty that the intercorporeal space provides the conditions for the processes described by psychoanalysis. This leaves us no longer having to play at jumping over unbridgeable gulfs between discrete individuals.

Heidegger uses 'thrownness' to describe a radical kind of projection and, in light of Merleau-Ponty's description of bodily being in relation to others, he is referring not to geometric or Euclidean space, where the body is a dis-crete entity localized in space, but to an affective body spatiality. Interpersonal space is where I sense you and you pick up some vibes from me. It is where one person can walk into a room and affect the affective-somatic state of all the individuals within the group.

In relation the body surface, I would say it is not only localized in space, but situated in the field of surfaces. I join Lafrance (2009), Manning (2009) and Pile (2011) in referring to psychoanalysis and addressing the relation-ship between the skin and culture. Rather than assuming a literal border to the body, I suggest thinking about the body surface as a littoral border, which can be likened to an oceanic wave that rises and falls and is more protean in nature.

In this chapter, I have tried to draw out the implications of Freud's descrip-tion of the body ego as 'not merely a surface entity' but as 'itself a projection of a surface'. The skin as a surface exists not only as a place but outside in a field of surfaces. A skin surface which I try to call my own exists in its most radical state as a liminal zone, a threshold that is potentially shifting and is neither fully inside nor outside but on the borders of an inside–outside. It is precisely a border zone.

Manning (2009) takes this point further to spell out the radical possibili-ties, suggesting that the skin, in becoming the other projected surfaces, is no longer tied to a body ego self-reference but is truly situated in a social rela-tional field:

> What if the skin were not a container? What if the skin were not a limit at which self begins and ends? What if the skin were a porous, topological sur-facing of myriad potential strata that field the relation between different milieus, each of them a multiplicity of insides and outsides? (Manning 2009: abstract)

There are different possibilities. Manning refers to the radically social potential of the skin surface as situated in a field of surface relations. In contrast, when it is tied to the function of the skin ego gestalt at one extreme the skin boundary can appear to get lost in the other, for example in the climax of sexual intimacy. Or inversely, there can be a tendency to shore up the boundary, as in defensive behaviour.

15

Skin Narratives

The Mobile Skin and Matrix Structure

The argument I am developing is that the skin requires the skin matrix for relational structure and function, to feel alive as skin in a world. The skin matrix derived from the environmental field can develop in many different ways, showing neural plasticity and the possibilities of varied constructions and configurations. I hope to shift the understanding of brain–body maps and the plastic formations of the body ego away from a hypostatized brain approach and towards the body, to show how the bodily senses are environmentally patterned and relationally built.

The manifestation of ego construction as skin expression, in both sensory and motor terms, has indicated that a divide between thought and action is neither helpful nor applicable, nor is body image opposed to comportment and motility, for body memory and enactment can go together as can lived body perception and motor-neuromuscular performance. Changes in the brain–body maps generated in the area of the sensorimotor cortex strip and in dynamic brain–body processes can relate to lived body experience. I have suggested that these brain–body processes are influenced by the sensory semiotic constructs of the body derived from the interpersonal and social world. I shall show, by citing further clinical cases, how disturbances in relations including attachment, loss and trauma can have an impact on the actual skin as a matrix structure.

Anzieu refers to Bick's case of baby Alice who experienced a sudden change in the consistency of environmental care, with a move to a new house and the onset of her mother's depression, and the impact this had on the formation

Between Skins: The Body in Psychoanalysis – Contemporary Developments,
First Edition. Nicola Diamond.
© 2013 John Wiley & Sons, Ltd. Published 2013 by John Wiley & Sons, Ltd.

of her skin envelope. This impact was not solely a shift in mental container function but involved changes in the veritable sensory skin border.

To pursue this point, let us take the case of Sue, one of my patients when I worked as a clinician in child and adolescent psychotherapy.

> Little Sue had lost her father suddenly from a heart attack when she was seven, and was to describe him some two years later, rather suggestively, as her 'backbone'. The shock of the death was marked across her body: she spontaneously developed a repetitive spasm that would make her body jerk – a muscular, undulating, ripple-like movement running across her body, like a form of somatic slash, autonomic, neurological and muscular. In the girl's initial referral contact her mother reported the motility change after the loss; Sue herself did not indicate an awareness of the spasm and always acted as if nothing had taken place.
>
> Throughout the therapy it was plain to see that the jerking movements took place frequently to begin with, and then over the years became less regular and more intermittent. But they persisted, the loss having left its memory trace, marking her nervous muscular and neural set-up. It was not until two years into the therapy that it was brought up in a session, because a boy at college had commented on her 'weird' posture. Reaching pre-puberty, Sue had become increasingly aware of her body in relation to its significance for others, and the boy's comment had taken on a particular importance in this context.

Gallagher and Cole (1998 [1995]) would in this case regard the body schema as having been affected. However, what is interesting to me is how affective states such as loss, in this case relating to attachment, can alter motility function and procedural memory, living on as a pattern of behaviour. Like a memory, it can decrease in intensity over the years but not dissipate; the trace of the loss and the mark remain, the meaning of loss for bodily integrity seared into motor-neural pathways.

Skin Narratives and Trauma

I suggest ways to rework some of Anzieu's ideas about the skin ego, I shall flesh out the question of symbolic expression and the body. There has been some confusion in the psychoanalytic debates which still harbour dualist tendencies as to the symbolic capacity of the body symptom, if any, for the mind is said to symbolize, not the actual body. I approach this discussion from a different viewpoint to suggest that body symptoms tell a story and are a form of narrative expression instead of words. In the case below the body enacts a scene of what is going on before words are found and deployed. One of my claims in this book is that the body can tell stories about situations lived and set up by environmental relations that have not been subjectively and linguistically processed. In Chapter 18 I shall classify different modes of meaning articulation in somatic expression, in order to define the relation between body symptoms and symbolic capacity and offer a tentative clarification of the meaning of symbolization.

I have mentioned the sexually abused American adolescent, Daniel, in Chapters 5 and 9 (see also Diamond 2003):

Daniel presented as an overgrown schoolboy, dressed in clothes too tight for him. He crouched in a corner with his face buried, his posture saying 'shy and shamed'. There was no known aetiology for his extreme state of withdrawal. Initially his condition had been investigated as a medical problem, as I worked in a multidisciplinary team. Daniel suffered terrible headaches and would feel dizzy and lose his balance, and sometimes topple over. Middle ear conditions were investigated and he had a scan to check for a possible brain tumour, but nothing could be found.

These bodily symptoms continued in the first six months of therapy. A history of sexual abuse by his adopted elder brother began to emerge. As he remembered the experience in the sessions he felt threatened, would let out a yell and run out. He later explained that it felt like he was going to explode. Acknowledging the abuse that threatened his masculine sexuality and identity at core was simply intolerable. The experience could not be integrated into his conscious body ego self. Before the threat was even acknowledged, let alone put into words, the body was already enacting the narrative. The body gestalt was literally collapsing, toppling over; his motility function was unintegrated and under threat of fragmenting and falling apart or exploding, before the experience could be put into words and consciously acknowledged. The suggestion here is that body ego integrity and the corresponding fear of bodily disintegration are involved in the formation of the body ego and development of meaning around identity can be lived out in bodily ways pre-reflectively known before language-based processing.

However, as the therapy progressed, Daniel expressed more explicitly the nature of his relational disturbance and breakdown in somatic terms. As he shared the unbearable experience, he would remember the abuse as spontaneous sensations in his genital and related areas, which would take him by surprise and which he described as a feeling of being taken over: he would feel strange and not himself, as though a piercing object were prising him open and making him feel confused, happy and sad all at the same time. He would look in the mirror and in his 'misrecognition' see his brother before him. His visual and visceral states felt like a usurpation, the alien spine of the other in his flesh.

At worst, as we got closer to the threatened madness, Daniel would go out of control in the room and in a frenzy 'sexualize' tables, bottles, the wall without discrimination between animate and inanimate objects and regardless of whether he was on the side of the human or non-human. He would then collapse on the floor, amazingly and crucially, leaving me protected from the onslaught – both of us having survived the most terrifying enactments of a breakdown in actual and (metaphorical) body integrity.

Sexual abuse as an intrusion, of 'excess' stimulation which transgresses incest and Oedipal boundaries, confounds attachment with 'excess' sexual excitement in relation to a parental or other related figure. Ferenczi (1949 [1933]) refers to this as a confusion of tongues (tactile tongues) where the language of affection (attachment) and the language of passion (sexuality) confuse spatial sensibility.

While working with sexually abused adolescents I noted how in some cases an affectionate light touch would feel intrusive and penetrating to the person, too much proximity leading to hypersensitive reactions. In the case of the sexually abused young woman Emily, sitting in a room with a group was too much for her because she had no sense of a skin filter boundary. Her spatial relations would go haywire, and she would experience sensory states whereby she felt penetrated from all directions and would blush uncontrollably with shame, desire, inhibition, humiliation and the sense of violation. Or in inverse cases, adolescents would seek out sexual contact, becoming inappropriately touchy-feely and lacking any sense of acceptable conventional proximity.

Perturbing relational environments can produce a sensory skin matrix that is more disorganized and chaotic, slack and less cohesive, propping the skin only incoherently. In these cases the sensory skin matrix is open to greater failure; it cannot act as a protective relational shield or function as an interactive boundary and differentiating filter. However, even when the environmental matrix is more structured, this does not mean that everything is intact and shored up once and for all. A prop only acts tentatively as a support; as a scaffolding structure it is potentially fragile and essentially lacking in substance. Being frail, it is easily weakened and can collapse under duress. Lacan refers to the fundamental situation of the fragmented body in regards to the superficies of the gestalt effect. Here what is addressed is the sensory somatic and embodied state of this experience.

Even in circumstances where a 'good enough' nurturing environment provides skin support, but is later followed by extreme trauma, as in situations of war, abuse and torture, the skin function as a boundary and as consistent in sensation and responsiveness can all of a sudden crack and break down; in chronic circumstances it may never be rebuilt.

> Zara, a survivor of torture, was knifed in her arm, which caused her searing pain. The cruelty of the attack involved the knife being twisted inside the cut and it has left the arm permanently damaged. When she tries to use it, it will not bend properly and creates discomfort. The torture Zara suffered involved a threat not only to herself but also to her sister. Zara described her family life prior to her capture, where she was very protected by both parents. As a girl growing up in an African community, she was relatively restricted to the home and her dependency encouraged.
>
> When she came to see me, Zara could not wash or look after herself. She explained the burning pain that covered her whole skin surface every time she tried to move to wash, remove her clothes and so on. The burning sensation would persist despite her being able to walk around and engage in other activities. I observed that the searing pain became unbearable only when it related to looking after herself.
>
> It appeared that the burning pain of her knife wound was no longer localized in her arm but now spread across her entire skin surface, that it had gone 'polymorphously perverse'. She had gone to both dermatological and neurological experts but no one could discover the cause. In my analysis, Zara's ego collapse involved a regression to a dependent state which was expressed and lived out somatically. Like Daniel (above), she was expressing a fragile body ego, enacting a cry for help.

This failure of self-preservation should not be related to a more primitive fixed biological order, as Laplanche has suggested. *Rather it indicates that for even the most basic self-care some elaboration of a skin matrix is required.* When that elaboration falls short or is disrupted, the consequences of a lack of an adequate skin matrix structure are exposed and the necessity of such a structure becomes explicit. Early dependency on the other constitutes bodily care of the self in no way makes this development reducible to a predetermined set-up; what self-care is predicated on is the development of an auto-affective relation and a basic semiotic sensory skin matrix formation derived from the other.

There are a vast variety of skin border experiences involving alterations in sensation and somatic states. There is a habitual set-up whereby greater stability is maintained and fluctuations are relative to a norm baseline and more limited. In the case of the skin envelope, this would be a skin border habitual set-up, which enables a person to cope with everyday life and conventional encounters with others (skin border responses, on the other hand, can dramatically alter in intimacy). The more radical the somatic fluctuations and functional disturbances in skin experience the more likely it is that there is a disorganized attachment history, radical sexual perturbation and/ or an extreme environmental or relational trauma. In the conventional language of an ego psychology, reference can be made to weaker and stronger ego structures. The difference in my way of thinking is that this is directly related to the potential protean nature of the sensory skin boundary, and that emotional vulnerability with respect to resilience can be expressed somatically and is not innate but relates to adverse relational histories and the developmental attachment disturbances they cause.

In patients who are somatizing, their over-attentive focus on somatic symptoms alters the sensory body ego response. This attention is not simply conscious, although there is an obvious conscious preoccupation. The focus is not within the patient's conscious control and involves a profound affective investment which is activated outside the person's state of awareness. This type of 'concentration' on the somatic state exaggerates the sensation, making it seem larger than life so it takes over all other activities – significance is concentrated on the body 'problem'.

When there is less fear and a more open, affirmative orientation there may be a potential for play when body states err from their norm. This may permit sensory alterity as something to be engaged with rather than an experience to run away from. This can be seen, for instance, in sexual experimentation where loss of identity in somatic states can be ventured, where a temporary loss of a sense of skin boundary or perturbing but exciting sensations can be enjoyed and expressed in extreme sensory states of skin and orifice pleasure, pain and exaltation which one may not have previously thought somatically possible. Sometimes those who want to experiment sexually opt to do so in a secure relationship, so that the risk can be contained by the attachment relationship.

An examination of skin symptoms shows up how important the intervention from the other is and that when there are fundamental perturbations in the relation there will likewise be fundamental disruptions and somatic alterations in the very function of the skin and touch. The skin surface and sensation are open to erring from a presumed and predefined fixed order.

Skin States

The approach I have adopted takes on board Freud's observation concerning identification where he describes taking on another person's body symptoms, mirroring and simulating the other's somatic symptom as one's own in behaviour and gesture. This not only involves mirroring the external appearance of the body – another person's 'exterior' – but can include other subcutaneous skin tissue linings of the body, for example, in Freud's patient (1905) Dora her throat catarrh linked with her vaginal secretions and so on.

Freud describes how in a hysterical paralysis the mirrored limb loses sensation and is anaesthetized, that is, a sensory alteration takes on a metaphorical sense and affective investment. Examples from Freud and Breuer's (1893–5) early case studies on hysteria are suggestive of this, for example the facial neuralgia suffered by Frau Cecile M, which was associated with her husband's humiliation of her: 'It was like a slap in the face' (1893–5: 178). Or Elizabeth von R, who could not allow herself to walk to her forbidden lover (her sister's spouse), and whose leg pains resulted in her not having a leg to stand on. Or in the boarding school (Freud 1921) where a girl had a fit of hysterics on receiving a letter from her jilting lover and the other girls followed suit. These cases reveal the human ability to mirror and to emulate others sensorily and from there on to make our own the skin surface of others – although there is also the potential for vital processes to be likewise copied.

In the area of surface skin phenomena Dinora Pines (1980) and Jorge Ulnik (2008), both dermatologists and psychoanalysts, explore the phenomena of skin eczema and related conditions as emotional reactions to experiences with significant others. Pines examines the fraught disturbances in the relationship with the mother as a battle between self and other played out on the skin surface. In her work as a dermatologist she noted that the soothing relationship she had with her patients resulted in a calming of the skin condition and even the dissipation of the symptoms altogether in a number of cases.

In eczema and other skin surface eruptions and irritations, the threat to a body ego skin boundary can be enacted as a skin war: a conflict between self and other, and in the case of a poorly developed body ego (in fact, a poorly skin) the threat of usurpation. Both Pine's (1980) work on skin communication and Ulnik's *Skin in Psychoanalysis* (2008) describe how the drama of the appropriating maternal other and child are expressed in skin experience. They argue that eczema, when affectively activated, can be viewed as a kind of relational battle.

Pines (1980) describes a case where a woman on returning home found her son hanged in the hallway in an act of suicide. She broke out in a shocking, raging, weeping rash, a direct expression of her feelings for all to see. The suggestion is not simply that affect is discharged into the body (which begs the question how), for the weeping rash is simultaneously an affective semantic expression reiterating the shock of exposure, but this time as her own – for the raging rash displays her anger and shame/guilt for all to view. The skin condition acts as a metaphor for her pain, the somatic expression bound up with the relation with the other and the significance of the loss.

Ulnik (2008) provides numerous examples of skin eczema and allied skin conditions that somatically express the patients' fundamental relation to others and to themselves. Here the state of the skin ego is lived as skin irrita-tion, swellings, rashes, forms of eczema and lesions. These somatic states show up the way affective states also have a direct link to the vulnerability of the immune system (Martin 1997) in relation to both attachment and loss (see Taylor 1987: 57–59). The immunological system is affected by attach-ment and loss. Susceptibility to illness and heightened mortality risk have been shown to be linked to attachment disturbance, deprivation, privation and loss (Spitz 1946; Robertson 1953; Taylor 1987; Martin 1997). Attachment, loss and neglect relate to the lowering of the immune system and the exigent biological functions for life, as in marasmus (failing to thrive), a biological process that is not separate from relational development.

> Jane developed a shocking urticaria and arthritic symptoms after her lover left her suddenly. The profound significance of the loss for her life, the loss of her bodily sexual enjoyment with him and the recent depletion in her bodily narcissism rendered the skin boundary fragile and vulnerable, lowering her immunological resistance. It was a tem-porary auto-immune response, and after two weeks she recovered fully and continued to work through the meaning of the loss in therapy.

McDougall (1989) gives an account from her own experience of childhood of how an emotional allergy to a toxic other resulted in a somatic reaction. Every time when she visited 'Mater' in the countryside she would break out in an urticaria. It was not the rich dairy milk, nor a reaction to airborne aller-gens but her intolerance of and irritation with the noxious 'Mater', who liter-ally got under her skin. My reading goes against McDougall's early theory of psychosomatics. I do not view the urticaria simply as a somatic explosion due to a deficit in mentalization. Rather I interpret it more in terms of relations with others, in this case a fundamental perturbation in relation to 'Mater', the associated conflict being somatically expressed as a troubled skin.

> Carolyn, a middle-aged German woman, came to see me complaining of a lack of interest in sexual relations with her husband. She repudi-ated sex and would do anything to avoid contact. Her childhood had been spent with a series of foster parents, including a number of foster fathers who overstepped their parental boundaries by expressing sex-ual desire for her. She recalled how they voyeuristically devoured her with their looks and hands.
> She described her husband, who was in his sixties, as a caretaker and it was very clear that he was first and foremost a paternal figure.

She found the slightest touch from him unbearably ticklish. I pointed out to her: 'You have, it seems, married your father and when he makes sexual advances, you react with [hysterically] itchy skin, which responds as an intensely irritable surface, in effect repudiating him and acting as a barrier to ward off both touch and all other possible feelings [sensations] which could arise in you.'

She seemed to regard her husband as the father she never had, but when he desired her, she experienced it as a transgression and expressed it as hypersensitivity, which both harked back to bodily memories of the perversity of touch and look and re-evoked a retreat to childlike, excessive polymorphous, ticklishness. What this implies is that Carolyn felt overstimulated, and the excitement was too much to bear. The sensation had a prepubescent component. It was sexual but not clearly genital, and could occur in any part of the body where she happened to be touched.

The Case of Debbie

Last but not least, Debbie was a complicated case which I characterize as borderline. She had a very fragile skin–gestalt matrix formation where loss of boundary of the skin self dominated. It was only in the later years of therapeutic work that the skin began to form more fully. The discussion in Chapters 16 and 17 of the importance of touch can be related to this case, but it is relevant here as another, more detailed example of skin eczema. The case accords with Pine's and Ulnik's idea of skin eczema as a skin battle, a struggle (in this specific example for the most basic sense of aliveness) for existence in relation to the other in the form of a skin enactment.

Debbie had been fostered after being kept in an incubator for the first six months of her life. A year into life she developed an eczema condition that remains to this day. She has only recently discovered as an adult that her skin condition relates to a deficit in moisture production which prevents her skin forming an adequate film protective barrier.

This lack of barrier, literally a protective skin layer, could be related to the period of critical development where in the first six months of life Debbie had been placed in an incubator and was not held or touched. She had been abandoned by both parents and left in a busy and poor hospital in a small American town at a time when the neglect of babies born prematurely was common. Furthermore, this period of privation – which is more extreme than deprivation, for it means never having had provision – was exasperated by her eczema being so bad in the first 12 years of life both foster parents touched her as little as possible and later on her siblings and peers repudiated her, repelled by the terrible skin condition.

The eczema began the first year into fostering and did not shift from then onwards. It was as if leaving the sterile environment of the incubator and then the shock of encountering others, after all that isolation and lack of stimulation, was too much – that Debbie experienced it as a kind of invasion, a form of impingement in the context of earlier privation. This was compounded by the emotional poverty in the familial environment, where she received a poor quality of care.

In Debbie's attachment history with her foster parents, there was neglect. They were poor and their own and their foster children numbered seven in all. They lived in a small flat in the heart of the Bronx. Debbie was the youngest and spent most of the time soiled and dirty, lacking stimulation and ignored. The only attention she had was being picked on by the other children, and she ended up being bossed around and doing all the menial tasks when she was a bit older. As far as any adult response to the children and Debbie was concerned, everything was about shutting up and doing what they were told, that is complete compliance was expected of them.

In what can only be described as the worst years of her life, from her late teens into her mid twenties, Debbie enacted a lack of a skin barrier through a form of acting out. She acted as though she had no protective boundary whatsoever. In a dissociated state she left home and wandered through New York City, drifting into prostitution. What was so marked in this period was her complete lack of agency, her degree of dissociation and deficit in any skin ego function, which were shown in her total lack of feeling and any animated response to repeated penetrative invasion. Her case was one of the most extreme forms of dissociation that can be found in chronic trauma (complex traumatic stress disorder).

Retrospectively, after many years of therapy and as a woman in her late sixties, Debbie could look back and seek to explain her underlying motives. In her retrospective construction she was struck by how she repeated the response of absolute compliance imposed by her foster parents in her encounter with the male 'predators'. In looking back she saw how desperate she had been for any response and attention that she was prepared to do anything for it.

Such a view, however, necessarily implies a degree of agency in Debbie that from all accounts was simply not there. Strikingly, for this traumatic period of her life she cannot recall a subjective and embodied experience. It was as if she had been physically removed from the situation. In more technical terms, she had no recall of autobiographical memory or of a sensory skin boundary experience. There has to be a degree of narcissistic investment for some active drive to seek out the other, and during that period there was no narcissism in her at all. It was as though she had died. She felt, when she looked back at that time, that she was functioning as a 'zombie'. I told her that it was like being in a state of incubation.

In therapy Debbie explained to me how since she had been in therapy her 'terrible' skin condition had started to fluctuate. Whereas it had been in a constant chronic state for a long time, it now flared up only when she felt relational turmoil. Her eczema condition seemed to be reacting relationally to affective situations; the skin condition worsened when she was recounting the past and in particular when 'memories' about sexual invasions returned. I have placed quotation marks around 'memories' because Debbie could not clearly recall events, but had daytime associations that would include clips of happenings from the past and vivid dreams. Clearly traumatized, she had flashback-style recall. At these times the skin rashes would break out. The lack of moisture production to protect the skin, the skin eczema and, most of all, her lack of a sensory skin boundary experience and autobiographical 'I' in the years of prostitution and destitution can all be viewed as somatic expressions of disturbances in the skin gestalt. This relates to a deficit in her skin matrix, relating to deficits in early relational development. Fragility and a lack of any adequate protective skin boundary prevailed.

In the years of therapy Debbie began to form a skin in which to exist and on which her eczema could be played out in a more interactional way. As her skin experiences began to connect to mood states and memory, including what was evoked by the therapeutic exchange, her skin expression suggested that the somatic symptom could now join in more readily with the analytic and relational conversation.

16

Skin Relation

Touch and Attachment

Touch is fundamental in attachment. The early Harlow experiments, which were influential on attachment theory, observed the importance of the terry cloth for the baby monkey; this proximal contact with the skin is central for human infants and their development. Hormones are stimulated by touch and there is clear evidence that in animals touch stimulates growth hormones and genital activity. In attachment terms, proximity and touch are essential for the bonding process, the release of oxytocin being described as the 'love hormone' or the 'bonding hormone'. The hormones that are released in attachment bonding are also excited with sexual bodily caresses in later intimate relations.

Failing-to-thrive syndromes in humans are the result of privation of affective contact with the attachment figure. Privation of touch can be so total that the psychobiological consequences can be devastating, profoundly arresting affective relational and biological development. The results include fundamental deficits in brain neuronal functioning and in physiological and emotional maturation, leading to chronic affective and somatic dysregulation, and lower immune function and higher mortality rates (Spitz 1946; Robertson 1953; Schore 1994, 2003a, 2003b).

For touch to figure as significant there has to be some relation to separation and the meaning of loss: the play of absence and separation in the attachment experience and the field of sexuality are necessary. Affective sensitivity conveyed in the sensory communication gives rise to a quality attachment and sexuality, which would not be possible without the significance of separation in the attachment context and the sensual relation. It is with this *significance of separation* that nuanced and discriminatory expression

Between Skins: The Body in Psychoanalysis – Contemporary Developments,
First Edition. Nicola Diamond.
© 2013 John Wiley & Sons, Ltd. Published 2013 by John Wiley & Sons, Ltd.

through touch is possible both for the expression of attachment and for the sexual experience. When the entry of the other is fundamentally disturbed in development, either by privation or by the overwhelming nature of touch by the maternal other, real difficulties can arise. When the relationship provision is either too much or non-existent, this can foreclose separation and block the development of relation and differentiation.

Skin Relations

What are the conditions of development required for the skin to come alive in relation to the field of others and to act as a relational border surface? When there is privation of relation, extreme neglect – as in the case of Genie, who was left to auto-stimulate circularly – or other prohibited situations – as in the long-term incubation of infants – there are fundamental deficits in the formation of a relational skin.

At the other end of the continuum there is the 'too much' environmental provision, the smothering (m)other who overprotects the infant, usually to assuage her inability to deal with separation and loss in her own life, so the gap in experience is covered over for both her and the infant. Juliet Hopkins (1996) addresses this type of parenting in her paper on 'too good' mothering.

Of course, fathers can do this as well if they are the main caretakers, but even if they are not (which is the general cultural norm), I have observed another phenomenon, where fathers who are separated or divorced use the relationship with the child to fulfil their own undistinguished, narcissistic needs, to make up for their loss of a partner and family unit and to stop up their own gaps in the name of what the child needs. As this often occurs later, it does not have so profound an effect on the child's development, but it does inhibit the child's ability to mature emotionally.

Finally, foreclosure of loss and the effects of separation can occur in cases of psychogenetic autism and forms of chronic psychosis, where the relation to others and the environmental field is never adequately established, because the mark of loss that allows for a sense of the other and of a differentiated relation is blocked.

What Is Required for a Relational Skin?

In tracing the pitfalls of the main propping account in Anzieu, I have suggested an alternative, more viable account which shows what is required for a relational skin to emerge. Anzieu claims that direct skin-to-skin contact is the biological datum on which communication between skins (initially between mother and baby) is based. The massage he then adds becomes the message, forming the signifying marks left by others. The question I ask is: how does the massage become the message? If one begins with a biological substratum and unmediated, direct skin-to-skin contact, no relation between skins gets established; the model instead characterizes the common skin which does not give birth to communication between skins but precludes this possibility.

Tustin's (1988) analysis of psychogenetic autism provides a detailed picture of what it would be like if direct contact of skins could be maintained. Her depiction of the autistic skin does not yield distance and relation; a space for relation is simply closed off. She states that objects (for example, a toy used to indent the palm of a hand) are used to block off any 'disturbing sense of separateness' (Tustin 1988: 25), and as a result the child lacks adequate sensory awareness of a spatial relationship with others and with its own body. Tustin goes on to say:

> Autistic shapes . . . engendered from the feel of edges around flat surfaces. Whorls of tactile sensations are felt to flow around body surfaces in a comforting and soothing way. They are tranquillizers. Thus, painful awareness of body separateness is avoided. (1988: 20)

And

> Wrapped around by their own bodily sensations which constitute the illusion of an auto-generated shell, there is no awareness of being inside the shell, the autistic shell shuts out all awareness of other bodies, and also of their own. Thus, awareness of bodily separateness is blocked. (21)

Finally, Tustin makes clear and explicit that

> The long distance and visual modes of perception do not have anything like their normal importance . . . some autistic children are thought to be deaf, or even blind, since they walk through objects as if they did not exist, although when they are given tests for these disabilities, their physical apparatus is found to be intact. (25)

Touch in this scenario assures absolute proximity without distance, since there is no differentiation within the experience of touch; there is little or no relation to touch as other. Impairment here is not about the organic properties of the substratum, but is related to a fundamental deficit in affective and relational development. Such a development is required for touch to be touching.

Despite his claims in his main propping account, Anzieu (1989) also comes to the same conclusion, that direct skin-to-skin contact leads skins to remain literally stuck together, the external shield being stuck to itself, where the mother's and the inner surface of the child's envelope merge as one and the same – a skin indifferent to difference, an undifferentiated continuity of presence, rendering no space *between skins*. Direct unmediated skin-to-skin contact therefore does not lead to contact or communication. Instead what is required is mediation within a relationship. *So it is not the pre-existence of a biological substrate (as in the first propping account) but the entry of the other that acts as the founding condition for skin communication.*

In his second and more radical account Anzieu replaces direct contact with the 'prohibition on touching [that] contributes to the differentiation' (1989: 117). This is not to be confused with the biological bedrock account. Anzieu now refers to a primary prohibition, prior even to the incest taboo, indeed 'a double prohibition'. Such a prohibition prevents the mother insistently touching her child, and the child constantly touching himself or herself (as Genie and Tustin's autistic child did). According to Nicolas Abraham: 'If there is a prohibition, it does not, in the last analysis, concern incest . . . but rather the excessive prolongation of mothering' (Abraham and Rand 1979: 27). Anzieu comments: 'the interdiction is implicitly signified to the child in the active form of physical distancing' (1989: 143); 'The mother moves away . . . withdrawing . . . the breast, averting her gaze' (143), prohibiting 'the return of the maternal breast, a return which can now only be fantasized; this prohibition is not instituted in the case of the autistic child who continues to live in the mother's breast' (112).

Interaction implicitly signifies through little acts: mother gives baby her breast and later withdraws it; she touches the baby soothingly, then stops; she goes out of the room and then returns. The ebb and flow of feeling and particular nuances of affect are directly expressed in touch and its absence. In the context of maternal–infant experience, attachment and separation necessarily go hand in hand. So touch comes into being with some prohibition (no direct contact) as a condition of its social institution. It is not a matter of proximity to skin only, but the simultaneous impact of separation on tactile experience, which thus makes possible difference and otherness in the maternal relation, thus breaking symbiosis from the beginning. It is an instituted inhibition within the maternal sphere, necessarily operating therein, not wholly predicated on the entry of the paternal other but on the plethora of differences already in play which open up the maternal from within and which includes the paternal (in such an economy) but not as the only key signifier of difference.

If the primary prohibition of touch is prior to incest and relates to the mother's capacity to distance and to dis-identify with her child, it would, I suggest, imply that the maternal body can bring into play a fundamental differing (which even in a more phallic-based determination is arguably not simply reducible to the phallic 'third') that is to do with her quality of emotional maturation – her capacity to be in the depressive position – to acknowledge loss and difference which get expressed in the affective body know-how. I suggest that otherness can already be at work differentiating the maternal field.

What happens when in development the 'symbolic' process is disturbed?[1] It is not simply mother's literal comings and goings which makes a symbolic process possible, since all mothers do this (how many mothers can stay with the child physically at all times?). What is important is the affective quality or style of interaction, which facilitates a differential space for the child's body. The quality of separation and the institution of an experience of absence directly affect tactile-sensory body states and are not installed as a psychical abstraction. The skin ego does not just develop and become increasingly psychical in its non-materiality, a pure psychic ideation. The tangible and the intangible coexist, for the intangible exists in the tangible, in the somatic sensory states themselves.

Merleau-Ponty refers to an 'invisible hinge' at the heart of the touching–touched relation, an 'untouched touch' (Merleau-Ponty 1968: 151). It is not so much a deprivation of touch but more *a certain withdrawal within touch for touch to be touching*, a certain non-presence in touch and of touch. In other words, it is not a matter of absolutes, no touch in contrast to the presence of touch, but rather the absence of touch becomes part of the experience of touch. It is this absence in touch that brings touch to life.

Implied touch goes alongside literal touch, derived from the other and from past acts; the memory remains and the trace of repetition is already at work in a re-encounter with an actual stimulus. Metaphor and sense go together. Merleau-Ponty refers to the visible and the invisible, and the touched and the untouched of the auto-affective relation. In tactile mirroring, blind spots remain – there are gaps in vision: there is rhythmic touch and non-touch, smell with its simultaneous indefinable aspect, the flow of a voice and a resonating quality that fades away.

Touch with no punctuation would be a continuous presence, touch and skin as on a continuum. The spacing, the gap, the absence of touch, the mini-separations permit a rhythmic discontinuity, and here it is interesting to revisit Freud's statement 'that the sense organs register stimuli via an appropriation of period' (1895: 310). There are in the sensory proto-conversation rhythmic dissonance, temporal spacing and musicality, as Trevarthen reminds us.

In Summary

So far I have argued that the direct skin-to-skin contact outlined in Anzieu's first propping account does not yield skin relation but what emerges in the radical second account is that a certain prohibition is required for skin communication, for *a relation between skins*. The skin is not a closed-in biological system but is from the first open in relation to an environmental field and has the potential to come alive to self and to others.

Anzieu notes that the maternal function excessively prolonged is too successful in maintaining the illusion of a common skin – a direct skin-to-skin contact which effectively smothers the child's body with the illusion of the sufficient skin. The maternal envelope in this context works to close down any breathing space forged by the trace, shores up all gaps and does not allow any relational space for communication to take place. Caretakers in these scenarios often cannot deal with emotional pain and anxiety around separation deep within their own lives, and they use the child to attempt to stop up the gaps. Such parents overprotect and molly-coddle the child, wrapping it in cotton wool and over-identifying with it. By doing so they create an illusion of direct skin-to-skin contact which works to annul the experience of absence.

Pure continuity of touch does not bring the skin surface into play or to sense the other. For the other to figure as another, as other, there has to be a certain sensory registering of a withdrawal of touch. For touch to be affective, a space needs to be forged for a relationship with it.

Note

1   'Symbolic' refers to the psychoanalytic understanding of the registering of loss and absence as the basis for the emerging capacity to 'symbolize'. Across the psychoanalytic literature, most markedly in Lacan, 'symbolizing' has become associated with the ability to represent *in absentia* through speech and the word; the subject can do this only if loss and absence are acknowledged. In Anglo-American psychoanalysis this process is related to the way affects can be contained in speech and word through articulation that binds affect to sense; henceforth a subject can identify and express feelings in thought. As Lacan does not endorse a language of affects, he refers more to the lack that underlies the problematic of the subject and the symbolic linguistic field.

In this context, I refer to the general principle that in order to symbolize there is the registering of absence and hence the significance of relation based on separation and differentiation, not symbiosis or fusion. I do not locate this capacity to symbolize with the coming of the word or speech alone in so far as I have already identified the emergent symbol in the sensory and semiotic communicative exchange between parent and infant.

17

Skin Writing and Touch as Analogous to Language

Touch as a differentiated and nuanced sense can be considered fundamental for a relational connection of body with world. In Michael Ondaatje's novel *The English Patient* the character Almásy suffers terrible burns which leave him without the sense of touch. He is incapable of perceiving anything through his skin, non-existent as it is, though he can use his mouth, a vein in his arm and his wolf-grey eyes. Benthien (2002) observes that in this state of tactile deprivation Almásy gradually loses touch – all he has left are disconnected internal phantoms as his tactile relation with others and with the world gradually disintegrates. As Benthien observes:

> Here it becomes very clear that, in the final analysis, the skin ego is no visual image of the self (as psychoanalytic theory suggests) but instead a sensation ego that establishes and . . . sustains itself through tactile traces. (2002: 220)

As we have seen, it is the other that touches us, and the skin is brought alive only by being touched. In English 'to touch' means to 'put the hand or finger upon' or 'to affect with feeling and emotion' (Anzieu 1989: 143). For touch to touch us, it has to affect us, and for this to happen we have to have a relation with the other, which involves touching and being touched, whether I feel my own body as an object, as another for myself, or touch another's body as other. A sense of difference and relationship is required in order to truly feel the flesh as alive and for the flesh to feel the semiotic chain of language.

Anzieu's analysis claims that the massage becomes the message. He refers to the film *Johnny Got His Gun* (1971) where the nurse traces the outline of words on the skin. But if direct skin-to-skin contact does not lead to

Between Skins: The Body in Psychoanalysis – Contemporary Developments,
First Edition. Nicola Diamond.

differentiation and relation, how can the massage become a message? Anzieu describes how Helen Keller learned language through the simple tracing of outlines of words and objects on the skin. However, the presence of pressure on the skin does not in itself give rise to any symbolic or signifying mark.

While I shall consider touch as a style of writing, I shall argue that the metaphor of writing, taken literally as a concrete transcription of marks on the skin, a linguistic mode directly mapped onto touch, only leads up a blind alley and does not bring us any closer to an understanding of how significance is transmitted through touch. The literal translation of a writing on the page to a drawing on the skin has hampered an understanding of 'skin writing' in other related fields like social and cultural studies, where inscription has been understood in a reduced sense, as a literal transcription onto the skin, like a skin tattoo or a piercing.

Such social brandings of the skin, while highly relevant, do not in themselves help to explain adequately how tactile-sensory forms of signification transmit meaning. If the approach to transcription remains with the idea of the skin as a biological substratum and nothing more, then how do markings 'penetrate' the skin, given that a biological substratum is in itself immutable, literally impervious and simply indifferent to qualitative differences?

I address skin inscription by suggesting that Helen Keller learned language not through the tracing of outlines of words and objects on the skin but through an understanding of the *differences* between touches and the patterns of touch built into styles of touch: the difference and relation between one kind of touch and another, until a repertoire of small differences form systematic patterns of sense (Diamond 2006: 87). Physical pressure simply leaves a temporary indentation which fades. A pressure mark on the skin does not leave signifying marks.

Likewise it is not the electronic pulses impressed on the skin that enable blind people to receive messages in Braille. The alphabet is transmitted not via the electronic pulses per se, but rather through the rhythmic discontinuity, the relation between the pulses. These rhythmic modes then form patterns that convey specific meaning (Diamond 2006: 88). Rhythmic dissonance and relations of difference are set up between touches. This is required for relational patterns and their eventual formation into semiotic networks. Taking these points into consideration, we can now see that massage can turn into message, touch transformed into discriminate and meaning-giving sense. I regard touch as on the way to language and as functioning relationally like a language, where 'language' is not tied to a narrow linguistic definition.

There is a problem with literal marks on the skin or memory as footprint (see Freud 1920) which Plato observes in his *Theaetetus*, where memory is conceived as wax: 'We hold this wax under the perceptions and thoughts and imprint them upon it. Just as we make impressions from seal rings' (Plato 1921: 135–136). For Plato a memory that can be rubbed out cannot guarantee knowledge. However, when impressions are permanently retained as a substantive mark, indenting a wax surface, as on a signet ring, there is the problem of the quantitative mark imprinted upon a surface. This cannot open memory's writing mark as Freud shows in 'Beyond the pleasure principle' (1920). Freud depicts what can go wrong using his metaphor of the skin as the surface of the vesicle, which is literally trampled to death with the onslaught of stimuli. The surface becomes nothing more than a dried-up crust. As a crust trampled to death it is inert matter and can no longer function as a receptive surface.

It is not the indentation that leaves the trace, the mark of memory, for the physical mark leads to a dead end. In place of it there is a spacing, a certain absence of touch that already distances sensory touch in proximity, and allows for a *between* in touch and for in-between touches (Diamond 2006: 88). Freud's reference to sense organs registering stimuli via an 'appropriation of period' now makes even more sense, as 'appropriation of period' indicates a temporal delay, a rhythmic dissonance, making Trevarthen's stress on musicality and rhythmic spacing in the sensory proto-conversation most pertinent for the *language of affect*. The interruption of flow, the missteps of the dance, make up the sensory patterned choreography; here the affective-sensory 'disruption' is not opposed to language but makes sensory language a possibility.

For touch to begin to be touching, in the space of mini-separations a relation to the other is installed in one's own experience of touch, 'The other and world as third party having already entered' (Derrida 1976: 165) the auto-affective skin–touch relation, thus making Derrida's comments somewhat clearer:

> touching–touched admits the world as a third party . . . The exteriority of space is irreducible there . . . And the outside, the exposed surface of the body, signifies and marks forever the division that shapes auto-affection. (165)

What Derrida describes is the space of separation that differentiates touch, the non-presence in touch: the other as already there, at the very heart of auto-affective sensory states. This discussion starts to address touch as a discriminatory and meaning-giving sense. After all, touch can be discerning and subtle, and can express deep feelings and multiple possible meanings. In short, touch can be considered a form of language.

To refer back to the skin as matrix: it is a sensory set-up derived from the other which is already at work offering a map that functions as a grid, facilitating discrimination between touches and the sense receptor's capacity for differentiation. In tactile sensory experience there is 'the worldly residence of the signifier . . . that which is written remains' (Derrida 1976: 163). For Derrida writing is not reducible to the written word or language to speech and linguistics; it is the way the trace of the other, of history-memory and of culture is already there opening up matter, including the flesh and the senses, a 'violent spacing of nature' (Derrida 1976: 107).

According to this reading, the skin is already supplemented and supported by a sensory body matrix. In this reworked psychoanalytic formulation, there is the influence of the key caretaker and proximal others, and also of wider environmental influences. The skin matrix prop makes it possible for the skin to function as a bounded relational surface, albeit construed in varying ways according to the developmental relational trajectory and the culture in which we live.

What I am emphasizing is that the impact of separation and absence in the birth of the symbol (which has been associated with symbolization in speech and the linguistic sphere) likewise impacts on the formation of the skin and tactile-sensory experience, and that tactile-sensory communication is a form of language made so by the diacritical logic of setting up relational differences between elements in a sensory system. This basis for the construction of meaning in linguistic communication is found in different form in tactile-sensory communication.

Separation allows for relation and for the prop matrix (the sensory scaffold derived from the (m)other) to establish its signifying tactile marks, for the other to figure as another and for the possibility for differentiation in skin experience – so that the sense of touch can have a relation with the other and world. Touch can be more or less nuanced depending on the sensitivity and the style of touch that has been developmentally in play, the type of sensory matrix grid that is offered as the provision. Indiscriminate touch without relational sensitivity can eventually result in a less discriminate tactility; ongoing and later relations can and often do introduce greater nuance and subtler differentiation, but not always.

A person can come from a family where either minimal tactile affection is displayed, or touch is present but is, for example, made practical and pragmatic, where touch is all about efficiency and the purpose is the task. Touch can be rough, crude and so on, and such attributes are of course profoundly fashioned by the cultural values in specific contexts. Types of touch are what makes a 'good' or a 'bad' lover; a certain tactile development is required for the possibility of difference between kinds of touch, of discriminating and discerning touch.

Development is not simply linear, nor defined only by the maternal; there are fathers and siblings, relatives and peers. Development is ongoing and somatic memory involves retrospective reconstruction or construction, the effect of deferred action, sensory-based memory in temporal creation, memory shifts between present, past and future situations.

Trauma and Disturbances in Tactility and Differentiation

There is a basic fragility in skin integrity and none of us, however secure (or resilient) and shored up, is ultimately immune to the effects of trauma. Trauma is part of everyday life, but excessive traumatization can more obviously show up the fragility that is potentially there in us all.

I have had a great deal of experience working with severe trauma, including cases of chronic abuse, trafficking and torture, in my work as a staff psychotherapist at the Women's Therapy Centre and at the Helen Bamber Foundation (for victims of torture, abuse and human rights violations). The aftermath of highly abusive relations can leave the sense of skin boundary utterly precarious. Sensations are confounded as is discrimination between kinds of touch (see Chapter 15 where I identify somatic states that express the confusion of sensory tongues in the aftermath of chronic cases of sexual abuse). It is not only in early development, but also in later destructive relations, that the type of tactile relations can work to unmake touch and world. Later experiences of chronic sexual abuse can both over-sensitize and undo the subtlety of touch, so that numbness dominates as a form of sensory dissociation. Torture and abuse work to break down all body boundaries and differentiation and to destroy meaning, fundamentally affecting sensory skin-touch body states, sensitivity of touch and the reception of tactile stimuli.

Elaine Scarry (1985) describes torture as inflicting indescribable, all-consuming pain and unmaking language and world. Torture attacks the body, and all boundaries of the body are breached by the torturer, the appropriating other. At the extremity of such encounters discriminate tactile experience can be destroyed; where gross touch dominates, being is obliterated, where one is left alive but dead and no value or meaning is possible anymore.

This could be what Agamben (1998) refers to as 'bare life'. In the aftermath of torture, what remains are bare survival and pain. Where no known medical conditions can be discerned, organs, muscles, nerves and skin can flare up in pain. I mentioned Zara in Chapter 15 whose skin burned with searing pain. Such pain is chronic and unfathomable and endures for a long time post-trauma. Discriminate sense is consumed into the dominant sensation of pain. This pain is experienced as being 'done to' to the sufferer and is often experienced as an alien force taking a grip, as a form of body takeover.

The Alien Entity in the Skin: *Unheimlich* as the Skin

Laplanche refers to 'the veritable spine in the protective wall of the ego'. I interpret this 'spine in the flesh' as the sensory state of the other existing in tactility and skin border experience, an irreducible alterity in the auto-affective relation manifested as the 'disowned', 'alien body part', an other, an 'evil' force that enters as the appropriating other that threatens to usurp the body.

In torture and abuse the torturer-abuser lives on in the body like an alien entity in the form of perturbing sensory states that take over, appropriating body space and annihilating the body as its 'own' states. I gave the example of Daniel, the sexually abused adolescent who became so consumed by the abuser in his 'own' body that a frenzy would at times take him over transform him into the riotous other (see Chapters 5, 9 and 15). At those moments all sense of body 'ownness' was lost, as he rushed around the room out of control, 'sexualizing' everything in sight, a bottle, a table, the air. Or the case of Zara, the gash in her arm inflicted by the torturer lived on in the somatic symptom well after the event as a stabbing pain that had generalized and taken over her entire body surface, like a force coming from elsewhere. Zara's skin was so inundated with sharp stabbing pains that in effect the pain had supplanted her skin, a stabbing sensation for each and every pore so that no untainted space was left.

In extreme states the boundary between human and non-human breaks down (as in Daniel's frenzy) – from Tausk's 'influencing machine' to moments where all discrimination ceases to exist. These sensory configurations of the veritable and virtual other – as the spine in the wall of the ego flesh – in extreme form express themselves in states of *Unheimlich*. Clients complain of states that they liken to de-realization and depersonalization but as estranged flesh – the 'not me'.

Radical states of *Unheimlich* – not being at home in one's own body – are part of the somatic living on well after the fact of violation, abuse or torture. However, extremities of bodily experience show up most sharply what occurs in less overt ways in 'normal', everyday life. Creative media like film can explore such bodily possibilities vividly and dramatically. For example, *Being John Malkovich* (1999) explores states of body alterity and the uncanny in its play on fantasy and realism, to create the visual surreal which captures the unfamiliar familiar so well.

In 'The uncanny' (1919) Freud describes the state of *Unheimlich* and its opposite. As a brief reminder, *Heimlich* refers to homeliness and hearth, the familiar and the comforting, and the way which the German word simultaneously holds the opposite sense: strangeness and not being at home, the unfamiliar and the bizarre. Freud writes of his experience on a train. While in his cabin, he is shocked by the sudden entry of a stranger, who to his horror and surprise is no other than himself. The wash cabinet mirror has swung forth and the intrusive other is in fact his own reflection. The subject of the doppelgänger continues as Freud draws on E. T. A. Hoffmann's story 'The sandman' (1916) and the strange experiences of the lifelike doll which is not human but appears human for moments; in one of the macabre aspects of what I consider *Unheimlich* body states, the inanimate becomes animate.

Unheimlich depicts states of subjectivity and being where we become alien, strange and unfamiliar, to ourselves. Such states readily involve the body and are, I suggest, frequently experienced in somatic symptoms, I have linked these states to fragmenting alterations of the veritable body ego directly affecting bodily states. Even in everyday life, a bodily injury or change to body form or function can lead to an experience of estrangement and a fragmentary sense of the body. As Lacan so aptly observes, the fragmented body is paramount for us all, and form always involves some idealization which is imaginary, based on illusion. My focus is not only on the visual and the ideational body image, but on the sensory and veritable. I have also looked at extremes experiences of interpersonal trauma which have led to heightened states of sensory and somatic alterity and body fragmentation.

Flesh can be experienced as alien in body dimorphic states, or a sense of estrangement can be associated with organ pain and the viscera. Sensations can be experienced as strange and unknown, signalling danger. Flashbacks about the abuse make the body feel invaded, alien and taken over by the intruder.

Body Image and *Unheimlich*

The examples that follow are related mainly to body image and perceptual alterations. Here I explore the experience of the body after surgery or a routine operation and how it leads to associated states of *Unheimlich*.

One of my patients had a knee operation, after which she felt that everything had changed. She could not recognize herself: 'Something has changed about me, I do not feel the same.' She did not 'feel herself', she used to say, 'I feel a different person' – and described an unease and discomfort with her body. She had enjoyed lovemaking with her husband, but that had now stopped. She no longer felt attractive and indeed could not recognize herself as who she used to be. When she looked back to the time before the operation she saw her body and sexuality in an idealized way; after the operation her view changed to the opposite and she repudiated her body. There was a sense of irreparable damage and a fear and anxiety that she would never feel okay in her body ever again.

What was striking was her loss of sexual interest which was replaced by a detailed focus on her knee pain. The intensity circumference of the spatial region 'affected' would change and her mobility would be severely affected. Some days she would lie all day with her leg horizontal; with mobility the sensations increased, as did estrangement from her body. She felt that her gait was not her own and when she caught a glimpse of her shadow in the street she got a shock – it was as if a stranger were in her place. Her experience recalls Freud's when he realizes that the old man in the mirror was in fact himself.

Another of my patients, who had facial surgery to correct a protruding chin, experienced a similar alteration of bodily being. In this case, she experienced a narcissistic withdrawal from the world back into the body as an object of focus. Instead of an idealized imaginary identification with a body gestalt, she constructed before operation (BO) and after operation (AO) scenarios: before being the *Heimlich* body (self forever lost) and after an *Unheimlich* body, shattered and deformed. She could not recognize her face as her own, which was ugly and awful, and did not feel quite part of the human race any more. She seemed to have forgotten why she had had the operation in the first place now that she had lost the sense of who she was. She would look in the mirror every couple of minutes, and every time she saw her face she panicked, went into a sweat and wanted to jump out of her skin. She had strange sensations in the lesion area, which no neurologist found typical; every time a pang of pain hit her she would be thrown into a fragmented body state, where it felt like everything was collapsing and she was a physical mess.

There are the body dysmorphic states of everyday life. Eating disorders and conditions like bulimia are common, as are less severe forms of anorexia. In these conditions the person disowns 'unwanted flesh' and in more conventional language projects the unwanted parts of the self onto the disowned part of the body. In this case the 'unwanted flesh' is experienced as deforming the skin/border boundary, and becomes the disowned alien, the 'not me'. Alterity is displaced onto the 'disowned flesh' as if it could be removed and as if it were possible to achieve an ideal unity. The 'excess flesh' can take on an 'abject' status (Kristeva 1982), existing on the border, undecidable, between subject and object, me and not me.

In my understanding, this otherness in one's own body is related to a genuine and irreducible alterity, the installation of otherness in the heart of ownness, the inhabitation by another of our own skins, where borders are constantly negotiated, sometimes incorporating and other times attempting to exclude. The more alterity is embraced and not feared and defended against, the more we can let go of the symptom, while the more we hold on to and try to retain a pure and untainted 'me' skin, the greater will be our sense of the disowned flesh and the exaggeration of our discomfort and phobic response.

A Literal-Littoral Skin Surface

I have described how the viscera and brain do not inhabit a pure inside but are in a way turned outwards towards the external world; in turn the insides of the body have been turned inside-out. The skin, in failing to act as a container, allows for fundamental seepage. The self-contained body is now so deformed that it is no longer the same.

Merleau-Ponty pointed out that the skin envelope could be likened to a glove turned inside-out and outside-in, the other and world as installed therein, a form of invagination meaning to fold inward or to sheath, the outside=inside forming the folded envelope structure, with the inside=outside forming a rim always exposed to the other. Lacan refers to the Möbius strip as a topological and mathematical way of thinking about a boundary where there is an erasure of distinction between inside and outside, where the shape changes but maintains continuity, where the outside continues inside and the inside border turns outside (Figure 17.1). As a trope for body and field, the Möbius strip possesses a relational outside–inside movement which inscribes one figure in another and thus creates an alternative to a geometric model of physical space where never the twain shall meet. It also gives rise to uncanny effects in violating binary divides, fundamentally disrupting normative boundaries.

The Möbius strip not only describes the rims of body orifices as the drive circulates (Lacan), but to adapt Lacan, it can be used to depict the entire skin surface and its relational skin envelope structure. Furthermore its skin surface, as noted earlier, exists as a literal and littoral border, in its ability to function both as a protective habitual boundary and as a potential littoral zone which, like the shoreline, is in movement, liminal in being undecidedly inside–outside and precarious in identity in its openness to the possibility of change in the encounter with a shifting relational field.

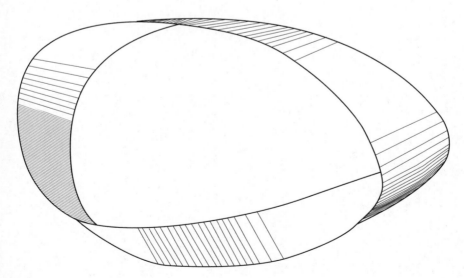

Figure 17.1   The Möbius strip.

What Is Between Skins?

In this book I describe a bio-life vital skin set-up as an inside–outside and outside–inside. The vital processes that first appear interior have already let the outside in, and the skin surface is directly exposed in its exteriority. There is an affective-relational semiotic structure which situates the brain and body in relation to others in a social field. This is my reading of Merleau-Ponty's glove turned inside-out and outside-in, a Möbius space that is seamless. There is fundamentally no binary dividing line between the body and the 'outside' world and this is the way to think of the border of the body as *between skins* for the fundamental opening of my skin and of other skins to world – as a skin enveloping structure.

18

Psychosomatics and Conversion
The Question of the Symbol

Body symptoms as a form of meaningful expression will be explored in greater depth in this chapter. In referring to the body and meaning, I have considered how absence and separation alter bodily experience and the fact that meaning also fails; where there is meaning there is also non-sense. However, because meaning has been allied to speech and thought, the relation between soma and meaningful expression has not been well understood. I have focused on how the soma has access to the symbolic dimension of human experience, but greater clarity as to the differences in symptom formation is required. I shall also define terms and styles of somatic expression.

Joyce McDougall: Psychosomatics versus Conversion

'Conversion' has gone out of favour and psychosomatic symptoms of the alexithymic kind are more readily identified by practitioners and in psychoanalytic writings. It has been claimed that psychosomatic symptoms of the more alexithymic type, somatic complaints which are not meaning-bound and which lack a symbolic dimension, are presenting in our clinics more readily now, and that conversion symptoms (which, in contrast to the alexithymic type, are rich in meaning and associative material) are presenting less often.

I would suggest that this turnaround, away from conversion and towards psychosomatics (lacking symbolic expression), is not simply a reflection of the changing maladies, but also to do with the limits in the current state of psychoanalytic (and related) understanding. In my view there has been too much generalization. A broad range of somatic symptoms have become defined as alexithymic when not all of them may fit within this category.

Between Skins: The Body in Psychoanalysis – Contemporary Developments,
First Edition. Nicola Diamond.
© 2013 John Wiley & Sons, Ltd. Published 2013 by John Wiley & Sons, Ltd.

By reducing symptoms of a somatic nature to a non-symbolic content, the shortcomings in the theory regarding somatization are easily avoided and go undetected. Since the majority of bodily symptoms by definition lack meaningful expression, there isn't the need to explain the relation between body and symbol. I have already suggested that a number of somatic symptoms that are viewed as lacking meaning and symbolic significance are arguably misdiagnosed. My argument is that a number of somatic complaints have a more symbolic dimension, but this goes unnoticed owing to the shortcomings in the current thinking about bodily symptoms.

In my discussion of Joyce McDougall's early work in Chapter 4, we saw that psychosomatic symptoms were considered alexithymic (no words for feelings) and therefore to lack symbolic content. However, in this chapter I shall examine McDougall's thinking and the shortcomings of the alexithymic approach in greater depth. McDougall's insightful work has been very important, and I shall revisit her approach to somatic symptoms as a way both to identify the issues at stake and to find a way to resolve them.

McDougall modifies her perspective in the later work, noting that not all psychosomatic patients express flatness of affect and lack of meaning in their symptoms. She thus starts to address a more complex somatic experience under the umbrella of psychosomatics. McDougall (1989) refers to archaic and primitive emotional states that relate to infantile experience, libidinal states, narcissistic longings, threats to survival and more significantly body integrity – including the fear of merging or disappearing, of being engulfed or abandoned, of the body holding in or letting go, of the emptying of content and so on. These 'experiences' relate to Kleinian phantasmagoria in 'primitive' states of 'mind'.

I have claimed that as we look closer at somatic expression, the body symptom can enact the threat to bodily ego formation before it can be put into words, my argument being that this involves a sensory elaboration – non-verbal sense-making – and is therefore related to some development of the skin matrix (for there to be a corresponding deformation). In each case there is a specific style of skin matrix and its demise which is the outcome of the particular relational developmental trajectory.

From my perspective, I embrace McDougall's later insights into the greater complexity of what is going on in the body symptom. However, I find that her attempt to explain such observations exposes the limits of her theory, based as it is in the mind/body split. Her language is revealing. She suggests 'that the mind sends primitive messages to the body and the body takes over' (McDougall 1989: 28). The meaning is in the message, the mind's work, but this begs the question, how so? How does the mind send messages to the body, and how does the body take up such messages if by definition it is not and cannot be in the sphere of meaning itself? To begin with, McDougall identifies how the body takes over in a number of ways. She refers to the flight/fight response, taking on board the psyche's message of danger, a primitive message of warning to the body which, she argues, 'bypasses the use of language'; therefore the danger 'cannot be thought about' (28). She thus reverts to a dualist vocabulary: the mind has thought, the body does not. Here only the psyche is capable of meaning, even if primitive, so it has to send messages to the body. But given the dualist split how does the message become somatic?

The flight/fight response McDougall mentions could be understood as an affective biological reaction of the autonomic nervous system and amygdala, which has been well studied in post-traumatic stress disorder. Most importantly, in the attachment research such a response has been related to the meaningful relational context of attachment and affiliation, and the radical perturbation of those relations, including the effects of traumatic separation. The flight/fight autonomic reaction therefore develops in connection with affective attachment states that are meaning-laden. The somatic response I suggest is much more complex than a simple reflex-type response, for the affective soma is embedded in relational being.

McDougall (1989) states that the body goes into overdrive and appears to go mad, which can result in violent skin reactions; a rise in the metabolic rate and/or blood pressure; holding of the breath, as in asthma; emptying of the stomach contents, as in ulcerative colitis; or dysfunctions in sleeping and eating. In McDougall's thinking, this body takeover is reduced to a kind of mindless biological overdrive, but my exploration of the vital order as vital process and as a vital set-up suggests otherwise. I have attempted to address the more complex picture, exploring further what Merleau-Ponty calls extasis, or what is referred to in psychoanalytic and contemporary neurobiological explorations as *plasticity*, that is how neurological processes and biological functions can be open to alteration and development – radical deregulation and the marginal effect, and sensory semiotic formations.

In the formulations I have suggested here, I have linked soma to semiotic processing, to a type of somatic unbinding and binding that cannot be distinguished from the formation of skin body mapping. For example, spilling contents relates to a definite body figure, a sense of inside and an enclosing body envelope, albeit labile and destabilized in the symptom, or to a skin war response which may be related to a traumatic loss or a fundamental perturbation with the other which disrupted the formed body ego states, exposing their fragility.

As McDougall develops her observations, she finds that she has to concede that there is more to the body than her mind/body divide allows for. She then states: 'The body, like the mind, is subject to the compulsion to repeat' (1989: 28). She argues that in the body a repetition of painful sensory states is the result of a complex mind–body reaction and destructive tendencies, which she suggests arise 'when certain relations with significant others are felt to be threatened' (28). However, she again insists that this is a non-symbolic process, for it bypasses 'the code of language which would have allowed the affect laden representations to be named, thought about and dealt with by the mind' (28–29): an emotion is aroused but not in a symbolic way. Note here that McDougall's definition of symbolic process is highly meta-reflective.

So now the body, like the mind, is capable of something as nuanced as repetitive compulsion, which I would argue links somatic states directly to the re-enactment of trauma based on the memory trace, to loss and significant others, a theme of this book. However, in reverting to the typical mind/body vocabulary, McDougall's question of how the soma can be taken up and articulate such processes as 'the compulsion to repeat' is left unanswered.

McDougall refers to 'non-verbal "signifiers"' (1989: 10) but then argues that 'the mind is making use of the body in order to communicate something, to tell a story' (16). For her, somatic states are ultimately without thought and reveal 'an archaic form of mental functioning that does not use language' (10). McDougall's terminology acknowledges that the body communicates and tells a story, but she then underplays this and says that it is the mind that does it all; her point is therefore somewhat confused and contradictory. Within the terminology of mind versus body (rather than brain–body which would be better), there is little understanding of how the mind could access and thus *use* the body; or, if it is in fact possible to develop 'non-verbal signifiers', then why are somatic states only and necessarily reduced to the archaic?

Beyond these inconsistencies in her argument, there is something more interesting: as McDougall details her observations and expands her understanding, she has to concede that somatic symptoms take on more meaning than she had first thought. She ends up describing different kinds of somatic manifestations, of varying complexity. Her first claim, that psychosomatic symptoms are not meaningful, is thus moderated; psychosomatic symptoms *can* be 'primitively' meaningful. Her expanding take on psychosomatic symptoms suggests that the mind/body division, which still underlies her thinking, cannot adequately account for the rich variety of somatic states that she comes across. So McDougall finds herself grappling with message and meaning and its translation into the body.

What McDougall helpfully highlights is how different somatic processes occur, the alexithymic type of somatic expression at one end of the spectrum, which I would agree presents with flatness of affect and little or no metaphorical expression, in contrast to other forms of psychosomatic symptoms that can arise, when fundamental perturbations around bodily self and others emerge, or somatic dysfunctions occur, such as overdrive or the body's compulsion to repeat and tell (bodily narrate) a story. The psychosomatic symptom in her characterization of it is now starting to share features with conversion phenomena (in regard to a meaning–soma connection). The distinction between the two types of body symptom starts to develop fuzzy edges. Despite this, McDougall has to find a way to establish the clear distinction between psychosomatic and hysterical body symptoms, so she states that conversion symptoms are not real but imaginary, in contrast to psychosomatic symptoms which involve organic changes to the 'real' body. This view, I would argue, can be challenged in so far as conversion symptoms can and do bring about alteration in sensation and functional changes which, in spite of having no known underlying organic pathology, nevertheless directly involve the body in that motility, movement and somatic and sensory processes can be affected.

Organic changes are not necessarily found with psychosomatic symptoms. There are many clients who present with body symptoms like migraine, muscular spasms, weakness, burning and other skin sensations, digestive and excretory disorders, sleeping disorders, organ pain without developing any identifiable organic condition, while the sensory and functional alterations are very much present. Only certain patients develop chronic and irreversible states that are known medical syndromes.

I understand and agree with McDougall's point when she implies that in cases of chronic alexithymia or equivalents, where there is an absolute poverty of meaning elaboration across the board, the patient is more likely to develop an organic condition or illness eventually. This contrasts with the person who is meaningfully and affectively engaged with their affective-somatic states. In such cases the symptom may therefore not remain fixed but possibly shift in affect and meaning.

Divisions into different types of somatic formation do not stay clear-cut. In reality patients can sometimes present with a combination of somatic phenomena, where in one patient meaning elaboration can be marked in some body symptoms but not in others. Body symptoms do not always fall into neat categories, although there may be a tendency in one direction rather than another, just as individuals do not fall into one attachment category but may present a number of attachment styles, while showing a greater tendency for a dominant attachment disturbance over others.

What the discussion on symptom formation has thrown up are several key issues. (1) A body/mind split cannot account for the way a somatic symptom can be meaningfully expressive. (2) What exactly is meant by symbolic capacity and processing? (3) Traditional definitions of the symbolic process and what language means exactly are limited. (4) There are different kinds of body symptoms with varying degrees of meaning elaboration. It may be helpful to categorize these different types of body symptoms, their symbolic abilities and the way their symbolic capacities vary.

Symbolic Processing

McDougall defines the symbolic process as 'the code of language which would have allowed the affect laden representations to be named, thought about and dealt with by the mind' (1989: 28–29). In my view this definition describes a very developed ability, where representations can be named and then addressed in mental activity. A definition of the symbolic that involves naming and reflecting on meaning, I suggest, is a specific outcome of a developmental achievement that is certainly required for a successful analysis and is nurtured by the process, but I do not think that accessing the symbol requires such an elaborate symbolic process. In Chapter 3 I made a distinction between somatic access to rudimentary symbol capacity and complex symbolic processing. McDougall appears to advocate what in my view can only be defined as advanced symbolic processing, which is related to higher cortical activity, where integration takes place and, arguably, involves a greater conscious awareness as part of the process, or at least the unconscious made conscious by effortful work. I think this type of symbolic processing is an 'advanced' state and that there is a more basic symbolic capacity that has been left out of the picture.

McDougall's model of symbolic ability is a linguistic thought- and speech-based process understood as a mental activity alone. She conceives of the mind and body in dualist terms, for in her view it is only the mind and not the body that can access ideation; it is only the mind that accesses the symbol, which is understood as 'non-material', the symbol representing the object *in absentia*. The representation *in absentia* ventures into the more abstract and thereby constitutes an ideational process. The degree of reflective capacity defined here is very developed and relates to 'mentalization', arguably under the influence of Pierre Marty and Michel de M'Uzan (1963; Marty *et al.* 1963). There may be even a cognitive idea of 'processing thought' detectable in McDougall's definition. The kind of reflective process McDougall is talking about (and which relates to much written in psychoanalysis about the symbolic process) is, of course, important but it is only part of the story. Furthermore, where the understanding is still based on a persistent mind/body duality, it is not helpful and inevitably leads to impasses.

There is another way of defining the symbol. One way is to redefine exactly what is meant by processing. Peter Fonagy and Mary Target (1997: 680–681) state at one point that affective processing relates to a more pre-reflective process which has to link to non-verbal interpersonal experience. I have argued that ways of reworking experience relate to a development of a kind of procedural know-how, which involves a shift in interpersonal body models, and that this coincides with changes brought about in affective somatic-semantic states. As we have seen, the pre-reflective embodied mode is worked through in doing and action. This implies that an acting out need not be negative and regressive, for a different style of re-enactment can be considered, which involves some change and reorganization.

Schore (1994, 2003a, 2003b, 2011) crucially emphasizes right brain–body affective meaning-processing for actual change in experience and attachment. He emphasizes revising the pre-verbal body-based working models of self and others. In my view, these models are not reified representations but are brain–body experiences. I have argued that brain–body experiences are formed by sensory-semiotic vital and skin matrix sets-ups, which derive from communication with significant others. Here a broadening of language takes place to include semiotic expression.

The field of language, I would argue, includes the somatic and procedure-based processing. This type of processing, of course, cannot ultimately be separated from speech- and thought-based reflective work and, indeed, integration is the key. However, the soma cannot be left out of the picture; the somatic-sensory level is profound and should not be viewed as existing outside language and as therefore incapable of symbolic access or of any symbolic processing potential. In my definition, symbolic processing requires both bodily procedural processing and what McDougall relates to a language-based linguistic process.

Most people are probably familiar with pseudo-analysis. The impressive person who has been in analysis for many years is, to all accounts, capable of a high level of symbolic reflection in the sense of effectively linking affect to ideation, and of elaborating to some extent consciously unconscious material. He or she can make connections to dream life and other related non-conscious states, referring to various meanings, associations and metaphors. In spite of all this, there is no shifting of deep-seated difficulties in such a person. As you hear more about their life, what becomes clear is that they keep getting into relations where the destructive cycle is repeated. It is like an anti-know-how which stops them from moving on procedurally. All the alpha processing in this context is only transforming meaning at the level of ideas and speech and words, but does nothing effective to alter the somatically felt action-based meanings. Unless there is a reworking of these beta elements, affective change will not occur.

Bodily Enactment

McDougall's linguistic and ideationally based symbolic process has led to the procedural bodily mode of being not been adequately understood. Balint's (1992 [1968]: 205) analysand, who did a somersault in the consulting room, was benefiting from talking analysis, but the somersault genuinely facilitated a shift from a childhood impasse of failure and giving up to a small 'jump ahead'. It represented a form of procedural body know-how that ever so subtly re-patterned 'non-verbal signifiers' (McDougall 1989: 10).

The model I have proposed in this book attempts to address how a compulsion to repeat can be expressed in bodily terms and how the enactment can be a form of narration. I have noted that Fonagy argues that non-verbal memory cannot be accessed in analysis and agreed that such a memory cannot be accessed verbally; however, I believe that non-verbal memory reveals itself in bodily expression and in enactments of transference and counter-transference. Phil Mollon (1998) gives an example of a small child who enacts a non-verbal memory of an abusive relation with a doll before it is put into words. I believe that the body can express sensory meaning even when insight and awareness are lacking.

Enactment is the action of doing. As with procedural memory, the know-how lies in the action itself; in driving the car, dancing the dance, doing the physical act, the body just *does* it. My hypothesis is that a story can be told by the body before words are found or before the person puts feelings into conscious thought or speech. Here affect is bodily embedded in somatic experience and involves a semiotic process. What is being played out is the bodily know-how, which by being bodily expressed in the doing can render the sense of the action which continues to go unrecognized on a reflective level. This is why, at this stage, talking about the meaning necessarily leads to a dead end. This has been misinterpreted by some to conclude that there is no meaning or symbolic significance.

Merleau-Ponty notes that in the somatic symptom the body can transform relational phenomena, for example a 'refusal of others or of the future' into a '*de facto* situation'; the body can only 'symbolize existence because it realizes it and is its actuality' (1962: 164). In this context, the transformation of relational being into a thing like body phenomena does not help a person to make relational links because all appears de facto, but the somatic field has already enacted a non-verbal sense. The body can do this because it is in fact relationally embedded.

Somatic access to the symbol is related to the broadening of language to encompass extra-linguistic modes of expression and sensory and gestural forms of communication that engage the soma itself. In this context there are varying degrees of pre-reflective and reflective processing and modes of awareness. This is a very different take to an approach which views 'concrete' forms of somatization as necessarily indicative of a symbolic deficit. In my view, even when the somatic expression concerns fragile ego states, threats to the body gestalt, there is still at work a skin matrix formation effected by perturbations in relation to the other. For a deformation of the body ego to take place and to be expressed somatically, there has to be a manifestation of the semiotic skin set-up, however fragile.

I do not regard the body gestalt as an a priori given nor do I think there is a preconstituted 'phantasy' body derived from insular instinctual urges. Instead I would emphasize that the developments of bodily processes in a relational context are already underway, even with 'primitive' body states. In this sense my approach here differs fundamentally from earlier Kleinian thinking and therefore also from some of McDougall's presuppositions. Sensory, non-verbally based meaning is in my view rooted in right brain–body processes and in pre-reflective and procedural modes of body memory. The body know-how may in fact be destructive, even a form of anti-knowledge, where there have been perturbed relations constituting the know-how which render the re-enactment a form of locked-in compulsive repetition. Depending on the relational patterning, the know-how can be organized, or at the other end disorganized, leading in some cases to greater chaos and mayhem. In the latter context meaning becomes more scrambled and confused and there is a greater tendency to unbinding, such as can be observed in disorganized attachment bodily enactments and multiple dissociative symptom formation and phenomena.

So even when meaning is not shored up and coherency is somewhat lacking, there is still symbol access in so far as meaning and disruptive body set-ups are being played out. However, the breakdown of structure and meaning becomes more dominant in these disorganized set-ups, where the sense of fragmentation and of being uncontained by bound meaning are to the fore. Although when there is a breakdown of meaning this is in reference to what has been meaningful, there are nevertheless moments when bodily experiences cannot be bound at al and fall out of the field of the symbol and meaning. This experience – Lacan's 'encounter with the real' or Bion's 'nameless dread' – is traumatic.

The Body Speaks the Subject

Who is doing the narration when the body expresses significant experiences through enactment before words are found? It does seem that in higher symbolic processing, where reflective processes are active, the shift from una-wareness to greater awareness is more fluid and that a more active relation to experience is possible. In this context a person can actively intervene, reflect upon affectively somatic states and try to rework them in a chosen direction. This contrasts with extremely traumatized persons, whose intrusive and destructive relations with others overwhelms and devastates them. Working with chronic cases of sexual abuse, torture and loss, I have come across strik-ing similarities in body symptom formation. In all cases there is an entirely passive relation, as if the sensory change in the body 'does it' to them and narrates them, as though an other is orchestrating the body. In such cases, a story is played out in the sensory reliving, where the perturbed relation with the other, the body environment set-up, speaks the soma; even though there is a marked failure of procedural *processing*, the enactment shows a scene.

The enactment depicts the perturbed relation with the other and/or nar-rates aspects of the micro or wider environmental set-up. In my view, this is because the body in this context accesses the symbol but has no capacity to process it symbolically. Here the use of the term 'symbol' covers a broad spectrum; *there is no processing in the somatic procedural action*, but sym-bol access exists in so far as a set of semiotic relations are somatically mapped despite the fact that agency in such cases is radically undermined and is out of action.

The traumatic situation is the introduction of a disruptive set of relations which subjugate and create states of helplessness. Abuse and torture very often occur over a period of time and organize specific self–other relations, conveyed qualitatively in the tactile acts, mirrored and sensed, in what is said and how it is said. In Chapter 17 I discussed how gross acts can work to annihilate tactile differences by overriding everything with pain and by confounding sensory discrimination. The disruption of the somatic matrix is such that it can result in debilitation, long-term somatic discomfort and deformations of the skin experience in sensation and failing skin boundary states.

The interpersonal environment set-up is never unmediated. The situation involves the established meanings and social relations that already exist and the particular attack on those meanings and reinstitutions of sense that have created a perverse set-up. The denigrated other can be treated as an object, made to feel like a 'thing', or more a 'piece of shit'; every vile projective communication can be pushed onto the other to defile and attachments develop along disorganized paths. Sensory flashbacks retell the scene; body memory vividly relives not only the vision but the smells, the taste, the sensation. Memory does not get laid down accurately and is always infused with the historical phantasmagoria already circulating in experience.

In addressing the profundity of effects on bodily states that cannot be verbally accessed and the body phantasmagoria that circulate in dreams and the like, it may be more relevant to refer to Freud's 'thing representation' in the unconscious. However, Laplanche and Pontalis remind us that thing presentation is related to preverbal signifiers and that it reinvests and revives the memory trace (1983: 448). Things have semiotic configuration and should not be understood as unmediated entities 'in themselves'.

It is evident from psychoneurological trauma studies that brain processing is affected by trauma, as for example Yovell (2000) points out, that in states of overwhelming shock, stress hormones flood the brain, affecting Broca's speech area and the hippocampus, declarative event-based memory, while stimulating the amygdala and the affect of intense fear. Van der Kolk states that what exists is 'speechless terror' and 'the body holds the score' (in Kolk *et al.* 1996: 289). It is well known that in relation to severe traumatic experience memory is liable to greater distortion, gap, confabulation and greater confusion between the imagined and actual.

In Chapter 15 I described the case of a sexually abused boy who was investigated for middle ear problems and a brain tumour, who continued to complain of dizziness and lost all motor coordination. He would topple over, enacting his body disintegration. The threat to his body ego integrity from the abuse and the implied accusations of homosexuality were expressed in action before the associative links could be consciously thought and put into words. He did not feel that he had any control over his body and described the experience in terms of an alien other taking over his body. The recurring sensations in his mouth and genitals would happen by surprise, taking him unawares; it felt to him as if a force or someone else was doing it to him. The sensation was of a piercing, a prising him open. The scene was relived as a sensory mapping on the body, incarnating the appropriation by another. He would look in the mirror and see his brother looking back at him, a visual usurpation of his body identity.

Pierrette illustrates the olfactory envelope described by Anzieu:

Pierrette produced a smell, which was focused on and amplified in her experience. She described it as a foul smell emanating from her back. People would stop and stare, and ridicule her, she told me: 'It is this terrible smell that comes from my back. It is like pooh.' 'How do you know about the smell'? 'Because people react in the streets,' she grimaces, showing me how they look.

Pierrette had suffered multiple anal penetrations under torture. The smell was the legacy of the torturer under her skin who had put bad things inside her – sperm, which had mingled with her excreta. The rapists had contaminated her with their being and sperm, and this had got inside, been implanted in her body space. They did things from behind; she had not wanted to see what had happened, but other people would find out what she had not wanted to see – they could sniff it out, and she was ashamed. The smell would betray and reveal her shameful secret for all to know.

The back told of her behind, where she was repeatedly raped by the torturers, and the foul smell was her rotting inside, as she believed she had been polluted. The belief was so powerful that her sweat glands and genitals produced a persistent unnatural smell. The olfactory sensory projection was the means whereby her body told the story and 'keeps the score' (Kolk *et al.* 1996), betraying her consciousness. Her shame was expressed in the emanating smell for all to sniff out, and it would expose her. Pierrette's body was expressing in itself, rather than in words, a fundamental perturbation of relation, a usurpation by an other.

The cultural meaning of intense shame and exposure to the gaze of others is central in this example. In many parts of Africa rape is seen to sully the woman and to stain her for life, as it is in parts of India too, where the raped woman can be regarded as an untouchable. Pierrette felt cursed; this is her explanation for why she suffered. Beliefs are powerful and, as Penny Woolley and Paul Hirst (1982) point out, using the example of voodoo. The belief in voodoo can lead to biological death, for voodoo can kill.

There is a much stronger belief in fate in some non-Western cultures than in our rational Western one, and many of my African patients speak of being cursed. For some cultures the idea of processing and reflecting on feelings or of expressing them is entirely foreign. People from other cultures do not necessarily think about their experiences in the same way as we do in the West, where we can be ethnocentric. It is important to be aware of cultural differences, and we need to be careful that our presuppositions do not lead us to assume that those who do not respond as we do are less intelligent or less able, whereas they are just different.

In Chapter 15, I described Zara's case, where the cutting of her arm and the twisting of the knife in the wound led to the development of generalization whereby her entire skin surface felt like it was burning and being punctured by stab wounds. She felt it was being done to her all over her body, the surface that had been exposed to the breaching cut reminding her insistently that the aggressor had supplanted and taken over every part of her skin surface. Zara had been brought up to be a human rights activist by her parents, and, having experienced torture and the loss of loved ones, she felt survivor's guilt. Her somatic symptom became a means by which she tortured herself for being the survivor when others had died. At the same time, her suffering was senseless and represented the meaningless acts of violence gratuitously inflicted on her and on those she loved.

Somatic Access to the Symbol and Symbolic Processing

Where the somatic symptom is in the grip of a compulsive repetition arrested and stuck therein, and the body know-how is in the grip of an anti-knowledge, where symbolic processing either procedurally or in the higher-order linguistic reflective mode is not taking place or is doing so very inadequately, there is nevertheless still somatic access to the symbol, in that the sensory and somatic can still narrate a story, express a meaning, even though there may be no conscious understanding or working through of what is being communicated.

I have argued that somatic access to the symbol should be addressed via loss and absence, which leaves its mark as a memory trace, thereby facilitating sensory semiotic patterning. This somatic access allows for sensory and somatic enactment as a form of simple story-telling. That there is no symbolic processing (reworking on a procedural or mentalized level) does not leave the body without symbol.

In this context there is a distinction between *somatic access to the symbol* and *symbolic processing*. Within symbolic process there is both procedural right brain–body processing, which is fundamental, and more reflective linguistic processing, which can involve a meta-reflective dimension. In optimal lived experience the procedural and linguistic modes are interwoven. Thus I propose a different notion of the symbol, for in terms of the most basic definition there is no (or very little) symbolic processing but the body is still capable of expressing affectivity and meaning.

In crude neuroscientific terms the subcortical brain and brainstem could be described as generating basic emotions and fundamental body processes, and undergoing a process of formation under intercorporeal and environmental influences. Later development involves higher cortical activity, which includes linguistic and cognitive processes. In development there is then the integration of bodily processes and emotions with cortical activity.

The more reflective symbolic processing involving higher cortical activity could be related to what has been termed 'mentalization'. However, what is important here, as Schore points out, is the underlying right brain–body development and ultimately right and left brain integration.

Symbolic Categories: Different Types of Somatic Symptom Formation

I suggest that McDougall identifies certain affective developmental pathways in the early relationship which result in different types of somatic symptom formation. I shall look at these in turn, with reformulations in each case where necessary, in order to avoid a mind/body dichotomy.

Failure and deficit in symbolic access and processing

Alexithymia has its place in understanding a certain type of body symptom disorder, where there is a failure in language of metaphorical relational expression in symptom formation. Chronic psychosomatic conditions are often linked to this type of problem, where there is an obsessive preoccupation with illness and sometimes the development of a downward spiral. Here there is a problem with both somatic access to the symbol as well as processing, including processing in procedural mode and affective-linguistic expression.

Rather than adopting a dualist ontology, I view this condition as entirely the result of a developmental deficit relating to disturbances in the early relation with the other. There is a deficit in response, both in affective attachment terms and in instigating a response to separation, which prevents an adequate relation to otherness and difference, and there is a failure to forge links between the infant's affective-somatic expressions and the other's sensory matrix set-up, which prevents a conjoining of somatic affective states with a semiotic set of relations; in other words, a fundamental decoupling takes place between soma and semiosis.

According to this view, the extreme of the continuum, the example of alexithymia, expresses a perturbation in symbol formation because *access to a certain relational sensibility has been barred*. I agree with Schore's explanation that the infant's affective somatic states are not adequately articulated in the sensory dance. There is a fundamental failure between (m)other and baby to connect affectively. Where a caretaker is not affectively sensitized to the infant, the affect-soma states of the infant cannot find association with the non-verbal signifiers derived from the other. The affective soma is hence not processed in the proto-conversation. When linguistic acquisition comes into play, there is a deficit in right brain–body relational development: words are used but in a logical and rational manner, devoid of affective charge and emotive sense, and qualitative relational affectivity is impoverished.

In cases when there has been either privation, as in circumstances of excessive neglect, or, at the other end of the continuum, a prolongation of mothering, overprotection, which attempts to foreclose separation (because the (m)other cannot tolerate the experience of loss and therefore attempts to cover it over by a form of smothering), there will be problems in accessing the symbol, which profoundly impacts on somatic development. Reference has been made to autistic and related states, where the inability to experience and tolerate separation and to be aware of difference and a sense of otherness do not only affect overall behaviour and emotional response but also the sensory field and tactility itself.

Freud's early understanding of actual neurosis and neurasthenia provide useful insights into underdeveloped affective somatic states. From a contemporary perspective, these are seen in terms of a fundamental impairment in the other, in the latter's failure to offer responses that will facilitate the infant's affective somatic links and semiotic development. Deploying Lacan and attachment thinking, Verhaeghe and Vanheule argue that the problem lies in the inability

> to process the arousal coming from the drive in a symbolic way. The reason for this impossibility is sought in the failure of the primary caretakers in presenting the child with the necessary symbolic tools for drive regulation. (2005: 493)

They present an argument that post-traumatic stress that lives on as a somatic disorder well after the event is not an automatic response to trauma but relates to earlier relational deficits that precede the trauma and result in the persistent inability to process affective somatic responses; the person the develops, or is left with, an actual neurosis similar to what McDougall describes in relation to chronic psychosomatics, when everything is reduced to a physical build-up state.

While I agree with Verhaeghe and Vanheule in the way they explore the impact of the other on development and locate the difficulty in the other, the approach I take differs in a number of fundamental ways. Verhaeghe and Vanheule generalize about post-traumatic symptom formation, whereas I regard post-traumatic stress as somewhat of an umbrella term covering a variety of phenomena and aetiologies, and while I agree that in certain cases the link between post-trauma response and actual neurosis is valid, it is, however, also important not to overgeneralize and simplify.

First, I would say that the prolongation of post-traumatic symptoms can be the result of the traumatic situation itself and need not only relate to earlier developmental deficits in the other. Having worked with the worst cases of abuse, trafficking and torture, I have found that social reality can prove unbearable. The extremity and duration of adversity matters and the consequent disruption and entire devastation of relational structures should not be underestimated. It can so fundamentally impair and rock to the core any vital and skin ego set-ups that symptomatic trauma response can happen to any one of us and potentially override any developmental history.[1]

Secondly, Verhaeghe and Vanheule take the mainstream view that the advent of linguistic structures opens symbolic possibilities and hence it would follow for them that, if the soma becomes the dominant form of symptom expression, then by definition it indicates a problem of symbolization. I would question too ready assumptions of this sort. In my experience somatic symptoms following trauma can tell an unspeakable story through enactment, expressing somatically what cannot as yet be put into words.

However, in the chronic cases where the compulsive repetition is caught in a time warp and processing and insight are barred in the long term, the somatic symptoms are likely to develop into a form of actual neurosis and chronic psychosomatic illness. In such cases reworking procedural experience may not occur, and the soma enacts the subject in a repetition of the same. This type of somatization can turn into a kind of chronic psychosomatic illness and eventually atrophy will occur. This has happened with some of my patients who have been in the throes of being passively acted upon and who have resisted bearing or facing the pain and recreating links. This is because re-owning their history has proved to be unbearable: the only way out for them is to opt for crippling physical illness.

In cases where actual neurosis dominates – and there are patients who are all aches and pains and nothing else – there is consumption by physical pain. Verhaeghe and Vanheule are right: the deficit in the early developmental other is evident, and there the therapist meets an impasse, where no links between the somatic and the traumatic relational history can be forged. However to further complicate matters, actual neurosis is hard to find in pure form. In life situations, where the other is inadequate in their response, it is often inconsistently so, so there is uneven development and neurotic anxiety revolving around loss and separation and elements of actual neurosis coincide. Here there can be a mixture of types of symptom formation. Some somatic symptoms bear witness to barely elaborated alexithymic states and others to meaningful expression: these are the clients for whom there is some hope, for the more neurotic side of the personality and symptom formation can be utilized in the analysis.

Body symptom formation with rudimentary meaning

Psychosomatic symptoms which do not conform to the alexithymic and related types express meaning and narrate. Here there is not such a marked deficit in development, but more a trajectory with limitations lacking complexity, where some meaning and metaphorical significance exists in the somatic symptom, but not in an elaborated way. Procedural know-how, however, also exists in a circumscribed way.

In this type of symptom formation, reflective processing (in the McDougall sense) is often lacking, so there may be little or no insight into what is going on in the symptom. The crucial question is whether or not there is some form of procedural processing at work. Where there is some reworking of procedural experience, it is helpful, even if it is circumscribed. In such cases there is more scope for flexibility and some hope of shifting the symptom.

Possible scenarios in developmental terms are where the caretaker has responded to the baby's states but his or her affective sensory communication is deficient in nuanced sensibility or lacking in elaborated affective sensory-emotional contact and sensitivity; where there are features of neglect and limited responses relating to avoidant or preoccupied attachment difficulties; where pragmatic responses fails to articulate and differentiate feeling states (see Bruch 1973).

Here we can include McDougall's revision of psychosomatic symptoms which go far beyond a conventional biological understanding of body processes. McDougall identifies how the drive is expressed somatically in the compulsion to repeat and in states of somatic overdrive. It is also possible to include specific sensory alteration in organ experience and functional processes that are not indicative of an underlying organic pathology but are expressive, are a form of communication. This type of symptom occurs when the soma is engaged in a meaning-making process and can include bodily enactment as narratives in action.

A semiotic-somatic articulation is not necessarily conscious but exists pre-reflectively. Although it is not symbolic in terms of a state reflected upon, linguistically named and processed, the somatic articulation nevertheless accesses the symbol in as far as the somatic process is always linked to what lives on in the aftermath of absence and sensory body memory, and this is what gets revivified and expressed in every somatic reiteration.

Under this rubric we can add a broad category of body symptoms induced by environmental trauma. These clients can appear a bit alexithymic, 'concrete' and somewhat preoccupied with body states; they complain of somatic pain rather than elaborate on the emotional nature of the pain; are fairly resistant to psychoanalytic observations, reflective process or interpretation; and are commonly lacking in insight. Despite this, their somatic symptoms express meaning and present a mini-narrative. The symptoms described have somatic access to the symbol. Some have procedural processing but this varies from case to case. Reflective insight and verbal thought process-ing are lacking or underdeveloped in this category.

Procedural and linguistically based symbolic processing

The third category of symptom type is the more elaborate symbolic and 'hysterical' style of symptom, the elaborated symbolic body symptom par excellence. However, if the elaboration is attributed to mind as opposed to soma, it remains a mystery how the body takes over in the expression of meaning or how sensory alteration occurs. This involves symbolic process-ing and elaboration in McDougall's sense, but I would emphasize proce-dural processing and re-enactment as a form of working through and of altering semiotic-sensory set-ups. There is, of course, linguistic processing, which enables the client through association to identify and reflect verbally. This is important but it is only part of the process.

No Neat Compartmentalization

Meaning-laden and alexithymic-based somatic states are not necessarily dis-crete conditions and can overlap in complex ways in lived experience. The potential is sometimes there for greater elaboration but it is not till the anal-ysis that the ball gets rolling.

> Melanie had come to see me suffering from panic attacks and was very concrete about her symptoms. She was unable to express her feelings; her only outlet was to cry on occasion while watching a soap drama. This was odd, for the intensity of her tears were in stark contrast to the superficiality of the melodrama.
>
> After the start of the therapy there was a turn for the worse when her body symptoms started to manifest in public places. There was an occasion where her knees were like jelly and she almost had to crawl to the public toilets. That this began to happen in a public place meant that she was seen by many in a helpless state.
>
> She described herself as 'like an invalid'. Through historical recon-struction and enactment in the transference, it all came out. One morn-ing the bell was not working, so I arrived minutes late to open the door. Her anger and frustration were palpable and she was shaking as she entered the consulting room. The affective intensity far outweighed any rational justification, and this indicated a transference reaction. As I probed, she burst out, 'I hated waiting for my sister. Every time I went out with the family we all had to wait.'

Her jealousy of her younger sister became obvious. The sister was handicapped at birth, and the only way Melanie could get attention and cry out for help was to swap her 'able' body (which had been neglected as she was considered healthy in comparison to her sister) for her sister's 'disabled' one. All this was enacted in the body symptom before being put into words, but the meaning discovered and reflected upon began in our co-construction of the meaning of her life and in the living out of her past attachment relations in the transference, a form of procedural processing in re-enactment. The reflection that followed, which was verbal, was important, but was only a part of a procedural-based symbolizing process.

The Body and the Hole in the Symbolic

I have been largely concerned with broadening the meaning of language and addressing the somatic field. In this chapter I have explored the different types of somatic symbol relations, and in this I have been concerned with soma and meaning. However, throughout the book I have explored imaginary and symbolic failure, the fragile and precarious body, the unbinding and deregulating of vital processes and the return of the fragmenting skin and its failure to act as a shored-up border, the hole in the skin matrix and the skin surface structure. I have focused on the alien, unknown flesh and the fact that the body is not under our control, in life and in illness, that the gap in experience is fundamental to bodily being and that the relation to the invisible and to non-touch in touch is basic to bodily existence. The encounter is with inevitable alterity and that which cannot be owned, had or known and which returns as the hole in the fibre, the gaping wound, the alien and irreducible other and in unbound phantasmagoria.

Summing Up

In the psychoanalytic literature symbolization has been linked to language as speech and linguistic signification. In this regard Anglo-American psychoanalysis, like Lacan, prioritizes language as rooted in speech-word and linguistic access. In this tradition of psychoanalysis symbolization has been understood as the capacity to register lack reduced to a psychic-mental feat and as related to a developed form of reflecting on experience that is located in thought-mind where ideation and affect link and a level of abstraction is possible. I regard such a model as identifying the mere tip of the symbolic iceberg.

I have broadened the term 'language' to include sensory–semiotic relations and the way somatic processing is marked by absence and memory trace. I have addressed somatic access to the symbol and distinguished this symbol access from symbolic processing. Symbolic processing is aligned with higher-order symbolic ideational processing, but not exclusively, for pre-reflective somatic procedural processing or right brain processing (Schore) is seen as fundamental for working through compulsive repetition and to find a reworked body know-how. Of course procedural processing and the higher cortical linguistic mode of reflection are to be integrated to work together, but this does not always happen.

To finally sum up the various meanings of symbol: I draw a distinction between symbol access which can include the somatic field; this is the registering of the memory trace and enables the sensory and somatic to partake in meaning and its failure. I refer to a form of sensory-somatic narrative enacted in the symptom, but this is to be differentiated from a second and fundamental level of symbol coming into process, which involves affective somatic and relational processing that is bodily and procedural in nature. This is then followed by a third and more refined mode of processing which is ideational-affective and is associated with reflective function and mentalization, which results in finding words to identify and name and to linguistic understanding to interpret and meta-process.

This third mode of symbolization would be the outcome of certain kinds of rearing practices, psychotherapeutic interventions and psychoanalysis par excellence. This is arguably very much a Western mode of making sense of experience which relates to a certain form of subjectivity. In my experience of working with individuals who have been brought up in different parts of the world, I have often found this kind of thinking to be alien and to lead to an impasse in the work. In this regard the ethnocentric aspect of understanding has to be constantly scrutinized and addressed.

Note

1   Although greater resilience or vulnerability is, of course, related to developmental history, the point I am making here is that devastating experiences over time, which involve excessive, perverse relations can result in fundamentally disrupting vital processes and skin expression in any one of us. Underlying fragility is potentially there in us all.

Conclusion
Have We Reached a Destination?

The Body as Interface

Starting with a figure of the organism with its insides – viscera and internal processes – separated from the environment by a sealed-off skin sac, making the body a discrete unit, I have in this book set out to invert and open up this body, so that it does not stay intact. The body's interior spills into the other and is exposed from the first to an outside relational field predicated on responses from others. Likewise the skin border fails to hold fast but frays and shifts. As an exteriorized surface, mirrored and touched, the outside seeps in and the protective seal is forever breached. This is compared with Merleau-Ponty's description of the body as like a glove turned inside-out and outside-in. I also draw on Lacan's spatial metaphor of the Möbius strip, but as a way of describing the entire skin envelope structure.

This emergent, 'new' body figure is not a simple metaphor. The actual and lived experience of the body, the senses and the biological functions and processes are based on this inside-out/outside-in relational structure, a veritable trope indeed. The foundations for this relational body configuration exist as intercorporeality, which emerged from phenomenological descriptions in philosophy, was observed in developmental psychology, found ground in neurobiology and influenced areas in contemporary psychoanalysis.

Intercorporeality signals a paradigmatic shift from a one person-body perspective to a muilti-person-bodied approach in psychologically based disciplines. It signposts a move away from the isolated organism and towards an organism–environment model, flagged up at the turn of the century by biologists such as Jakob von Uexküll and later further developed in the neurosciences. Intercorporeality is the way the body is derived

Between Skins: The Body in Psychoanalysis – Contemporary Developments,
First Edition. Nicola Diamond.
© 2013 John Wiley & Sons, Ltd. Published 2013 by John Wiley & Sons, Ltd.

from the field of others. The body is observed and lived from the body space of the other. This is a sensory lived experience. Merleau-Ponty describes this phenomena as the child finding its body in the other's body. Neurobiologists refer to affective neural simulation from observing the bodily actions of others.

I therefore state that the other and the relational field comes first, implying that there is no a priori owned unity to the body. The bodily I ego develops later and only as the outcome of development. Cultural differences exist and I suggest that trajectories regarding body ego formation vary a great deal. For example, some contexts put much more emphasis on the body in relation to community and do not uphold the self-contained bodily I, which is so dominant in the Anglo-American and European world. Reference here is to the materially lived body and not only to body ego-I as a mental perception.

The intercorporeal field has suffered misunderstandings. It has been associated with unity, merging, symbiosis and harmony. Such an interpretation assumes a body identity and hence a bodily I function that can find wholeness in merging with others. Implicit here is the idea that the ego can extend into the world and subsume everything into itself. Or intercorporeality has been wrongly equated with only a positive relating, such as 'shared attunement' states (Stern) in mother–infant interactions.

Intercorporeality describes a bodily aperture to a field with others as a condition of existence. As such, intercorporeality is not a blissful state of oneness but is potentially and fundamentally disarming, opening up an irreducible alterity, an otherness that can never be incorporated into ownness. I explore how intercorporeal being can be experienced as an encounter with the uncanny, which Freud describes so well, and which can haunt and threaten the bodily I ego states and from which there is no ultimate refuge.

Modes of relating which are identified qualitatively as positive or negative are simply evaluations that can arise only in specific rearing contexts and are the outcome of different developmental situations. In all such cases intercorporeality is the precondition; therefore relations with others inevitably impact on bodily processes and skin experience. This is why others can get right inside and under our very skins.

Whereas intercorporeality is a general phenomenological description of being in the world, actual contexts vary and the specific relational situations that we are thrown into have a dramatic impact on how bodily being is lived and experienced. There are certain developmental trajectories which I identify as two opposing extremes on either side of a continuum. Where at one end, there is the 'too little' (not having a relationship – a state of privation), at the other end there is the 'too much' (m)othering (the state of being smothered). In either case the modes of non-relating as the quality of relating forecloses the gap that allows for a relational differentiation based on body (ego)/other differentiation. The result is disturbances associated with the psychogenic autistic spectrum. In such circumstances there are not only difficulties with affective embodied self–other relating but also with sensory body states and spatial awareness of other bodies.

I also explored other types of developmental pathways where the soma is not affectively linked to an empathic quality of relating (Stern's attunement) and how this can result in alexithymia (no words for feelings), where the body expresses affect in physical states but in this context lacks any connection to affective relational meaning.

In bringing to bear current understandings of intercorporeality, I have explored developments in psychoanalysis regarding the biological body and emerging psychical processes, and detected a dualism still at work which creates an impasse in thinking. According to this view, the body is governed by the laws of nature and embedded in a biological bedrock; it is therefore fixed and predetermined in structure and function. On the other hand, there is an emergent ideational realm where the sexual drive and body image/skin ego are open to imaginative changes but for the psyche only.

Propping is introduced as the border term (derived from Freud's *Anlehnung* which in German means to lean on or be propped up on) to refer to a way of overcoming dualism by linking body and psyche. Laplanche in *Life and Death in Psychoanalysis* (1985) explores propping in relation to the basic internal biological functions for life: digestion, excretion, secretion, homeostasis and so on. He argues that propping shows how sexuality and the drive emerge by at first leaning on the biological bedrock and then deviating from it. He describes a metonymic and metaphoric slide, whereby the psyche develops from the prototype but then, in being ideational, becomes protean and based in fantasy. Anzieu in *The Skin Ego* (1989) argues in the same vein, that the psychic skin ego derives from the organic skin and that propping accounts for how the actual skin has a relation with the mental skin ego as an ideational construct.

I have shown how propping according to the main account cannot create the link between soma and psyche. I locate the problem in the biological bedrock model which is so stuck in a predetermined, fixed biological order and identity that it will not budge. It is so stamped by nature, so located in a brute material presence that it has to be left out of a psychic order altogether, and an assumed dualist split sustained. This model of the body is simply unviable. Such an unhelpful model is not only to be found in part in Laplanche and Anzieu but also in other, more current models in psychoanalysis. For example, I have critically addressed problems with aspects of the mentalization model that has enjoyed popularity in recent years.

The impasse created by dualistic accounts and their assertion of a biological bedrock model has led to an unbridgeable gulf between the actual body, fixed by nature, and the protean body said to be of the psyche, the mental sphere alone. I have pointed out how this kind of model cannot account for the way in which a lived body is affected by an imaginary protean body.

Instead I have looked at how there is a direct relation between an affective imaginary body and alterations in actual body states. Drawing on examples of how a more imaginary body is expressed in a variety of bodily symptoms, where there is either an unknown organic aetiology, and of how the complexity of body phenomena cannot be explained by such causes, I have explored the interpenetration of an affective protean body and the changes that take place in sensory states, in motility and comportment, in body processes and in actual body gestalt formations.

A second and more radical understanding of propping emerges whereby the vital processes (basic bodily functions) do not have a fixed limit and route from birth but are considered premature and underdeveloped while in this immature state, dependent on the other. The vital processes have now been identified as insufficient in a variety of ways and thus necessarily pass through an intercorporeal exchange. In this way, the vital processes find a prop in the other and in the interventions derived from the other.

The response from the other, far from meeting a biological need, is imperfect. It is subject to temporal delay with the comings and goings of the other and thus mini-absences. The communication which replaces any immediacy of response provides what I have described as a semiotic, gestural, sensory, signifying set-up and which, it is suggested, functions like a language, bringing with it the adult world of meaning.

My analysis shifted from a model of the vital order (based on a fixed biology) towards what I referred to as the vital set-up, where there is a sensory semiotic proto-conversation (Trevarthen), whereby the body processes are structured in relation to others and the social situation, which makes up a vital field. Depending on the type of vital set-up, the body processes are regulated and/or deregulated.

Likewise, by radically rereading the meaning of propping, this time in Anzieu's work, I challenged the view that the skin is simply grounded in biology and derives all its properties from therein. I looked at the way the skin does not get its gestalt form from nature but from a mirroring environment. In this second model the skin is from the first propped by the look and touch which in turn derive from others and the way the gestural-sensory responses from the other form a type of skin matrix structure. This skin matrix provides the skin with a scaffold-like relational support structure. The skin is explored not as biological datum but as a surface bound to the field of others.

I addressed attachment and sexuality in relation to regulating and deregulatory body processes, including how secure styles of attachment set up ways of regulating body processes via the other. I showed that these practices also conform to habitual structures, whereas sexual practices and incitements can tend towards deregulation and states of excess that can tip into either the direction of play or be linked to traumatic deregulation. I also considered how traumatic somatic deregulation can occur in both the context of insecure attachment and fundamental disruption of affectionate bonds, as well as in the sphere of sexuality.

Due to constraints of space, I have not been able to adequately address the specificity of sexuality, and further discussion is required.[1] My general move is away from bio-logos and towards a bio-life, and I have drawn on recent developments in neuroscience regarding neural plasticity and memory as trace, to explore how bodily processes can be changed by experience with others. I extend the effect of an environmental field by considering the cultural organization of bodily rearing practices, social imaging of the body and styles of comportment.

A consideration of neural plasticity is central in the move away from a classic biological bedrock model. I have also drawn on neuroscience to challenge a divide between mind, body and world. According to contemporary understanding, there are brain–body dynamic relations while sensory information derived from others and the environment is received. Thinking involves brain–body dynamics and the processing of sensory information derived from the environment.

I explored the brain–body map where the representation of the homunculus is located, and relate this to Freud's body ego structure and formation. I look at the way brain–body maps are rooted in body processes and receive sensory information from the world of others, including how the body is mirrored and touched. I considered a complex model, drawing on neuroplasticity and the brain–body map from neuroscience, discussions from psychoanalysis and intercorporeal approaches that explore how body constructs and the motor functions involve unconscious and social input. I also addressed how psychoanalytic understanding of the complexity of the body ego and interpersonal semiotic configurations of the body may influence neural plasticity and brain–body mapping.

In this book I have fundamentally challenged the separation of a body semiotics from the field of language proper and explored how non-presence is endemic to somatic experience. I have argued that it is wrong to locate the registering of absence to a non-material mind and proposed a way of understanding skin inscription and of considering touch as a genuine form of language. By re-working a structural linguistic model, I suggested a way of conceiving language as differential elements in relation to a tactile writing. In order to show that bio-relations connect the body and other in a semiotic and social articulating field.

Somatization and the Symptom

Using many examples, I examined the complexity of somatic expression from body symptoms found in the consulting room to those that abound in everyday life. I explored how these body states are testimony to the inseparability of the body and relations with others, to intercorporeal existence and developmental modes of acquired relating. I looked at bodily states where the other is experienced as the flesh and where bodily alterity and the uncanny exist in somatic states. I suggested that extreme trauma and its effects in the body can show up more starkly what in fact goes on in everyday bodily experience.

I proposed, and gave examples to illustrate, how through the symptom the body narrates and enacts a meaning before it can be put into words. I refer to somatic access to the symbol which enables a sensory semiotics so that the body can express affective metaphors that depict (as the examples indicate) body ego states and perturbation in relations with the other. I drew a distinction between somatic access to the symbol and symbolic processing. With the latter, I broke this down further into different types. Somatic access to the symbol enables the body to tell a rudimentary story with sensory, non-verbal signifiers; at its most basic, body symptoms may not rework or work through experiences, nor will insight necessarily be gained. There is an enactment and in trauma this takes the form of an embodied 'compulsion to repeat'.

'Symbolic processing' in my use of the term involves precisely processing the affective semiotic material. Here I refer to procedural embodied processing where non-verbal relational sense gets reworked. This can be pre-reflective and based on body action; in such a case a re-enactment is not a repetition but brings about some change. Finally, there is a further symbolic process which resembles the meaning normally used in the psychoanalytic literature where affective states are articulated linguistically, through words and speech, enabling affects to be contained and represented in thought, named, identified and elaborated upon so that reflection (including meta-cognitive processes) becomes possible. In this sense, processing affect and ideation come together and there is a transformation of affective states into reflective states that are attributed to 'mind'.

In this formulation I put forward different types of symbolic processing. In lived experience they are not discrete processes. Procedural and linguistic processing can be coterminus. In the neuroscience attachment literature, Schore would refer to this as the necessary integration of left and right hemisphere brain processes. What is important is the integration of bodily based subcortical functions with higher, complex cortical processing.

Effective integration is a developmental feat and in actual life there is a great deal of uneven development. There is also no universal or cultural agreement as to what integration is or should be, so any interpretation of what is integrated and how to value such integration is context-bound and socially dependent.

It is clear that my model of symbolic processing also includes the more traditional word-speech-based symbolic process but I see that as more the tip of the iceberg. I contend that procedural enactment shifts are required to bring about more fundamental changes in somatic-affective states.

The discussion which relates the somatic to symbolic processes included a look at the possible shortcomings of particular aspects of the mentalization model, specifically the way this approach has influenced the analysis of somatic symptom formation. I address the limitations in the contemporary use of the term 'psychosomatics' (understood as a failure of symbolization and an expression of concrete functioning), citing Joyce McDougall's work.

I suggested that we have seen the demise of what Freud referred to as the 'conversion' or 'hysterical' body symptom. I argued that conversion symptoms have gone out of fashion not simply because they present less frequently in the consulting room, but more because current models cannot address such symptoms, and contemporary definitions of 'psychosomatics' are more popularly used. It is necessary to have a better understanding of body symptoms which allows for their greater complexity, the meanings the body symptom can express and the stories they tell. I hope this book will be regarded as a contribution to this understanding.

The discussion of the body and symbolic access is evidently an address to Bion's beta and alpha functioning and the way his thinking has been taken up in Anglo-American psychoanalytic debate. In a reading of Bion that retains a residual dualism, beta elements can only be understood in a debased sense as raw affective-somatic states that in themselves remain so. In contrast to these beta elements, the alpha, higher order is responsible for mental processing and can transform these elements into thought, both in terms of transforming affects into containing ideas and by making it possible to hold 'abyssal experience' in thought. If the beta elements are simply by definition unprocessed archaic bodily states, then they remain so and any transformation takes place only in the alpha, ideational domain. The body in this sphere becomes effectively pure ideation and not body, while the body in its brute being remains a different order of reality. It is important to account for how affective somatic states and alpha capacity can be fundamentally linked together and how alpha function is also rooted in beta processes, otherwise alpha processing leaves the actual body out of the account.

Have We Reached a Destination?

In the account of somatic access to the symbol, it was seen that the experience of absence and loss marks the body and that there is an intercorporeally based sensory semiotics. Such a semiotic somatic can offer a form of rudimentary narrative as a bodily enactment before anything can be put into words. I examined ways of redefining the symbol that no longer privileges speech, word, mind and argued that somatic symbol access is not the same as symbolic processing. I further identified different types of symbolic processing.

The outcome of this reconsideration of the somatic and sensory body is that we have ended up with a logic which refuses to set up an either/or situation or to think in absolutes. In the biological field it is not a matter of organic aetiology opposed to a protean nature and plasticity, but we must acknowledge the actuality of both processes and the fundamental openness of biological systems. Questioning the absolute, monolithic nature of bio-logos allows for bio-life as a more open field, and reveals how development, growth and change, and the profound influence of others, of culture and of memory and language (in its broader sense), can impact on body experience, process and expression.

Likewise there is no binary logic with regard to intercorporeal existence. Intercorporeality is not defined as an undifferentiated symbiotic field, but as a relational field of differences where otherness exists. There is no opposition between the body and the symbol; there is somatic access to absence and loss, the memory trace and semiotic process and this is the case for expression of meaning and also when meaning wavers and fails to be bound. Sense and non-sense coexist.

The aim is to uproot dualistic thinking, binaries and decisive absolutes. In contrast, my starting point is open to uncertainty and does not follow a track which is final and conclusive. This more open and fluid style of thinking is likewise thematically reflected in the fascination with opening up body borders and allowing for flow, and with fundamentally challenging rigid body boundaries. I characterize this style as more feminine rather than masculine, the masculine being aligned with claims for totalizing truths and body closure.

In proposing a model of bio-sociality, I have employed hypothetical constructs that are heuristic and refer to lived body states, to clinical realities and to research findings. In an approach that does not adopt the either/or, imaginative connections and scientific study are used together. I allow the line to become blurred between imaginative body geographies and evidence-based claims. This is with the aim of provoking debate and encouraging creative thinking between disciplines rather than of asserting any absolute truth or scientific knowledge.

Science is never free from theory and belief, and certainly requires imaginative exploration and sometimes wild hunches. It is particularly difficult when exploring interdisciplinary connections, since one has to be able to cut across fields and therefore have some sense of each domain without being a master of all. What I have hoped to do in this book is challenge the prohibition that has been established by traditional disciplinary divides and stir up, even incite, more lively debate and a greater licence to play productively across disciplinary lines and borders. This book promotes interdisciplinary developments and there is no possibility of this without risk.

Note

1 See my 'Exploring some vicissitudes in feminine sexuality' (forthcoming), where I focus on states of sexual excess and pleasuring, the significance of loss and the problematic of sexual identity and the body as expressed in the somatic symptom.

References and Further Reading

References

Abraham, N. and Rand, N. (1979) The tropology of Freud. *Diacritics* 9(1): 15–28.

Abraham, N. and Torok, M. (1994) *The Shell and the Kernel*, ed. N. Rand. Chicago: University of Chicago Press.

Agamben, G. (1998) *Homo Sacer: Sovereign Power and Bare Life*. Palo Alto, CA: Stanford University Press.

Alain-Miller, J. (1992) Lacanian psychoanalysis. Public talk, Centre for Freudian Analysis and Research, London.

Alain-Miller, J. (2012) Reading the symptom, trans. A. Price. Paper presented at the Tenth Conference of the New Lacanian School, 2011.

Ansermet, F. and Magistretti, P. (2007) *Biology of Freedom: Neural Plasticity, Experience, and the Unconscious*. London: Karnac Books.

Anzieu, D. (1989) *The Skin Ego*, trans. C. Turner. New Haven: Yale University Press.

Atwood, G. E. and Stolorow, R. D. (1984) *Structures of Subjectivity*. Hillsdale, NJ: Analytic Press.

Balint, M. (1992 [1968]) *The Basic Fault: Therapeutic Aspects of Regression*. Evanston, IL: Northwestern University.

Barthes, R. (1985) *The Grain of the Voice: Interviews, 1962–1980*. London: Jonathan Cape.

Benthien, C. (2002) *Skin: On the Cultural Border between Self and the World*, trans. T. Dunlap. New York: Columbia University Press.

Bick, E. (1968) The experience of the skin in early object relations. *International Journal of Psychoanalysis* 49: 484–486.

Bion, W. R. (1962) A theory of thinking. In *Second Thoughts*. London: Heinemann.

Bowlby, J. (1969) *Attachment and Loss*, vol. 1: *Attachment*. London: Hogarth Press.

Bruch, H. (1973) *Eating Disorders: Obesity, Anorexia Nervosa, and the Person Within*. New York: Basic Books.

Between Skins: The Body in Psychoanalysis – Contemporary Developments,
First Edition. Nicola Diamond.
© 2013 John Wiley & Sons, Ltd. Published 2013 by John Wiley & Sons, Ltd.

Callaway, E. (2010) Mirror neurons seen behaving normally in autism. *Neuron* 66(3): 461–469.

Casey, E. (1993) *Getting Back into Place*. Bloomington: Indiana University Press.

Casey, E. (2000) *Remembering: A Phenomenological Case Study*. Bloomington: Indiana University Press.

Cohen, N. J. and Squire, L. R. (1980) Preserved learning and retention of pattern-analyzing skill in amnesia: dissociation of knowing how and knowing that. *Science* 210: 207–210.

Damasio, A. R. (1994) *Descartes' Error: Emotion, Reason and the Human Brain*. London: Putnam.

Damasio, A. R. (2000) *The Feeling of What Happens: Body, Emotion and the Making of Consciousness*. London: Vintage Books.

Damasio, A. R., Tranel, D. and Damasio, H. (1991) Somatic markers and the guidance of behaviour theory and preliminary testing. In H. S. Levin, H. M. Eisenberg and A. L. Benton (eds.), *Frontal Lobe Function and Dysfunction*. New York: Oxford University Press, pp. 217–229.

Derrida, J. (1976) *Of Grammatology*, trans. G. C. Spivak. Baltimore: Johns Hopkins University Press.

Derrida, J. (1978) Freud and the scene of writing. In *Writing and Difference*, trans. A. Bass. London: Routledge & Kegan Paul.

Derrida, J. (1983) Geshlecht: sexual difference, ontological difference. *Research in Phenomenology* 13(1): 65–83.

Derrida, J. (1987a) Geshlecht II: Heidegger's hand. In *Deconstruction and Philosophy: The Texts of Jacques Derrida*, trans. J. P. Leavey, Jr, ed. J. Eliss. Chicago: University of Chicago Press, pp. 61–96.

Derrida, J. (1987b) The parergon. In *The Truth in Painting*, trans. G. Bennington and I. McLeod. Chicago: University of Chicago Press, pp. 17–147.

Derrida, J. (1993) Heidegger's ear: philopolemology (Geshlecht IV). In J. Sallis (ed.), *Reading Heidegger: Commemorations*. Bloomington: Indiana University Press.

Diamond, N. (1992) Biology. In E. Wright (ed.), *Feminism and Psychoanalysis: A Critical Dictionary*. Oxford: Blackwell, pp. 22–26.

Diamond, N. (1998) On Bowlby's legacy: further explorations. In M. Marrone, *Attachment and Interaction*. London: Jessica Kingsley, pp. 193–214.

Diamond, N. (2001) Towards an interpersonal understanding of bodily experience. *Journal of Psychodynamic Counselling* 7(1): 41–62.

Diamond, N. (2003) Attachment, trauma and the body. In M. Marrone and M. Cortina (eds.), *Attachment Theory and the Psychoanalytic Process*. London: Whurr, pp. 409–430.

Diamond, N. (2004) The phantom limb: body and language, cultural expression and difference. At http://www.artbrain.org/the-phantom-limb-body-and-language-cultural-expression-and-difference/, accessed 9 Jan. 2013.

Diamond, N. (2006) Between touches. In G. Galton (ed.), *Touch Papers: Dialogues on Touch in the Psychoanalytic Space*. London: Karnac Books, pp. 79–96.

Diamond, N. and Marrone, M. (2003) *Attachment and Intersubjectivity*. London: Whurr.

Dolto, F. (1984) *L'image inconsciente du corps*. Paris: Éditions du seuil.

Eagle, M. (2007) Attachment and sexuality. In D. Diamond, S. J. Blatt and J. D. Lichtenberg (eds.), *Attachment and Sexuality*. New York: Lawrence Erlbaum, pp. 27–57.

Edelman, G. (1992) *Bright Air, Brilliant Fire*. London: Penguin.

Federn, P. (1953) *Ego Psychology and the Psychoses*. New York: Basic Books.

Ferenczi, S. (1949 [1933]) Confusion of the tongues between the adults and the child: the language of tenderness and of passion, trans. M. Balint. *International Journal of Psychoanalysis* 30(4).

Flor, H. (2002) Painful memories. *EMBO Reports* 3(4): 288–291.

Fonagy, P. (2007) A genuinely developmental theory of sexual enjoyment and its implications for psychoanalytic technique. *Journal of the American Psychoanalytic Association* 56: 11–37.

Fonagy, P. (2011) Is psychoanalysis in danger of losing its mind by forgetting about the body? Paper presented at the Neuropsychoanalysis Conference, Berlin, June.

Fonagy, P. and Target, M. (1997) Attachment and reflective function: their role in self-organization. *Development and Psychopathology* 9: 679–700.

Fonagy, P. and Target, M. (2007) The rooting of the mind in the body: new links between attachment theory and psychoanalytic thought. *Journal of the American Psychoanalytic Association* 55: 411–456.

Fonagy, P., Gergely, G., Jurist, E. and Target, M. (2002) *Affect Regulation, Mentalization, and the Development of the Self*. New York: Other Press.

Fraiberg, S., Edelson, E. and Shapiro, V. (1975) Ghosts in the nursery: a psychoanalytic approach to the problems of impaired infant–mother relationships. *Journal of the American Academy of Child & Adolescent Psychiatry* 14(3): 387–421.

Freud, S. (1893) Some points for a comparative study of organic and hysterical motor paralyses. In *The Standard Edition of the Complete Psychological Works of Sigmund Freud*, vol. 1. London: Hogarth Press, pp. 157–172.

Freud, S. (1895) The project for a scientific psychology. In *The Standard Edition of the Complete Psychological Works of Sigmund Freud*, vol. 1. London: Hogarth Press, pp. 283–397.

Freud, S. (1905) Three essays on sexuality. In *The Standard Edition of the Complete Psychological Works of Sigmund Freud*, vol. 7. London: Hogarth Press, pp. 125–245.

Freud, S. (1914) *On Narcissism: An Introduction*. In *The Standard Edition of the Complete Psychological Works of Sigmund Freud*, vol. 15. London: Hogarth Press.

Freud, S. (1915) Instincts and their vicissitudes. In *The Standard Edition of the Complete Psychological Works of Sigmund Freud*, vol. 14. London: Hogarth Press, pp. 111–140.

Freud, S. (1919) The uncanny. In *The Standard Edition of the Complete Psychological Works of Sigmund Freud*, vol. 17. London: Hogarth Press, pp. 217–256.

Freud, S. (1920) Beyond the pleasure principle. In *The Standard Edition of the Complete Psychological Works of Sigmund Freud*, vol. 18. London: Hogarth Press, pp. 7–64.

Freud, S. (1921) Group psychology and the analysis of the ego. In *The Standard Edition of the Complete Psychological Works of Sigmund Freud*, vol. 18. London: Hogarth Press, pp. 67–143.

Freud, S. (1932–6) Femininity. In *The Standard Edition of the Complete Psychological Works of Sigmund Freud*, vol. 22. London: Hogarth Press and Institute of Psycho-Analysis, pp. 139–167.

Freud, S. (1937) Analysis terminable and interminable. *International Journal of Psycho-Analysis* 18: 373–405.

Freud, S. (1974 [1923]) *The Ego and the Id*, trans. J. Riviere. In *The Standard Edition of the Complete Psychological Works of Sigmund Freud*, vol. 19. London: Hogarth Press and Institute of Psycho-Analysis, pp. 3–66.

Freud, S. and Breuer, J. (1893–5) *Studies on Hysteria*. In *The Standard Edition of the Complete Psychological Works of Sigmund Freud*, vol. 2. London: Hogarth Press.

Gallagher, S. (1986) Body image and body schema: a conceptual clarification. *Journal of Mind and Behaviour* 7: 541–554.

Gallagher, S. (2005) *How the Body Shapes the Mind*. Oxford: Oxford University Press.

Gallagher, S. and Cole, J. (1998 [1995]) Body schema and body image in a deafferented subject. *Journal of Mind and Behavior* 16: 369–390. Repr. in D. Welton (ed.), *Body and Flesh: A Philosophical Reader*. Oxford: Blackwell, pp. 131–147.

Gallese, V., Keysers, C., Wicker, B., Gazzola, V., Anton, J.-L. and Fogassi, L. (2004) A touching sight: SII/PV activation during the observation and experience of touch. *Neuron* 42: 335–346.

Garland, C. (ed.) (1998) *Understanding Trauma*. London: Ducksworth.

Gasche, R. (1986) *The Tain of the Mirror: Derrida and the Philosophy of Reflection*. Cambridge, MA: Harvard University Press.

Gershon, M. (1999) *The Second Brain*. New York: HarperCollins.

Habermas, J. (1979) *Communication and the Evolution of Society*. Toronto: Beacon.

Hayman, A. (1994) Some remarks about the 'controversial discussions'. *International Journal of Psychoanalysis* 75(2): 343–358.

Head, H. (1920) *Studies in Neurology*, vol. 2. London: Oxford University Press.

Heidegger, M. (1962) *Being and Time*, trans. J. Macquarrie and E. Robinson. Oxford: Blackwell.

Heidegger, M. (1969) *Identity and Difference*, trans. J. Stambaugh. New York: Harper & Row.

Heidegger, M. (1982) *On the Way to Language*, trans. P. D. Hertz. New York: Harper & Row.

Hopkins, J. (1996) The dangers and deprivations of too-good mothering. *Journal of Child Psychotherapy* 22: 407–422.

Husserl, E. (1960) *Cartesian Meditations*, trans. D. Cairn. Dordrecht: Kluwer.

Iacoboni, M. (2005) Neural mechanisms of imitation. *Neurobiology* 15: 632–637.

Iacoboni, M. and Dapretto, M. (2006) The mirror neuron system and the consequences of its dysfunction. *Nature Reviews Neuroscience* 7: 942–951.

Isaacs, S. (1948) The nature and function of phantasy. *International Journal of Psychoanalysis* 29: 73–97.

Kinsbourne, M. (1998) Unity and diversity in the human brain: evidence from injury. *The Brain* 127(2): 233–256.

Klein, M. (1987 [1930]) The importance of symbol formation in the development of the ego. In *The Selected Melanie Klein*, ed. J. Mitchell. New York: Free Press, pp. 95–115.

Koch, S. C., Fuchs, T. and Summa, M. (eds.) (2012) *Body Memory, Metaphor and Movement*. Amsterdam: John Benjamins.

Kohut, H. (1971) *The Analysis of the Self*. Chicago: University of Chicago Press.

Kolk, B. A. van der, McFarlane, B. A. and Weisaeth, A. C. (eds.) (1996) *Traumatic Stress: The Effects of Overwhelming Experience on Mind, Body and Society*. New York: Guilford Press.

Kristeva, J. (1980) *Desire in Language: A Semiotic Approach to Literature and Art*. Oxford: Blackwell.

Kristeva, J. (1982) *Powers of Horror: An Essay on Abjection*. New York: Columbia University Press.

Kristeva, J. (1984) *Revolution in Poetic Language*. New York: Columbia University Press.

Lacan, J. (1977a [1936]) Aggressivity in psychoanalysis. In *Ecrits*, trans. A. Sheridan. London: Tavistock Publications, pp. 8–29.

Lacan, J. (1977b) The mirror stage as formative of the function of the I. In *Ecrits*, trans. A. Sheridan. London: Tavistock Publications, pp. 1–7.

Lacey, J. I. and Lacey, B. C. (1978) Two-way communication between the heart and the brain: significance of time within the cardiac cycle. *American Psychologist* 33(2): 99–113.

Lafrance, M. (2009) Skin and the self: cultural theory and Anglo-American psychoanalysis. *Body and Society* 15: 3–24.

Lakoff, G. and Johnson, M. (1999) *Philosophy in the Flesh: The Embodied Mind and its Challenge to Western Thought*. New York: Basic Books.

Laplanche, J. (1985) *Life and Death in Psychoanalysis*, trans. J. Mehlman. Baltimore: Johns Hopkins University Press.

Laplanche, J. (1989) *New Foundations for Psychoanalysis*, trans. D. Macey. Oxford: Blackwell.

Laplanche, J. (2002) Sexuality and attachment in metapsychology. In D. Widlöcher (ed.), *Infantile Sexuality and Attachment*, trans. S. Fairfield. New York: Other Press, pp. 37–54.

Laplanche, J. and Pontalis, J. (1983) *The Language of Psychoanalysis*, trans. D. Nicholson-Smith. London: Hogarth Press and Institute of Psycho-Analysis.

LeDoux, J. (1996) *The Emotional Brain: The Mysterious Underpinnings of Emotional Life*. New York: Simon & Schuster.

Lemma, A. (2010) *Under the Skin: A Psychoanalytic Study of Body Modification*. London: Routledge.

Levi-Strauss, C. (1968) *The Savage Mind*. Chicago: University of Chicago Press.

Leys, R. (2011) A turn to affect: a critique. *Critical Inquiry* 37(3): 434–472.

Lingis, L. (1985) *Libido: The French Existential Theories*. Bloomington: Indiana University Press.

Lorimer, D. (ed.) (2001) *Thinking beyond the Brain: A Wider Science of Consciousness*. Edinburgh: Floris Books.

Lyons-Ruth, K. et al. (1998) Implicit and relational knowing: its role in development and psychoanalytic treatment. *Journal of Infant Mental Health* 19(3): 282–289.

Manning, E. (2009) What if it didn't all begin and end with containment? Towards a leaky sense of self. *Body and Society* 15(3): 33–45.

Martin, P. (1997) *The Sickening Mind*. London: HarperCollins.

Marty, P. (1990) *La Psychosomatique de l'adulte*. Paris: Presses universitaires de France.

Marty, P. and M'Uzan, M. (1963) La Pensee operatoire. *Revue française de psychanalyse* 27: 345–356.

Marty, P., M'Uzan, M. and David, C. (1963) *L'Investigation psychosomatique*. Paris: Presses universitaires de France.

Massumi, B. (2002) The autonomy of affect. In *Parables for the Virtual: Movement, Affect, Sensation*. Durham, NC: Duke University Press, pp. 23–45.

Mauss, M. (1936 [1934]) Les Techniques du corps. *Journal de Psychologie* 32(3–4). Repr. in *Sociologie et anthropologie*. Paris: Presses universitaires de France.

McCraty, R. (2004) The energetic heart: bioelectromagnetic communication within and between people. In P. J. Rosch and M. S. Markov (eds.), *Clinical Applications of Bioelectromagnetic Medicine*. New York: Marcel Dekker, pp. 541–562.

McDougall, J. (1982) *Plea for a Measure of Abnormality*. London: Routledge.

McDougall, J. (1986) *Theatres of the Mind: Illusion and Truth on the Psychoanalytic Stage*. London: Free Association Books.

McDougall, J. (1989) *Theatres of the Body*. London: W. W. Norton.

Meltzoff, A. and Moore, M. (1977) Imitation of facial and manual gestures by human neonates. *Science* 198(4312): 75–78.

Melzack, R. (1999) Pain and stress: a new perspective. In R. J. Gatchel and D. C. Turk (eds.), *Psychosocial Factors in Pain*. New York: Guilford Press, pp. 89–106.

Merleau-Ponty, M. (1962) *The Phenomenology of Perception*, trans. C. Smith. London: Routledge & Kegan Paul.

Merleau-Ponty, M. (1964) The child's relations with others. In *The Primacy of Perception*, ed. J. M. Edie. Evanston, IL: Northwestern University Press, pp. 96–155.

Merleau-Ponty, M. (1968) *The Visible and the Invisible*, trans. A. Lingis. Evanston, IL: Northwestern University Press.

Mitchell, A. (2008) Contamination essence and decomposition: Heidegger and Derrida. In D. Pettigrew and F. Raffoul (eds.), *French Interpretations of Heidegger: An Exceptional Reception*. Albany, NY: SUNY Press, pp. 131–151.

Mollon, P. (1998) *Remembering Trauma: A Psychotherapist's Guide to Memory and Illusion*. Chichester: Wiley.

Ogden, T. (1992) *The Primitive Edge of Experience*. London: Karnac Books.

Panksepp, J. (1998) *Affective Neuroscience*. New York: Oxford University Press.

Perry, B., Pollard, R., Blakely, I., Baker, W. and Vigilante, D. (1995) Childhood trauma, the neurobiology of adaptation and 'use-dependent' development of the brain: how 'states' become 'traits'. *Infant Mental Health Journal* 16(4): 271–291.

Pfeifer, R. and Bongard, J. (2007) *How the Body Shapes the Way We Think: A New View of Intelligence*. Cambridge, MA: MIT Press.

Pfeifer, R. and Hoffmann, M. (2010) Embodiment, morphological computation, and robot body schemas. Paper presented at Conference on Body Representation in Physical and Virtual Reality with Applications to Rehabilitation, Monte Veritá, Switzerland.

Pile, S. (2011) Spatialities of skin: the chafing of skin ego and second skins in T. E. Lawrence's *Seven Pillars of Wisdom*. *Body and Society* 17(4): 57–81.

Pines, D. (1980) Skin communication: early skin disorders and their effect on transference. *International Journal of Psycho-Analysis* 61: 315–323.

Piontelli, A. (2002) *Twins: From Foetus to Child*. London: Routledge.

Plato (1921) *Theaetetus*. Cambridge, MA: Harvard University Press.

Pontalis, J. (1981) *Frontiers in Psychoanalysis: Between the Dream and Psychic Pain*. London: Hogarth Press and Institute of Psycho-Analysis.

Price, E. H. (2006) A critical review of congenital phantom limb cases and a developmental theory for the basis of body image. *Consciousness and Cognition* 15(2): 310–322.

Ramachandran, V. S. and Blakeslee, S. (1999) *Phantoms in the Brain*. London: Fourth Estate.

Ramachandran, V. S. and Rogers-Ramachandran, D. (2000) Phantom limbs and neural plasticity. *Archives of Neurology* 57(3): 317–320.

Rizzolatti, G., Fadiga, L., Gallese, V. and Fogassi, L. (1996) Pre-motor cortex and the recognition of motor actions. *Cognitive Brain Research* 3: 131–141.

Robertson, J. (1953) *A Two-Year-Old Goes to Hospital (film)*. University Park, PA: Penn State Audio Visual Services.

Saussure, F. de (1916) *Course de Linguistique Generale*. Paris: Payot.

Scarry, E. (1985) *The Body in Pain: The Making and Unmaking of the World*. New York: Oxford University Press.

Schilder, P. (1950 [1935]) *The Image and Appearance of the Human Body*. London: Routledge & Kegan Paul.

Schore, A. (1994) *Affect Regulation and the Origin of the Self: The Neurobiology of Emotional Development*. Hillsdale, NJ: Lawrence Erlbaum.

Schore, A. (2003a) *Affect Dysregulation and Disorders of the Self*. New York: W. W. Norton.

Schore, A. (2003b) *Affect Regulation and the Repair of the Self*. New York: W. W. Norton.

Schore, A. (2011) *The Science and Art of Psychotherapy*. New York: W. W. Norton.

Sheets-Johnson, M. (2012) Kinesthetic memory: further critical reflections and constructive analysis. In S. C. Koch, T. Fuchs and M. Summa (eds.), *Body Memory, Metaphor and Movement*. Amsterdam: John Benjamins, pp. 43–73.

Shouse, E. (2005) Feeling, emotion, affect. *M/C Journal* 8(6). At http://journal.media-culture.org.au/0512/03-shouse.php, accessed 28 Jan. 2013.

Siegal, D. J. (1999) *The Developing Mind: Toward a Neurobiology of Interpersonal Experience*. New York: Guilford Press.

Siegal, D. J. (2012) *Pocket Guide to Interpersonal Neurobiology*. New York: W. W. Norton.

Spitz, R. A. (1946) Hospitalism: a follow-up report on investigation described in volume I, 1945. *Psychoanalytic Study of the Child* 2: 113–117.

Stern, D. (1977) *The First Relationship*. Cambridge, MA: Harvard University Press.

Stern, D. (1985) *The Interpersonal World of the Infant*. London: Karnac Books.

Tausk, V. (1933) On the origin of the influencing machine in schizophrenia [1919], trans. D. Felbenbarn. *Psychoanalytic Quarterly* 2.

Taylor, G. (1987) *Psychosomatic Medicine and Contemporary Psychoanalysis*. Madison, CT: International Universities Press.

Trevarthen, C. (1978) Secondary intersubjectivity: confidence, confiding and acts of meaning in the first year. In A. Lock (ed.), *Action, Gesture and Symbol: The Emergence of Language*. London: Academic Press, pp. 183–229.

Trevarthen, C. (1979) Communication and cooperation in early infancy: a description of primary intersubjectivity. In M. Bullowa (ed.), *Before Speech: The Beginning of Interpersonal Communication*. Cambridge: Cambridge University Press, pp. 321–347.

Trevarthen, C. (1990) Signs before speech. In T. A. Sebeok and J. Umiker-Sebeok (eds.), *The Semiotic Web*. Berlin: Mouton de Gruyter, pp. 689–755.

Trevarthen, C. (1993) The function of emotions in early infant communication and development. In J. Nadal and L. Camaioni (eds.), *New Perspectives in Early Communicative Development*. London: Routledge, pp. 48–81.

Trevarthen, C. (1994) Infant semiosis. In W. Nöth (ed.), *Origins of Semiosis: Sign Evolution in Nature and Culture*. Berlin: Mouton de Gruyter, pp. 219–252.

Trevarthen, C., Aitken, K., Papoudi, D. and Robarts, J. (1998) *Children with Autism*, 2nd edn. London: Jessica Kingsley.

Tulving, E. (1972) Episodic and semantic memory. In E. Tulving and W. Donaldson (eds.), *Organization of Memory*. New York: Academic Press, pp. 381–403.

Tustin, F. (1981) *Autistic States in Children*. London: Routledge & Kegan Paul.

Tustin, F. (1984) Autistic shapes. *International Review of Psychoanalysis* 11: 279–290.

Tustin, F. (1988) 'To be or not to be': a study of autism. *Winnicott Studies* 3: 43–55.

Uexküll, J. von (1926) *Theoretical Biology*. New York: Harcourt, Brace.

Uexküll, J. von (1957) A stroll through the worlds of animals and men: a picture book of invisible worlds. In C. H. Schiller (ed. and trans.), *Instinctive Behavior: The Development of a Modern Concept*. New York: International Universities Press, pp. 5–80.

Ulnik, J. C. (2008) *The Skin in Psychoanalysis*. London: Karnac Books.

Verhaeghe, P. and Declercq, F. (2002) Lacan's analytical goal: 'Le Sinthome' or the feminine way. In L. Thurston (ed.), *Essays on the Final Lacan: Re-Inventing the Symptom*. New York: Other Press, pp. 59–83.

Verhaeghe, P. and Vanheule, S. (2005) Actual neurosis and PTSD: the impact of the other. *Psychoanalytic Psychology* 22(4): 493–507.

Weber, M. (1982) *The Legend of Freud*. Minneapolis: University of Minnesota Press.

Winnicott, D. W. (1971) The mirror role of mother and family in child development. In *Playing and Reality*. London: Tavistock Publications, pp. 130–138.

Woolley, P. and Hurst, P. (1982) *Social Relations and Human Attributes*. London: Tavistock Publications.

Young, I. (1990) *Throwing Like a Girl and Other Essays in Feminist Philosophy and Social Theory*. Bloomington: Indiana University Press.

Yovell, Y. (2000) From hysteria to posttraumatic stress disorder: psychoanalysis and the neurobiology of traumatic memories. *Neuropsychoanalysis* 2: 171–181.

Further Reading

Bergson, H. (1988) *Matter and Memory*, trans. N. M. Paul and W. S. Palmer. New York: Zone Books.

Callaway, E. M. (2009) Laminar specificity of functional input to distinct types of inhibitory cortical neurons. *Journal of Neuroscience* 29: 70–85.

Deleuze, G. (2005) *The Logic of Sense*. London: Continuum.

Diamond, N. (2005) When thought is not enough. In J. Ryan (ed.), *How Does Psychotherapy Work?* London: Karnac Books, pp. 113–135.

Diamond, N. (2009) Between the body and social trauma: working with the aftermath of torture. In S. D.-Sclater *et al.* (eds.), *Emotion: New Psychosocial Perspectives*. Basingstoke: Palgrave Macmillan, pp. 227–241.

Eco, U. (1979) *A Theory of Semiotics*. Bloomington: Indiana University Press.

Fonagy, P. (1999) Guest editorial: memory and therapeutic action. *International Journal of Psychoanalysis* 80: 215–221.

Grosz, E. (1994) *Volatile Bodies: Towards a Corporeal Feminism*. Bloomington: Indiana University Press.

Heidegger, M. (1995) *The Fundamental Concepts of Metaphysics: World, Finitude, Solitude*, trans. W. McNeill and N. Walker. Bloomington: Indiana University Press.

Krell, D. (1992) *Daimon Life*. Bloomington: Indiana University Press.

Kristeva, J. (1990) *Abjection Melancholia and Love*, ed. J. Fletcher and A. Benjamin. London: Routledge.

Lacan, J. (2004) *Four Fundamentals in Psychoanalysis*. London: Karnac Books.

Lackner, J. R. (1988) Some proprioceptive influences on the perceptual representation of body shape and orientation. *The Brain* 11(2): 281–297.

Mollon, P. (2000) The recovered memories controversy. *International Journal of Psychoanalysis* 81: 167–169.

Mollon, P. (2001) *Releasing the Self: The Healing Legacy of Heinz Kohut*. London: Whurr.

Peirce, C. S. (1951) *Collected Writings*. Cambridge, MA: Harvard University Press.

Penfield, W. (1958) *The Excitable Cortex in Conscious Man*. Liverpool: Liverpool University Press.

Penfield, W. (1962) Sir Charles Sherrington, O.M., F.R.S. (1857–1952): an appreciation. *Notes and Records of the Royal Society* 17(2): 163.

Pfeifer, R. and Leuzinger-Bohleber, M. (2011) Minding the traumatized body: clinical lessons from embodied intelligence. Paper presented at the Neuropsychoanalysis Conference, Berlin, June.

Segal, N. (2009) *Consensuality: Didier Anzieu, Gender and the Sense of Touch*. Amsterdam: Rodopi.

Sherrington, C. E. (1975) Charles Scott Sherrington (1857–1952). *Notes and Records of the Royal Society of London* 30(1): 45–63.

Solms, M. and Turnbull, O. (2002) *The Brain and the Inner World*. London: Karnac Books.

Tustin, F. (1969) Autistic processes. *Journal of Child Psychotherapy* 2: 23–39.

Tustin, F. (1972) *Autism and Childhood Psychosis*. London: Hogarth Press.

Tustin, F. (1980) Autistic objects. *International Review of Psychoanalysis* 7: 27–40.

Uexküll, J. von (2011) *A Foray into the Worlds of Animals and Humans, with A Theory of Meaning*, trans. J. D. O'Neill. Minneapolis: University of Minnesota Press.

Index

absence
    attachment and sexuality, 113–116
    memory trace, 84–87
    skin relations, 173–174
    skin writing and touch, 181–182
    symbol formation theory, 42–43
    temporal delay, 83–84, 107
    vital biological–psychic order
        division, 75
abuse
    the body speaking the subject,
        198–200
    skin narratives, 164–165
    skin writing and touch, 183, 184–185
    somatic access to the symbol, 203
affect(s)
    alexithymia, 54–55, 96–99, 189–190,
        201–202, 205–206
    attachment, 110–112
    body image acquisition, 132
    body/language relation, 38–39,
        40–42, 45, 47–49nn, 95–99
    body memory, 102, 103, 104–105
    intercorporeality, 92–93, 209–210
    mind/body dualism, 54–55,
        56–57, 97
    nurture/nature, 30–33, 36–37
    skin relations, 173–174, 176–177

skin states, 168–169
skin writing and touch, 181
somatic access to the symbol,
    200–203
symbolic processing, 194–195,
    201–203, 213
Alain-Miller, J., 58
alexithymia, 54–55, 96–99, 189–190,
    201–202, 205–206
alien entity, 71–72, 117–118, 183–186,
    206
alpha and beta functioning, 54, 56, 97,
    214
alterity see other/otherness (Other/
    Otherness)
anaclisis see propping
Ansermet, F., 86–87
anti-knowledge, 103–105, 196–197
Anzieu, D., 121–122, 126, 137–146,
    147–148, 154–159, 174–176
attachment, 31–34
    cultural differences, 100n
    erring biological functions, 67
    fight/flight response, 191
    mirroring, 131
    and sexuality, 1–3, 36–37, 58n,
        109–118, 211–212
    skin states, 169, 171

Between Skins: The Body in Psychoanalysis – Contemporary Developments,
First Edition. Nicola Diamond.
© 2013 John Wiley & Sons, Ltd. Published 2013 by John Wiley & Sons, Ltd.